C000095145

STREET ATLAS

Hertfordshire

First published in 1993 by

Philip's, a division of
Octopus Publishing Group Ltd
2–4 Heron Quays, London E14 4JP

Second colour edition 2000
Third impression with revisions 2002

ISBN 0-540-07684-8 (pocket)

© Philip's 2002

Ordnance Survey®

This product includes mapping data licensed
from Ordnance Survey® with the permission
of the Controller of Her Majesty's Stationery
Office. © Crown copyright 2002. All rights
reserved. Licence number 100011710

Printed and bound in Spain
by Cayfosa-Quebecor

Contents

III Key to map symbols

IV Key to map pages

VI Route planning

VIII Administrative and Postcode boundaries

1 Street maps at 2½ inches to 1 mile

177 Index of towns and villages

178 Index of streets, hospitals, industrial estates, railway
stations, schools, shopping centres and universities

Digital Data

The exceptionally high-quality mapping found in this book is available as
digital data in TIFF format, which is easily convertible to other bit-mapped (raster)
image formats.

The index is also available in digital form as a standard database table. It contains
all the details found in the printed index together with the National Grid reference
for the map square in which each entry is named.

For further information and to discuss your requirements, please contact Philip's on
020 7531 8439 or ruth.king@philips-maps.co.uk

(22a)	**Motorway** with junction number
	Primary route - dual carriageway and single
	A road - dual carriageway and single
	B road - dual carriageway and single
	Minor road - dual carriageway and single
	Other minor road - dual carriageway and single
	Road under construction
	Pedestrianised area
DY7	**Postcode boundaries**
	County and Unitary Authority boundaries
	Railway
	Tramway, miniature railway
	Rural track, private road or narrow road in urban area
	Gate or obstruction to traffic (restrictions may not apply at all times or to all vehicles)
	Path, bridleway, byway open to all traffic, road used as a public path
	The representation in this atlas of a road, track or path is no evidence of the existence of way
126 / 94	**Adjoining page indicators**

Walsall	**Railway station**
	London Underground station
	Private railway station
	Bus, coach station
	Ambulance station
	Coastguard station
	Fire station
	Police station
+	**Accident and Emergency entrance to hospital**
H	**Hospital**
+	**Places of worship**
i	**Information Centre** (open all year)
P	**Parking**
P&R	**Park and Ride**
PO	**Post Office**
X	**Camping site**
	Caravan site
	Golf course
X	**Picnic site**
Prim Sch	**Important buildings, schools, colleges, universities and hospitals**
River Medway	**Water name**
	Stream
	River or canal - minor and major
	Water
	Tidal water
	Woods
	Houses
House	**Non-Roman antiquity**
VILLA	**Roman antiquity**

Allot Gdns	**Allotments**	Meml	**Memorial**
Acad	**Academy**	Mon	**Monument**
Cemy	**Cemetery**	Mus	**Museum**
C Ctr	**Civic Centre**	Obsy	**Observatory**
CH	**Club House**	Pal	**Royal Palace**
Coll	**College**	PH	**Public House**
Crem	**Crematorium**	Recn Gd	**Recreation Ground**
Ent	**Enterprise**	Resr	**Reservoir**
Ex H	**Exhibition Hall**	Ret Pk	**Retail Park**
Ind Est	**Industrial Estate**	Sch	**School**
Inst	**Institute**	Sh Ctr	**Shopping Centre**
Ct	**Law Court**	TH	**Town Hall/House**
L Ctr	**Leisure Centre**	Trad Est	**Trading Estate**
LC	**Level Crossing**	Univ	**University**
Liby	**Library**	Wks	**Works**
Mkt	**Market**	YH	**Youth Hostel**

■ The dark grey border on the inside edge of some pages indicates that the mapping does not continue onto the adjacent page

■ The small numbers around the edges of the maps identify the 1 kilometre National Grid lines

The scale of the maps is 3.92 cm to 1 km
2¹/₂ inches to 1 mile 1: 25344

0	¹/₄	¹/₂	³/₄	1 mile
0	250 m 500 m	750 m 1 kilometre		

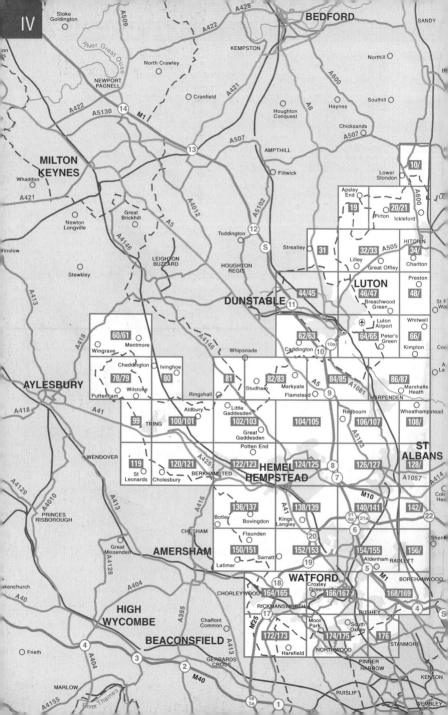

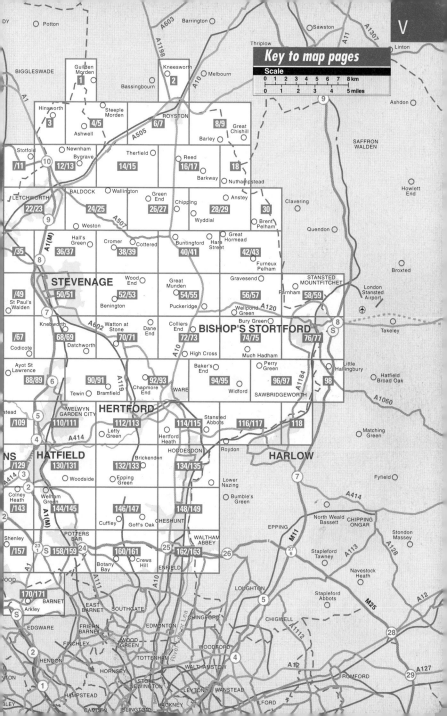

Key to map pages

Scale

0 1 2 3 4 5 6 7 8 km
0 1 2 3 4 5 miles

V

Potton
Barrington
Sawston
Thriplow
Linton
A11307
BIGGLESWADE
Kneesworth
Melbourn
Ashdon
Guilden Morden **1**
Bassingbourn
2
SAFFRON WALDEN
Hinxworth
Steeple Morden
ROYSTON
Great Chishill **8/9**
3
4/5
6/7
Ashwell
Barley
Howlett End
Stotfold
Newnham
Therfield
Reed
18
/11
10
12/13
14/15
16/17
Nuthampstead
Bygrave
Barkway
LETCHWORTH
BALDOCK
Wallington
Green End
Chipping
Anstey
Clavering
22/23
24/25
26/27
28/29
30
Quendon
Weston
Wyddial
Brent Pelham
Broxted
Hall's Green
Cromer
Cottered
Hare Street
Great Hormead
/35
36/37
38/39
40/41
Buntingford
42/43
Furneux Pelham
STANSTED MOUNTFITCHET
Wood End
Great Munden
Gravesend
London Stansted Airport
STEVENAGE
Farnham
58/59
/49
50/51
52/53
54/55
56/57
St Paul's Walden
Benington
Puckeridge
Wellpond Green
A120
Takeley
Knebworth
Watton at Stone
Dane End
Colliers End
Bury Green
8
/67
68/69
70/71
72/73
74/75
76/77
Codicote
Datchworth
BISHOP'S STORTFORD
High Cross
Much Hadham
Little Hallingbury
98
Ayot St Lawrence
Baker's End
Perry Green
Hatfield Broad Oak
88/89
90/91
92/93
94/95
96/97
Tewin
Bramfield
Chapmore End
WARE
Widford
SAWBRIDGEWORTH
A1060
HERTFORD
WELWYN GARDEN CITY
Stansted Abbots
/109
110/111
112/113
114/115
116/117
118
Letty Green
Hertford Heath
Matching Green
A414
Roydon
HATFIELD
Brickenden
HODDESDON
HARLOW
/129
130/131
132/133
134/135
Fyfield
Woodside
Epping Green
Lower Nazing
A414
Colney Heath
Welham Green
Bumble's Green
North Weald Bassett
CHIPPING ONGAR
/143
144/145
146/147
148/149
Stondon Massey
Cuffley
Goff's Oak
CHESHUNT
EPPING
Stapleford Tawney
A113
Navestock Heath
Shenley
WALTHAM ABBEY
Stapleford Abbots
/157
158/159
160/161
162/163
POTTERS BAR
Botany Bay
Crews Hill
ENFIELD
LOUGHTON
M25
Arkley
170/171
CHIGWELL
A12
BARNET
EAST BARNET
SOUTHGATE
CHINGFORD
A1112
EDGWARE
FRIERN BARNET
EDMONTON
WOODFORD
ROMFORD
A127
FINCHLEY
WOOD GREEN
A12
HENDON
TOTTENHAM
WALTHAMSTOW
HORNSEY
STOKE NEWINGTON
LEYTON
WANSTEAD
ILFORD
HAMPSTEAD
CAMDEN
ISLINGTON
HACKNEY

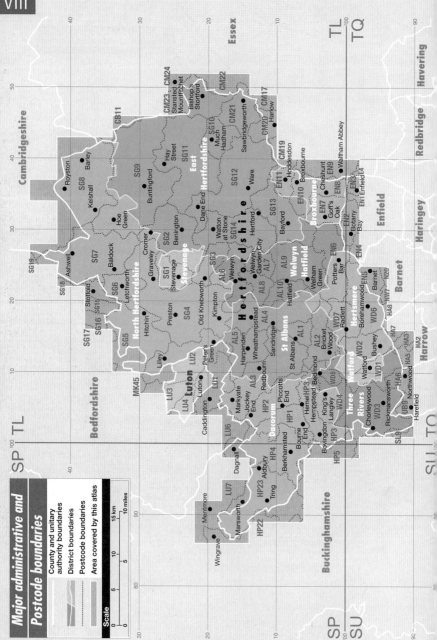

VIII

Major administrative and Postcode boundaries

County and unitary authority boundaries
District boundaries
Postcode boundaries
Area covered by this atlas

Scale
0   5   10   15 km
0   5   10 miles

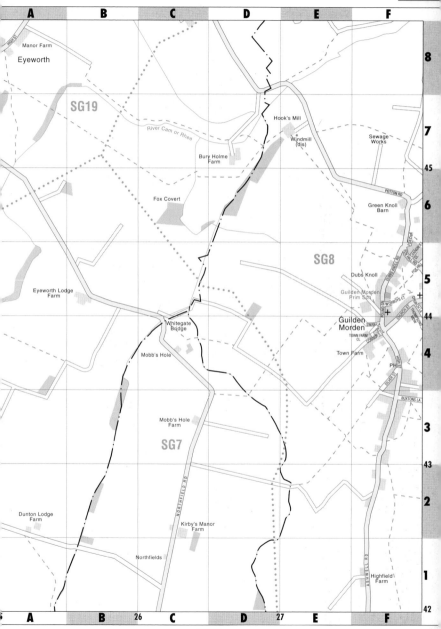

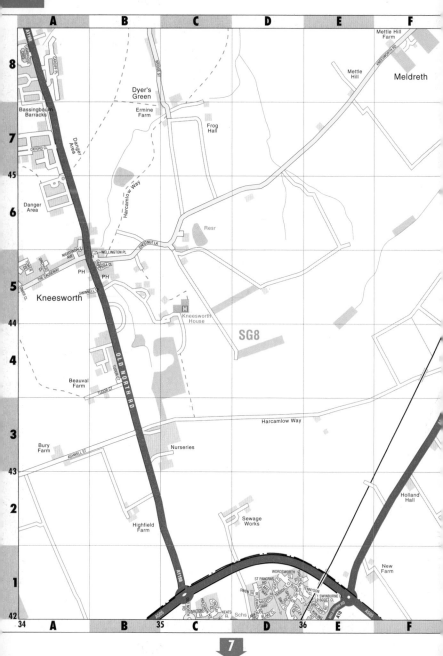

Meldreth

Mettle Hill Farm

Mettle Hill

Dyer's Green

Ermine Farm

Frog Hall

Bassingbourn Barracks

OXFORD CL

Danger Area

Harcamlow Way

Resr

Danger Area

NIGHTINGALE AVE

WELLINGTON PL

THE CAUSEWAY

PH

PH

GWINNELL CL

CHESTNUT LA

Kneesworth

SG8

Kneesworth House

H

OLD NORTH RD

Beauval Farm

TUDOR CT

Harcamlow Way

Bury Farm

ASHWELL ST

Nurseries

Holland Hall

Highfield Farm

Sewage Works

A1198

New Farm

A505

MILTON CL

KEATS CL

ST PANCRAS HO

WORDSWORTH

OWEN

BLAKE

TENNYSON CL

SWINBURNE CL

SCOTT CL

WELLINGTON RD

A10

A505

Schs

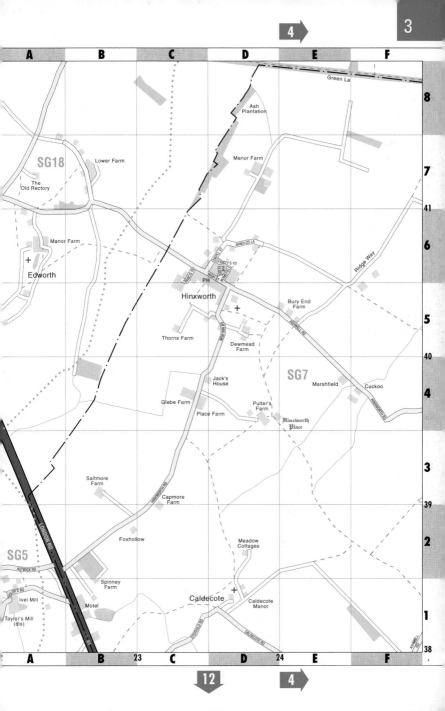

4

Green La

8

Ash
Plantation

SG18

Lower Farm

Manor Farm

7

The
Old Rectory

41

Manor Farm

6

Edworth

ARNOLDS LA

FRISTY'S YD

PH

Ridge Way

Hinxworth

Bury End
Farm

5

Thorns Farm

ASHWELL RD

Dewmead
Farm

40

Jack's
House

SG7

Marshfield

Cuckoo

4

Glebe Farm

Pulter's
Farm

Place Farm

Hinxworth
Place

3

Saltmore
Farm

HINXWORTH RD

Capmore
Farm

39

Foxhollow

Meadow
Cottages

2

SG5

LONDON RD

ASTWICK RD

Spinney
Farm

TAYLOR'S RD

Ivel Mill

Motel

Caldecote

Caldecote
Manor

1

Taylor's Mill
(dis)

STUDIO RD

CALDECOTE RD

ASHWELL RD

38

A   B   23   C   D   24   E   F

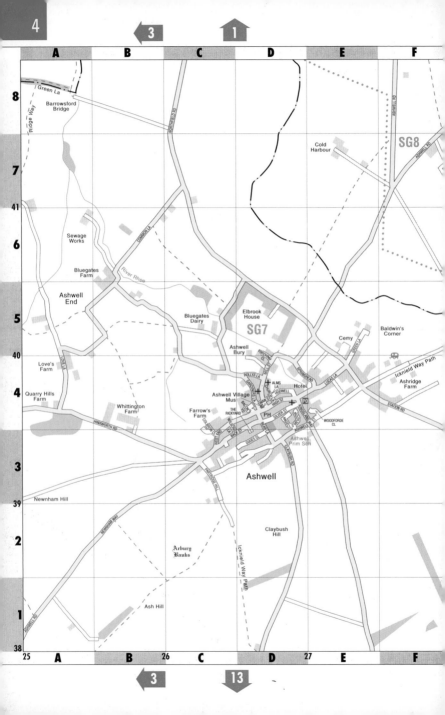

	A	B	C	D	E	F

Icknield Way Path

8

Limlow
Limlow
Hill

7

41

Highfield
Cottages

6

Highfield
Farm

5

LC

SG8

40

Therfield
Heath

Pen
Hills

4

Gallop

Hertfordshire Way

Church
Hill

Fordhams
Wood
(Nature
Reserve)

BALDOCK RD

Horse & Groom
(PH)

Kings
Ride

The
Thrift

3

Thrift
Farm

39

A505

Lower
Coombe
Farm

Chain Walk

2

Pantile
Farm

COOMBE RD

Thrift
Hill

1

38

A505

BALDOCK RD

P

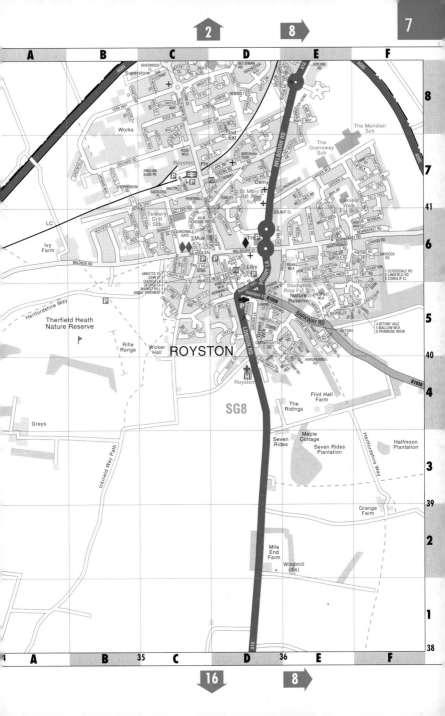

7

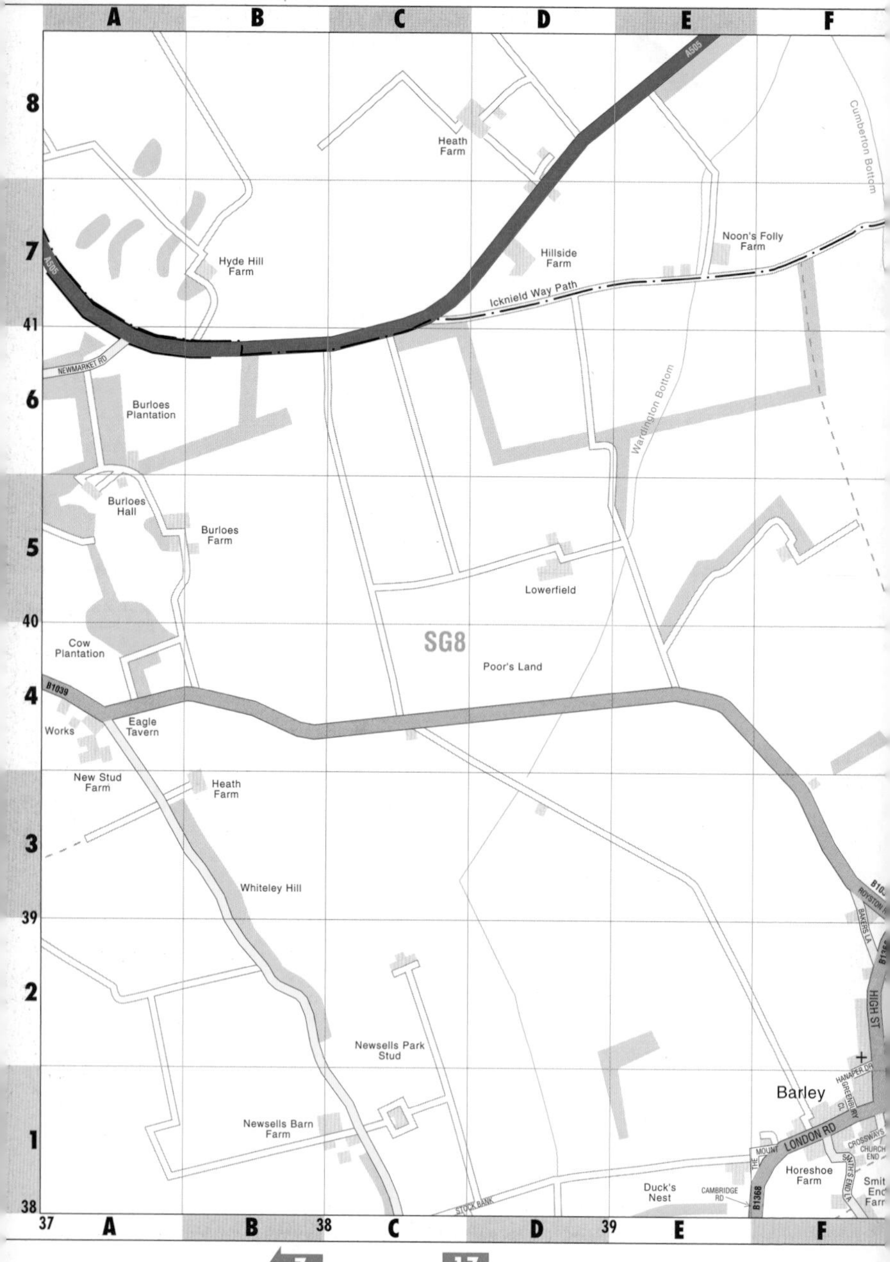

A B C D E F

8

Heath Farm

7

Hyde Hill Farm

Hillside Farm

Noon's Folly Farm

Icknield Way Path

Cumberton Bottom

A505

41

NEWMARKET RD

6

Burloes Plantation

Wallington Bottom

Burloes Hall

5

Burloes Farm

Lowerfield

40

Cow Plantation

SG8

Poor's Land

4

B1039

Works

Eagle Tavern

New Stud Farm

Heath Farm

3

39

Whiteley Hill

2

Newsells Park Stud

HIGH ST

Barley

1

Newsells Barn Farm

LONDON RD

Horseshoe Farm

Smit End Farr

38

STOCK BANK

Duck's Nest

CAMBRIDGE RD

B1368

37 A B 38 C D 39 E F

7
17

A B C D E F

8

7

41

6

5

40

4

3

39

2

1

38

North Hall Farm

Harcamlow Way

Icknield Way Path

BARLEY RD

B1368

Sells Close Farm

Harcamlow Way

Icknield Way Path

Green Ditch

New Buildings Farm

Clay Hill

NEW RD

Rectory Farm

SG8

Cumberton Bottom

New Hill

Lynchets Farm

Lime Farm

CHISHILL RD

BEDLAM PURLIEU

THE PINGGOT

GEDSTON RD

Great Chishill

BARLEY RD

CAMBRIDGE RD

PICKNAGE RD

CHISHILL RD

B1039

Chishill Windmill

Hill Farm

PLANTATION WAY

PH

MAY ST

MALTINGS LA

COL STAR CROFT

HALL LA

Barley C E F.I. Sch

PO

PICKNAGE CNR

CHURCH END

SHAFTENHOE END RD

COLLEGE LA

CHURCHGATE RD

May Street Farm

The Hall

B1039

Standard Hill

BOGMOOR RD.

LITTLE CHISHILL RD

40 A B 41 C D 42 E F

A B C D E F

NEW RD
A507

THE GARDENS
ARLESEY RD
PH

ARLESEY RD

A507

Henlow

Arlesey
Bridge

SG17

Old Manor
Farm

Cityfield
Farm

7

Westfield
Farm

Middlefield
Farm

37

Henlow Airfield

HITCHIN RD

Middle
Water

6

River Hiz

Sewage
Works

SG16

5

Camp

Playing
Field

Derwent
Lower
Sch

SPREEKLEY

WHITWORTH JONES AVE

Laurels
Grove

SG15

36

WHITTLE CL

Susans
Grove

4

Greyhound
Stadium

AARON RD

OLDFIELD FARM RD

Oldfield
Farm

STRAW
PLAIT
WAY

STATION RD

PH
PECKWORTH
IND EST

AVON RD

OLDFIELD FARM RD

MILL LA

Lower
Stondon

ASTRAL CL

Playing
Field

CHESTNUT AVE

THE OVAL

Lindas
Grove

Works

3

Cherry Tree
Nurseries

APPLECROFT

ORCHARD AVE

NORTHERN AVE

NORTHERN AVE

SOUTHERN AVE

BEDFORD RD

35

Wr
Twr

TSAR TREE
CL

Old
Ramerick

2

Holwellbury
Farm

Holwell Bury
House

Ramerick
Bottom

Holwellbury

1

Ramerick
Nursery

A600

SG5

LC

34

16 A B 17 C D 18 E F

4   14

A   B   C   D   E   F

The Knoll

8

Cat Ditch

Pembroke
Farm

Pembroke
Cottages

7

37

Gravelpit
Hill

Mitchell
Hill

Icknield Way Path

Bygrave
Plantation

6

Sewage
Works

SG7

Manor
Farm

Park
Wood

Bygrave

5

Old
Rectory

Manor
House

36

ASHWELL RD

4

Red
Cottages

WEDON WAY

Bygrave
Common

3

35

The Firs

ROYSTON RD

Half Way
Farm

2

BYGRAVE RD

Warren
Farm

WALLINGTON RD

Warehouses

ASHWELL WAY

1

SALE DR

THE SPRING

CONSTANTINE

MALTING

BLUE SPRING

MERCHANTS WLK

34

A   B   26   C   D   27   E   F

24   14

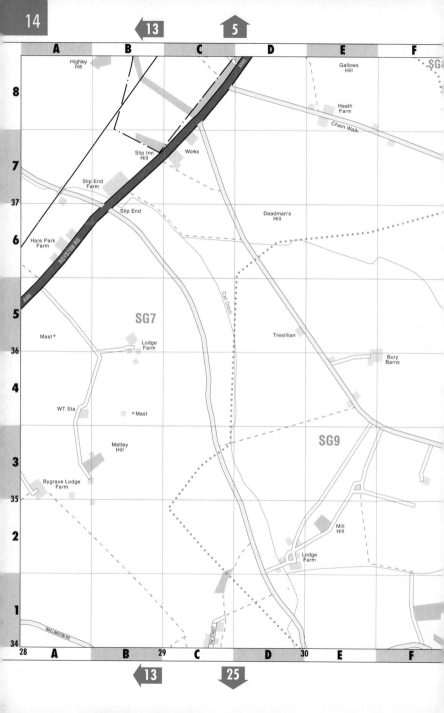

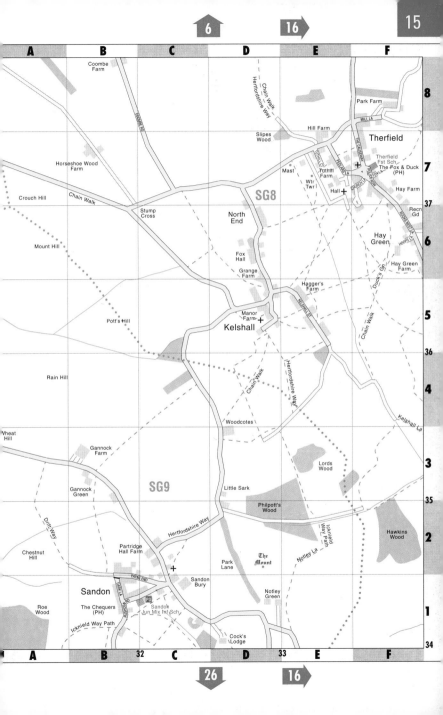

A B C D E F

Coombe Farm

Park Farm

Hill Farm

Slipes Wood

Therfield

Therfield Fst Sch.
The Fox & Duck (PH)

Horseshoe Wood Farm

Mast

Wtr Twr

Tuthill Farm

Hay Farm

Crouch Hill

Chain Walk

Chain Walk
Hertfordshire Way

MILL LA

THE CAUSEWAY

TUTHILL LA

PEDLARS LA

CHURCH LA

POLICE ROW

Hall

Recn Gd

ROOKS NEST LA

SG8

North End

Hay Green

Stump Cross

Mount Hill

Fox Hall

Grange Farm

Hay Green Farm

Duck's Gn

HOOPS LA

Pott's Hill

Hagger's Farm

Chain Walk

Manor Farm

Kelshall

KELSHALL ST

Rain Hill

Chain Walk

Hertfordshire Way

Woodcotes

Kelshall La

Wheat Hill

Gannock Farm

Lords Wood

SG9

Little Sark

Gannock Green

Philpott's Wood

Hawkins Wood

Drift Way

Chestnut Hill

Hertfordshire Way

Partridge Hall Farm

Park Lane

The Mount

Ickneild Way Path

Notley La

PAYNE END

Sandon Bury

Sandon

The Chequers (PH)

DUCK LA

THE SLIP

PO

Sandon Jun Mix Inf Sch

Notley Green

Roe Wood

Ickneild Way Path

Cock's Lodge

8

7

37

6

5

36

4

3

35

2

1

34

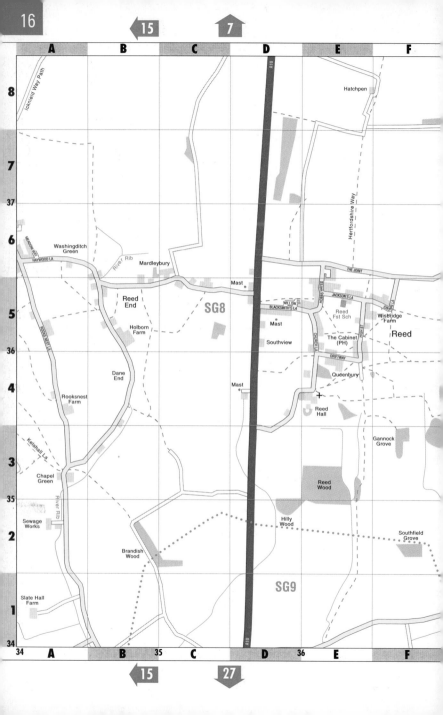

A   B   C   D   E   F

8   Hatchpen

Icknield Way Path

7

37

6   Washingditch Green   River Rib   Mardleybury   Hertfordshire Way   THE JOINT
MEADOW WAY   HAYWOOD LA

Mast

5   Reed End   SG8   Mast   WILLOW   HOBBS HAYES   JACKSON'S LA   COLES LA
BLACKSMITH'S LA   Reed Fst Sch   Wisbridge Farm

Holborn Farm   Mast   The Cabinet (PH)   Reed

ROOKS NEST LA   Southview   CHURCH LA   HIGH ST

36   Dane End   DRIFTWAY   Queenbury

4   Rooksnest Farm   Mast   +   Reed Hall   Gannock Grove

Kelshall La

3   Chapel Green   Reed Wood

River Rib

35   Hilly Wood   Southfield Grove

2   Sewage Works   Brandish Wood

SG9

1   Slate Hall Farm

34   A   B   35   C   D   36   E   F

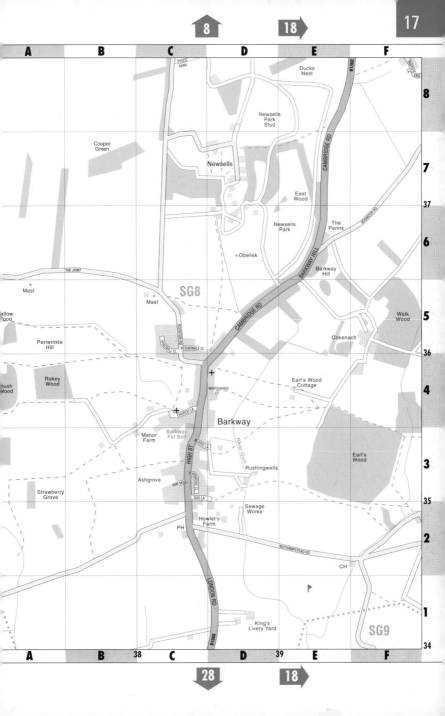

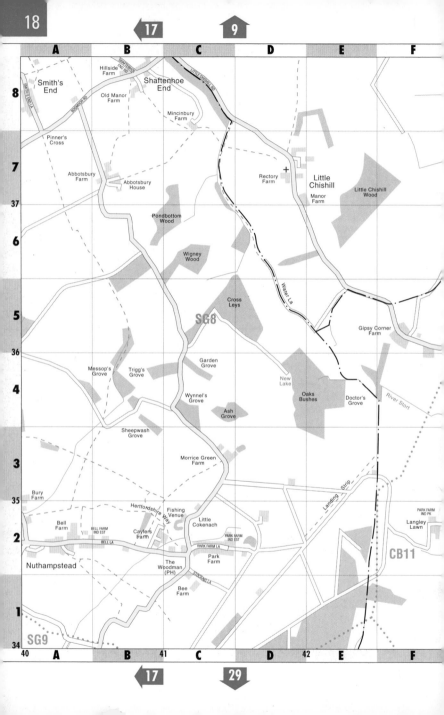

A B C D E F

8 Smith's End
Hillside Farm
Shaftenhoe End
Old Manor Farm
Mincinbury Farm
ROOKWOOD RD
BURY LANE
SHAFTENHOE END RD
LITTLE CHISHILL RD

Pinner's Cross

7 Abbotsbury Farm
Abbotsbury House
Rectory Farm
Little Chishill
Manor Farm
Little Chishill Wood

37

6 Pondbottom Wood
Wigney Wood
Water La

5 Cross Leys
SG8
Gipsy Corner Farm

36 Messop's Grove
Trigg's Grove
Garden Grove
New Lake

4 Wynnel's Grove
Ash Grove
Oaks Bushes
Doctor's Grove
River Stort

Sheepwash Grove

3 Morrice Green Farm
Landing Strip

35 Bury Farm
Hertfordshire Way
Fishing Venue
Little Cokenach
Park Farm Ind Est
Langley Lawn
PARK FARM IND PK

2 Bell Farm
BELL FARM IND EST
Caylers Farm
BELL LA
PARK FARM LA
Park Farm
CB11

Nuthampstead
The Woodman (PH)
STOCKING LA
Bee Farm

1

34
SG9

40 A B 41 C D 42 E F

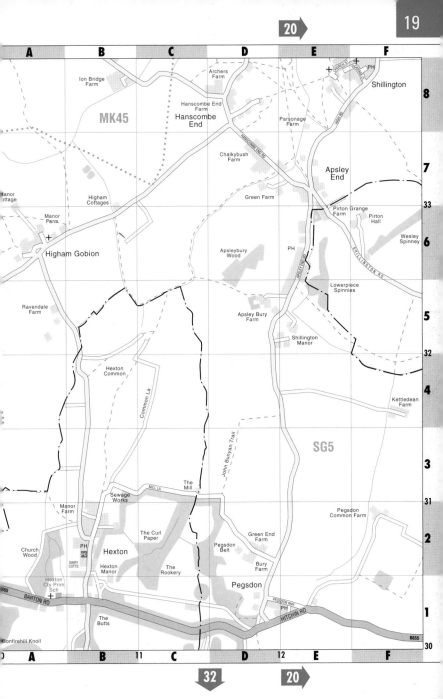

A B C D E F

8

Ion Bridge Farm

Archers Farm

Church St PH
Shillington

MK45

Hanscombe End Farm

Hanscombe End

Parsonage Farm

7

Chalkybush Farm

Apsley End

33

Manor Cottage

Higham Cottages

Green Farm

Pirton Grange Farm

Pirton Hall

Manor Farm

Wesley Spinney

6

Higham Gobion

Apsleybury Wood

PH

Lowerpiece Spinnies

Ravendale Farm

5

Apsley Bury Farm

32

Shillington Manor

Hexton Common

4

Common La

Kettledean Farm

John Bunyan Trail

SG5

3

The Mill

MILL LA

31

Sewage Works

Manor Farm

Pegsdon Common Farm

2

The Curl Paper

Green End Farm

Church Wood

PH
PO

Hexton

Pegsdon Belt

DAIRY COTTS

Hexton Manor

The Rookery

Bury Farm

Pegsdon

Hexton Cty Prim Sch

A455

BARTON RD

PEGSDON WAY

PH

HITCHIN RD

1

Bonfirehill Knoll

The Butts

B655

30

A B 11 C D 12 E F

19

8

Rosehill
Farm

SG16

7

33

6

New Wrights
Farm

HOWELL RD

Burge End
Farm

Burge End

Hammonds
Farm

West Lane
Farm

5

SHILLINGTON RD

Rectory
Farm

32

BURGE END LA

WEST LA

COLEMANS
CL

Pirton
Jun Mix Inf
Sch

ST MARY'S

FRANKLIN CL

SHED RD

BURY END

BRIDGE CR

Pirton

4

Wr Twr
Hill Farm

PRIORS HILL

DANEFIELD RD

POLLARDS WAY

GREAT GREEN

CRAB TREE LA

GREAT GREEN

CAMBRIDGE WAY

Toot
Hill

Icknield Way Path

THREE CLOSES

Hill
Farm

WALNUT TREE

HASTINGS BIRCH

3

Icknield Way Path
Wood La

SG5

Walnut
Tree
Farm

Knocking
Knoll

31

2

Highdown
Farm

HITCHIN RD

Tingley
Wood

High Down
House

Lower
Plantation

Highdown
Plantation

1

Tingley Field
Platation

Hanginghill
Plantation

Punch's
Cross

30

B655

Shrub
Wood

B655

19
33

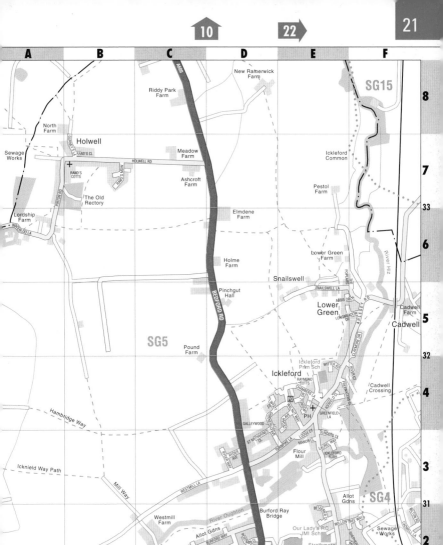

A B C D E F

SG15

8

North Farm

Holwell

Sewage Works

RAND'S CL

Riddy Park Farm

New Ramerwick Farm

Meadow Farm

Ickleford Common

7

HOLWELL RD

RAND'S COTTS

Ashcroft Farm

Pestol Farm

33

The Old Rectory

Lordship Farm

Elmdene Farm

6

Holme Farm

Lower Green Farm

River Hiz

Snailswell

BEDFORD RD

Pinchgut Hall

SNAILSWELL LA

Lower Green

Cadwell Farm

5

SG5

ABBIS ORCH

Cadwell

Pound Farm

Ickleford Prim Sch

32

Ickleford

WITTER

Cadwell Crossing

4

Hambridge Way

RAYMOND COTTS

PH

GREENFIELD LA

GALLEYWOOD

Icknield Way Path

ST KATHARINE

MANOR CT

ICKLEFORD BURY

3

Mill Way

WESTMILL LA

Flour Mill

Allot Gdns

SG4

31

Westmill Farm

River Oughton

Burford Ray Bridge

Our Lady's RC JMI Sch

Sewage Works

2

Allot Gdns

WESTMILL LA

BURFORD WM

Strathmore Inf Sch

The Priory Sch

King George V Playing Field

Westmill

MICHAEL MUIR RD

HITCHIN

Oughtonhead Common

Schs

TA Ctr

GLOVERS CT

STRATHMORE CT

1

BEARTON RD

BALMORAL RD

MARK'S CL

BEARTON AV

JAMES FOSTER HO

KIWI ALEXANDRA

30

A B C 17 D 18 E F

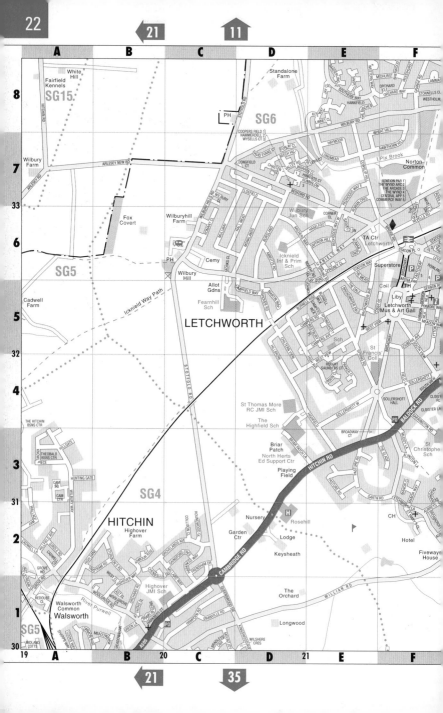

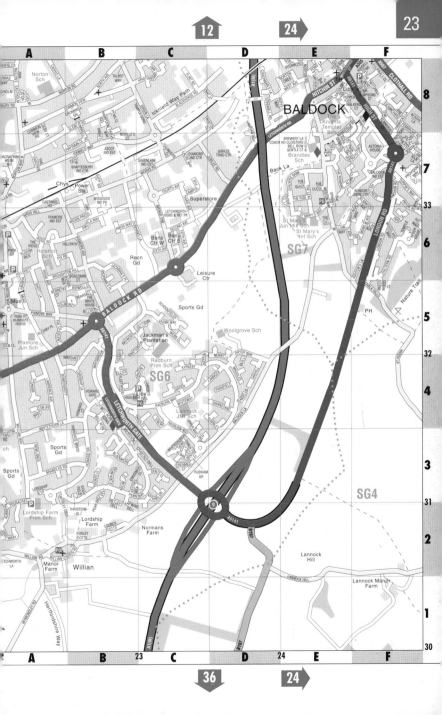

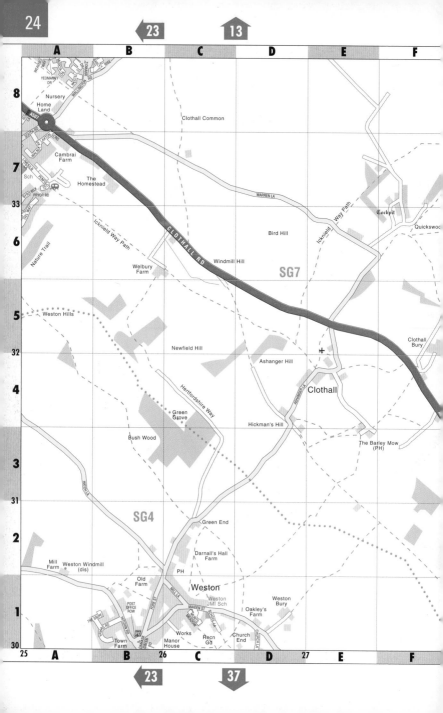

A   B   C   D   E   F

WEARE FARM

YEOMANRY DR

MASTROGE DR

JOHNSON DR

WALLINGTON RD

8

Nursery

Home
Land

A507

Clothall Common

7

Cambrai
Farm

The
Homestead

Sch

PRYOR RD

WARREN LA

33

Cockpit

Quickswood

Ickfield Way Path

Bird Hill

6

Nature Trail

CLOTHALL RD

Ickfield

Ickfield Way Path

Welbury
Farm

Windmill Hill

SG7

5

Weston Hills

Clothall
Bury

32

Newfield Hill

Ashanger Hill

4

Hertfordshire Way

Green
Grove

Hickman's Hill

Clothall

ASHWELL LA

The Barley Mow
(PH)

Bush Wood

3

31

SG4

Green End

2

Mill
Farm

Weston Windmill
(dis)

Darnall's Hall
Farm

PH

Weston
Bury

MAIDEN ST

PIKE ST

MILL LA

Old
Farm

Weston

Weston
JMI Sch

Oakley's
Farm

1

THE SHOTT

WARDEN RD

WESTON RD

POST
OFFICE
ROW

PO

Works

Manor
House

Recn
Gd

Church
End

CHURCH LA

CROSS LA

30

25   A   B   26   C   D   27   E   F

Town
Farm

MAIDEN ST

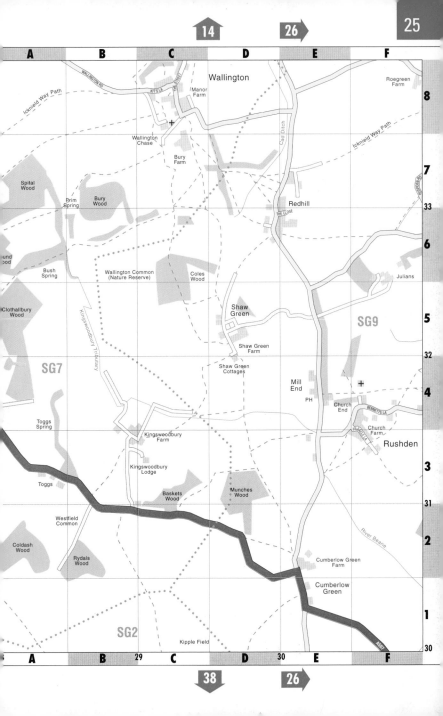

14 26

A B C D E F

8

Icknield Way Path

WALLINGTON RD
KIT'S LA
THE STREET

Wallington

Roegreen
Farm

Manor
Farm

Cald Ditch

Icknield Way Path

Wallington
Chase

+

Bury
Farm

7

Spital
Wood

Prim
Spring

Bury
Wood

Redhill

THE CLOSE

33

ound
od

Bush
Spring

Wallington Common
(Nature Reserve)

Coles
Wood

Julians

6

Clothallbury
Wood

Shaw
Green

SG9

5

Kingswoodbury Tributary

Shaw Green
Farm

32

SG7

Shaw Green
Cottages

Mill
End

PH

+

4

Church
End

BENNETTS LA

Toggs
Spring

Kingswoodbury
Farm

BRACES LA

Church
Farm

Rushden

Kingswoodbury
Lodge

Toggs

Baskets
Wood

Munches
Wood

3

31

Westfield
Common

River Beane

2

Coldash
Wood

Rydals
Wood

Cumberlow Green
Farm

Cumberlow
Green

SG2

A507

1

Kipple Field

30

A B 29 C D 30 E F

38 26

A   B   C   D   E   F

8

Icknield Way
Path

Killogs
Farm

Roe
Green

Tichney
Wood

Rockells
Jersey Farm

SG8

Five House
Farm

Wes
Woo

7

Beckfield
Farm

Green
End

Green End
Farm

Nursery

Chain Walk

BECKFIELD LA

RIDGERS RD

River Beane

33

Friars
Grange

Friars
Wood

Friars La

Doebridge
Farm

Bird's Nest
Farm

Mill End

6

Offley
Green

Chain Walk

Wood
Farm

Mill End
Farm

5

Bachelor's
Wood

Chain Walk

Lye End
Farm

32

Southern Green
Farm

Little Manor
Farm

Whitehall

Burgess La

4

Southern
Green

Broadfield Lodge
Farm

SG9

Park
Wood

Ellen
Green

3

Lodge
Farm

Chapel
Wood

Middle
Wood

Great
Wood

Bush
Wood

Chain Walk

Steward's
Ley

Chain Walk

31

Hall
Farm

Broadfield
Hall

Needle
Spring

Bolde ro's
Wood

2

Foxholes
Wood

Southfields
Farm

1

Horneywood La

Little
Wood

Throcking

Water
Tower

Throcking
Hall

COTTERED RD

30

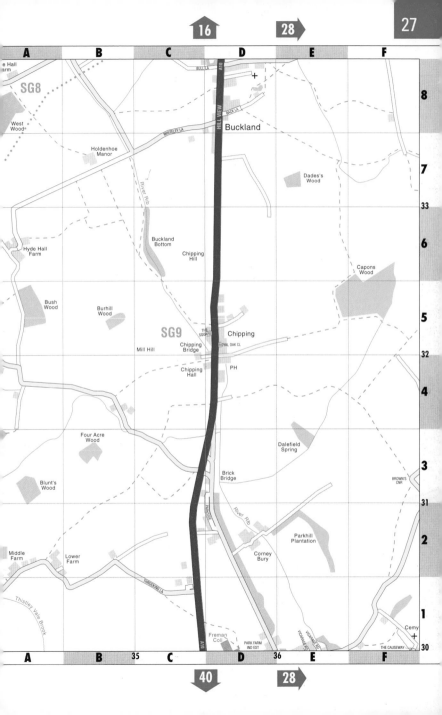

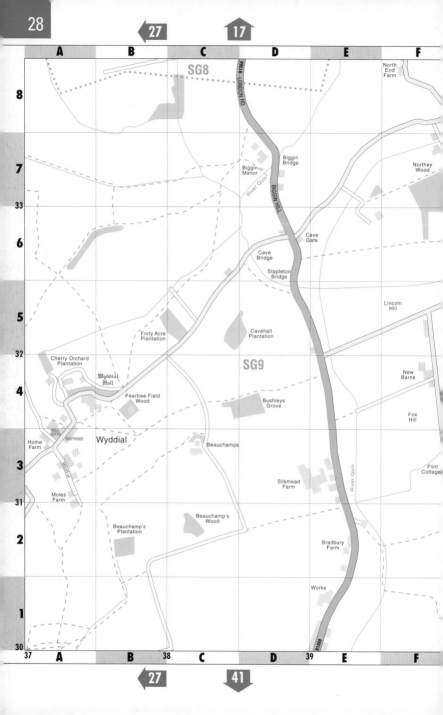

SG8

SG9

North End Farm

Northey Wood

Biggin Bridge

Biggin Manor

Cave Gate

Cave Bridge

Stapleton Bridge

Lincoln Hill

Forty Acre Plantation

Cavehall Plantation

New Barns

Cherry Orchard Plantation

Wyddial Hall

Peartree Field Wood

Bushleys Grove

Fox Hill

Home Farm

ROSE COTTS

SOUTHSIDE

Wyddial

Beauchamps

Flint Cottage

Moles Farm

Silkmead Farm

Beauchamp's Plantation

Beauchamp's Wood

Bradbury Farm

Works

River Quin

LONDON RD

BIGGIN HILL

CB11

SG8

Scales Park

White Hill

Bandons Farm

Pain's End

Two Acres Farm

Northey Wood

Cheapside

The Chequers (PH)

Anstey Castle

The Hale

Lower Green

Meesden

Anstey

Anstey Fst Sch

Snow End

The Fox (PH)

LINCOLN HILL

Roger's

Daw's End

Coltsfoot Farm

Manor Farm

River Ash

Anstey Bury

Hertfordshire Way

Puttock's End

SG9

Mill Mound

Brick House Farm

ANDERSON'S LA

HALL COTTS

Hormead Hall

Black Ditch

CONDUIT LA

Dane End House

Three Acre Wood

B1038

Borley Green Cottage

A B C D E F

8

7

33

6

5

32

4

3

31

2

1

30

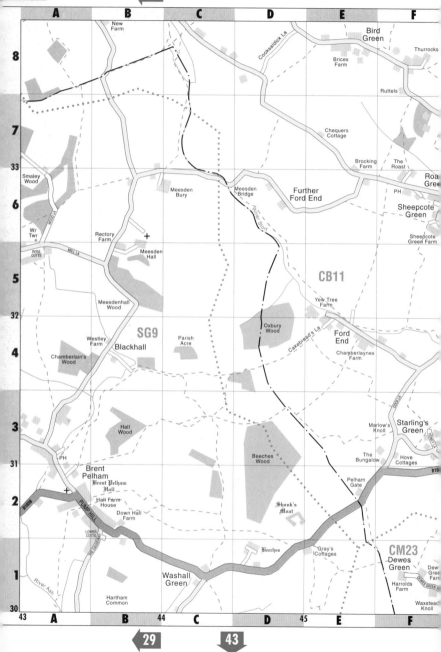

	A	B	C	D	E	F

New Farm

Bird Green

Cooksaldick La

Thurrocks

8

Brices Farm

Ruttels

7

Chequers Cottage

33

Brocking Farm

The Roast

Smaley Wood

Meesden Bury

Meesden Bridge

Further Ford End

Roa Gree

PH

6

Wr Twr

Rectory Farm

Meesden Hall

River Stort

Sheepcote Green

ROSE COTTS

MILL LA

Sheepcote Green Farm

5

CB11

Meesdenhall Wood

32

Yew Tree Farm

Westley Farm

SG9

Parish Acre

Oxbury Wood

Cakebread's La

Ford End

Blackhall

Chamberlaynes Farm

4

Chamberlain's Wood

Marlow's Knoll

Starling's Green

3

Hall Wood

COLT LA

HREE

31

PH

The Bungalow

Hove Cottages

Brent Pelham

Beeches Wood

B10

Brent Pelham Hall

Pelham Gate

2

Hall Farm House

Down Hall Farm

River Ash

PUMP HILL

Shonk's Moat

CM23

Dewes Green

LOWER COTTS

Beeches

Gray's Cottages

Dew Gree Farm

DEWES GREEN RD

1

Washall Green

Harrolds Farm

Waxstead Knoll

30

43	A	B	44	C	D	45	E	F

Hartham Common

A   **B**   **C**   **D**   **E**   **F**

8

Church Hole

Claypit
Plantation

Lion
Hill

Moor
Hill

Butts
Hill

Clark's
Hill

Deacon Hill

7

Cank
Hill

Claypit
Hole

Burwell
Platation

Gravel
Hill

The Meg

Devil's
Ditch

SG5

Pegdons
Spring

Wicks
Spring

29

Fairy
Hole

Hoo Bit

Icknield Way Path

Telegraph
Hill

Nature
Reserve

Muzzleford
Wood

6

Wasgrove
Wood

5

Mortgrove
Farm

John Bunyan Trail

Staple
Knoll

Brogsdell
Plantation

Brogsdell

Lilley Hoo

Newfield
Wood

Wasgrove
Plantation

28

Walk
Spring

Lilley Manor
Farm

Kingshill
Plantation

Mazebeard
Spring

4

LU2

Burnwell
Spinneys

HEXTON RD

Kingshill La

3

Ward's
Spring

Pond
Farm

Ward's
Farm

Stockinghill
Plantation

Lilley Hoo
Farm

27

Ward's Wood

Wardswood La

John Bunyan Trail

Lilley

HEXTON LA

GREEN ACRES

RUTLEY DELL RD

EAST SIDE BAULK

Hollybush
Hill

2

LILLEY HOO

SG5

1

George's
Plantation

Lilleypark
Plantation

PH

Lilley
Park

Church Farm

WEST ST

LILLEY BOTTOM

Ralphs
Farm

A505

INTERVESTHILL

26

Mushroom
Elders

Lilleypark
Wood

Allot
Gdns

A   **B**   **C**   **D**   **E**   **F**
10   **11**   **12**

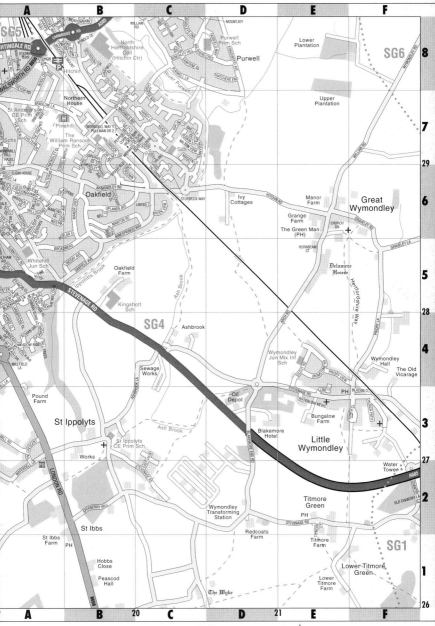

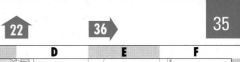

SG5

WALSWORTH RD

NIGHTINGALE RD

CAMBRIDGE RD A505

MEADOWBANK

WILLIAM RD

MOUNTJOY

North Hertfordshire Coll (Hitchin Ctr)

Purwell Prim Sch

Purwell

Lower Plantation

SG6

8

Hitchin

River Purwell

St Andrew's CE Prim Sch

Northern House

Upper Plantation

7

Pinehill

The William Ransom Prim Sch

WORDSELL WAY 1
PULLMAN DR 2

29

ELGIN HOUSE

Oakfield

STURROCK WAY

Ivy Cottages

HITCHIN RD

Manor Farm

Grange Farm

The Green Man (PH)

Great Wymondley

6

WYMONDLEY RD

BROADMEAD

CHURCH GN

GRAVELEY LA

HORNBEAM CT

GRAVELEY LA

Whitehill Jun Sch

Ippollitts Brook

Oakfield Farm

Ash Brook

Delamere House

Hertfordshire Way

5

STEVENAGE RD

Kingshott Sch

SG4

Ashbrook

28

Sewage Works

Wymondley Jun Mix Inf Sch

Wymondley Hall

The Old Vicarage

4

MILLFIELD

Pound Farm

Oil Depot

STEVENAGE RD

WATERLOW MEWS

PH   BLADON CL

CHURCH PATH

3

St Ippolyts

Ash Brook

Bungalow Farm

Little Wymondley

BLAKEMORE END RD

Blakemore Hotel

St Ippolyts CE Prim Sch

Works

Water Tower

A602

27

LONDON RD A600

SPERBERRY HILL

Wymondley Transforming Station

STEVENAGE RD

Titmore Green

PH

OLD CHANTRY LA

2

SG1

St Ibbs

Redcoats Farm

Titmore Farm

St Ibbs Farm   PH

Hobbs Close

Lower Titmore Green

1

Peascod Hall

The Wyke

Lower Titmore Farm

26

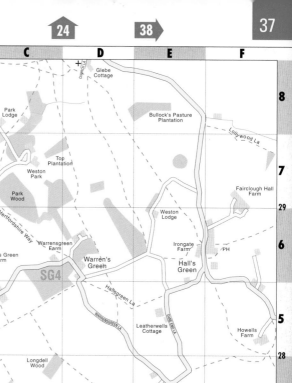

A B C D E F

8

Town MARLBOROUGH
Farm WOODLANCE
MEADE
ROWAN
CL
DAMASK
CL

Damask
Green

Park
Lodge

Glebe
Cottage

Bullock's Pasture
Plantation

Lollywood La

7

Top
Plantation

Weston
Park

Park
Wood

Fairclough Hall
Farm

29

Hertfordshire Way

Warrensgreen
Farm

Weston
Lodge

6

Friend's Green
Farm

Warren's
Green

Irongate
Farm

PH

SG4

Hall's
Green

Claypits
Wood

Hallsgreen La

5

Tilekiln
Farm

WARRENGREEN LA

Leatherwells
Cottage

LANE END LA

Howells
Farm

28

Longdell
Wood

Tilekiln Wood

New
Spring

Newberry
Grove

4

Dane End

The Warren

Brooches
Wood

Great Ashby

GREAT ASHBY WAY

Sheepleys
Spring

3

WHITWORTH RD

The Leys
Prim Sch

SALISBURY RD

LINCOLN RD

WEDGWOOD CT

BOULTON RD

GRISMORE

NEACHELLS

LOWES CL

SLEAPSHYDE

Claypithills
Spring

Wychelms
Spring

27

SG1

WINCHESTER
CL

BEVERLEY RD

WEDGWOOD

P

WEDGWOOD WAY

PARSONS GREEN
EST

SE PEPPER CL

2

RIPON RD

St Nicholas

CANTERBURY WAY

PILGRIMS WAY

PIN GREEN
IND EST

ULLSWATER CL

THIRLMERE

CARTWRIGHT RD

SG2

Boxbury
Farm

WELLFIELD
CT

CHAWOOD CL

MARTINS WAY

Box Wood

1

ARTHUR
GIBBENS
CT

A1072

SEFTON RD

Martins Wood
Prim Sch

DERBY
WAY

BELMAY RD

Martin's
Wood

BEESLEY WAY

BEDALE WAY CL

Boxwood
Lodge

VERITY WAY

THE OVAL

PO

P

A1155

FAIRFIELD RD

SANDOWN RD

26

A B 26 C D 27 E F

A   B   C   D   E   F

8

Barnacks Hill Wood

Kipple Field

Dolls Field

Weston Tributary

7

Lolleywood La

Harveyshill Farm

Luffenhall

Swamstey Common

SG9

29

Luffenhall Common

Church Farm

NEWELL LA

6

SG4

Whitehall Farm

Manor Farm

Newell Common

Cromer Windmill

Hare Street

Bancroft Farm

Walnut Tree Farm

Cromer

Cromerfield Common

5

Hick's Grove Cottages

Hick's Grove

Cromerhill Common

Cromer Farm

The Ainage (Pearson's Char

28

SG2

Brookfield Comomon

4

Howell's Wood

Sloggar's Wood

Cornhill Common

Bury Grange

Markham's Wood

Ardeley

River Beane

Ardeley Brook

3

Churchend Common

The Bungalow

Ardeley Bury

Ardeley St Lawrence I CE Prim Sch

SCHOOL LA

CRES

27

The Old Rectory

WHITE HILL

2

Dovehouse La

Manor Farm

BEECHOLT LA

CHURCH END

+

Squitmore Spring

Nursery

HIGH ST

Bridgefoot Farm

HUNTERS LA

BUTS LA

Walkern Bury Farm

1

TROTGALL LA

BROCKHOLL SHOTT

NOBLE TREE TREE

PO B1037

+

The Yew Tree (PH)

Chancey Hall

Walkern

MOORS LEY

26

28   A   B   29   C   D   30   E   F

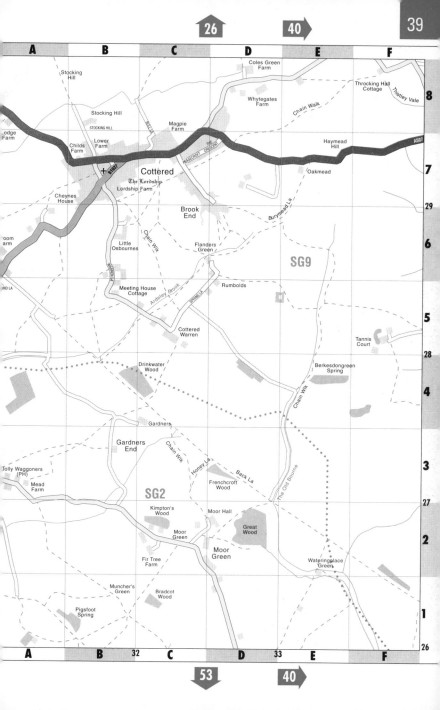

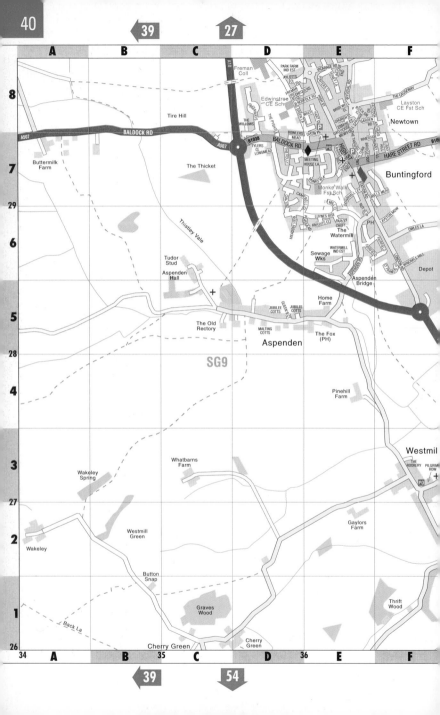

A B C D E F

8

HARE STREET RD
ALSWICK HALL COTTS
Alswick Hall Farm
Alswick Hall
Cemy
Alswickhall Wood
The Beehive (PH)
B1038
MOORFIELDS
Hormead CE Prim Sch
B1038
Great Hormead Brook
Hare Street
Swan La
Great Hormead Bury
Hertfordshire Way

7

Haley Hill Ditch
FAYLAND COTTS
WORSTED LA
Little Hormead Bury Farm
HORSESHOE LA

29

OWLES LA
Owles Hall
Owls Farm
Stonecross La
Hertfordshire Way
Little Hormead Brook

6

Haley Hill
Camp Wood
SG9
Bummers Hill

5

Stonebury Farm
Mutfords

28

Dogkennel Wood
Dassel's Hill
River Quin

4

Room Wood
ROSE MDW

3

estmill Bury
Langley Wood
Dassels
Dassels Bury

27

Westmill Lodge
River Rib
Sewage Works
SG11

2

Long Spring

A414

1

Millcroft Wood
Coles Park
Hay Lodge
Hay Street
B1368
Quinbury Farm

26

A B C D E F

38 55 42 39 42

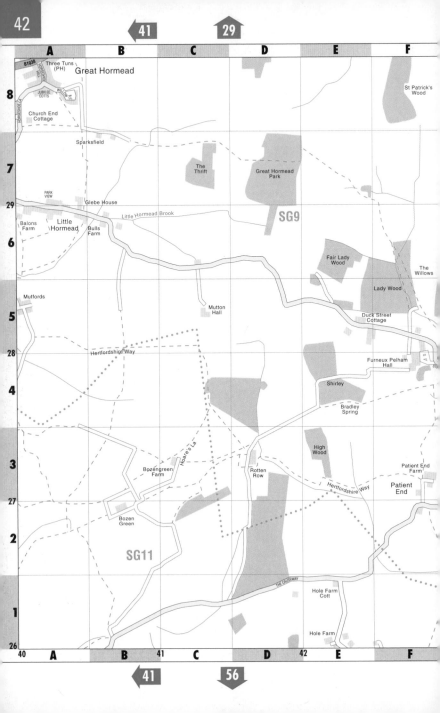

A   B   C   D   E   F

8

B1038

Three Tuns (PH)

Great Hormead

JUBILEE COTTS

Church End Cottage

Sparksfield

7

The Thrift

Great Hormead Park

St Patrick's Wood

29

PARK VIEW

Glebe House

Little Hormead Brook

SG9

Balons Farm

Little Hormead

Bulls Farm

6

Fair Lady Wood

The Willows

Lady Wood

5

Mutfords

Mutton Hall

Duck Street Cottage

28

Hertfordshire Way

Furneux Pelham Hall

4

Shirley

Bradley Spring

High Wood

Patient End Farm

3

Bozengreen Farm

Hoare's La

Rotten Row

Hertfordshire Way

Patient End

27

Bozen Green

2

SG11

1

THE CAUSEWAY

Hole Farm Cott

26

Hole Farm

40   A   B   41   C   D   42   E   F

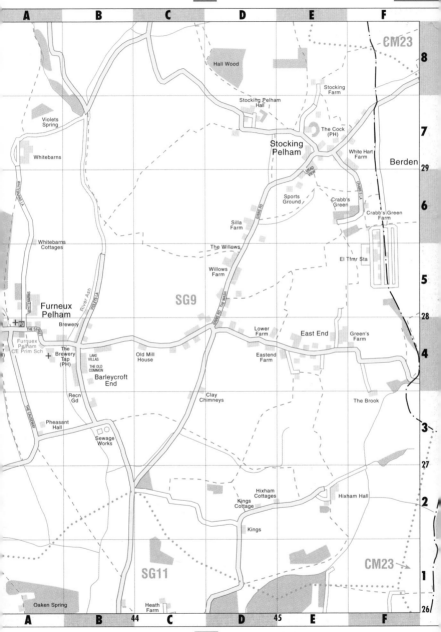

CM23

A B C D E F

8

Hall Wood

Stocking
Farm

Stocking Pelham
Hall

Violets
Spring

The Cock
(PH)

7

Stocking
Pelham

White Hart
Farm

Whitebarns

Berden

29

Sports
Ground

Crabb's
Green

6

Silla
Farm

Crabb's Green
Farm

Whitebarns
Cottages

The Willows

El Tfmr Sta

Willows
Farm

5

SG9

28

Furneux
Pelham

River Ash

Brewery

Lower
Farm

East End

Green's
Farm

Furneux
Pelham
CE Prim Sch

The
Brewery
Tap
(PH)

LAKE
VILLAS

Old Mill
House

Eastend
Farm

4

THE OLD
COMMON

Barleycroft
End

Recn
Gd

Clay
Chimneys

The Brook

3

Pheasant
Hall

27

Sewage
Works

Hixham
Cottages

Hixham Hall

2

Kings
Cottage

Kings

CM23

1

SG11

26

Oaken Spring

Heath
Farm

A B C D E F
44 45

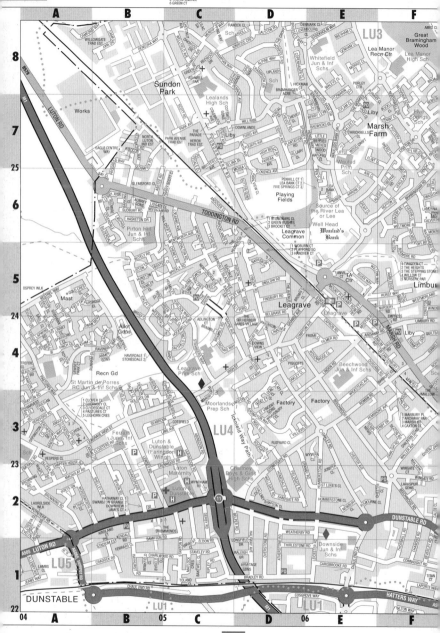

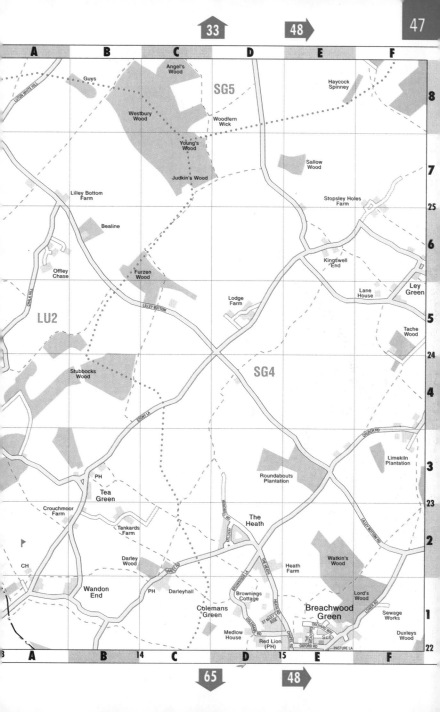

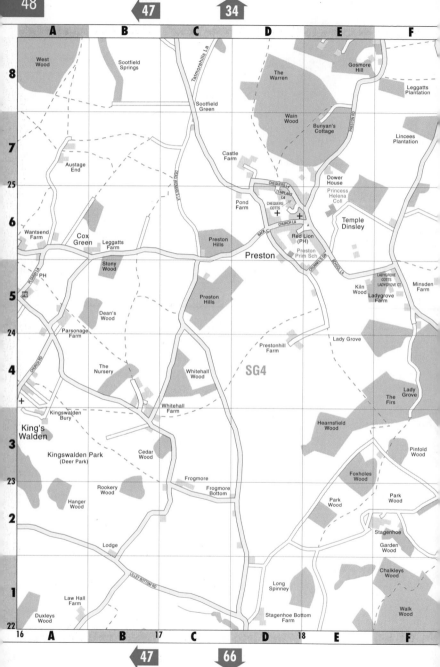

47

34

8

7

25

6

5

24

4

3

23

2

1

22

A   B   C   D   E   F

West Wood

Sootfield Springs

Tatmorehills La

Sootfield Green

The Warren

Gosmore Hill

Leggatts Plantation

Wain Wood

Bunyan's Cottage

Lincees Plantation

Austage End

Castle Farm

Dower House

Princess Helena Coll

Wantsend Farm

Cox Green

Leggatts Farm

Stony Wood

Pond Farm

CHEQUERS LA

TEMPLARS LA

CHEQUERS COTTS

CHURCH LA

Red Lion (PH)

Temple Dinsley

Preston Hills

Preston

Preston Prim Sch

DRUMMER LA

BUNYAN'S LA

Kiln Wood

Ladygrove Farm

LADYGROVE COTTS
LADYGROVE CT

Minsden Farm

PH

FOUNTAIN LA

Dean's Wood

Preston Hills

Parsonage Farm

Prestonhill Farm

Lady Grove

CHURCH RD

The Nursery

Whitehall Wood

SG4

Whitehall Farm

The Firs

Lady Grove

Kingswalden Bury

Hearnsfield Wood

King's Walden

Kingswalden Park (Deer Park)

Cedar Wood

Frogmore

Pinfold Wood

Hanger Wood

Rookery Wood

Frogmore Bottom

Foxholes Wood

Park Wood

Park Wood

Lodge

Stagenhoe

Garden Wood

VALLEY BOTTOM RD

Chalkleys Wood

Law Hall Farm

Long Spinney

Walk Wood

Duxleys Wood

Stagenhoe Bottom Farm

16   A   B   17   C   D   18   E   F

47

66

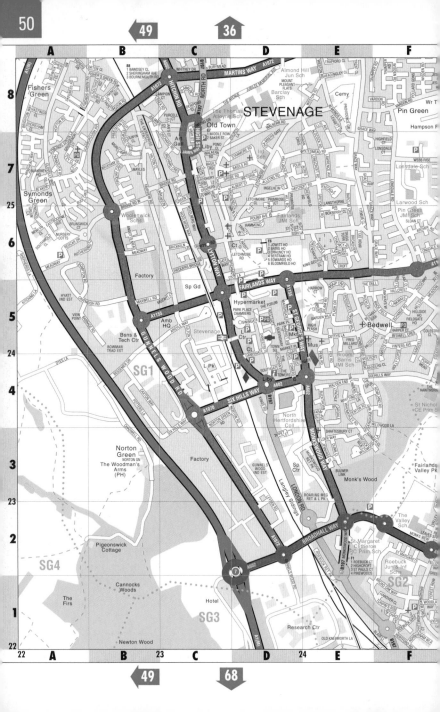

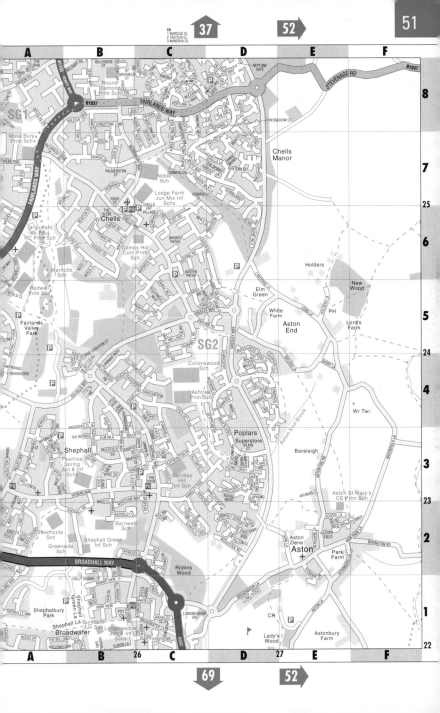

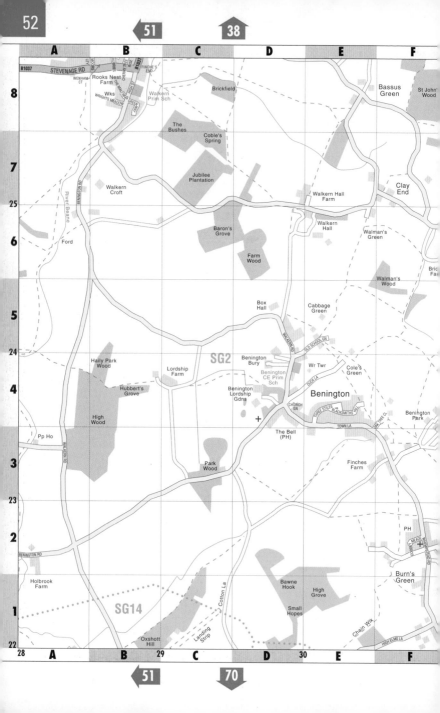

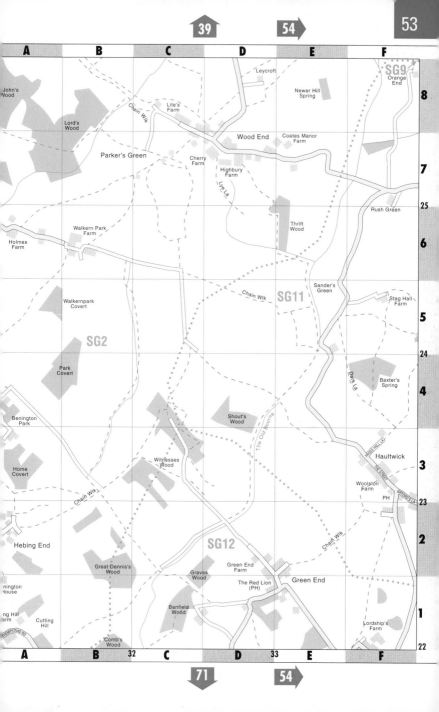

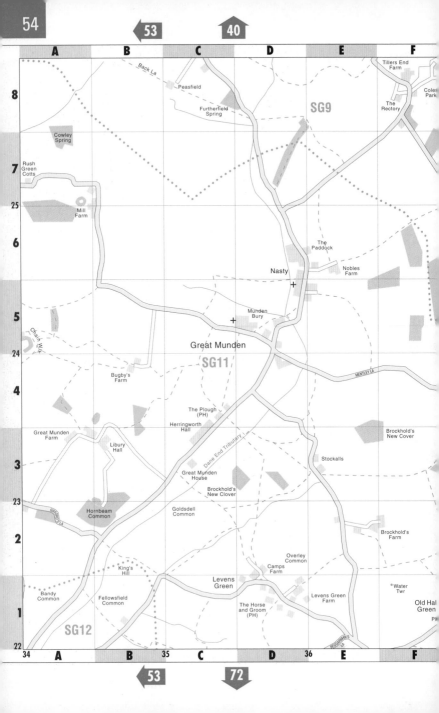

A   B   C   D   E   F

Tillers End
Farm

8   Peasfield   Coles
Park
Furtherfield   The
Spring   SG9   Rectory

Cowley
Spring

7   Rush
Green
Cotts

25   Mill
Farm
The
Paddock

6   Nobles
Farm
Nasty

Munden
Bury
5   Great Munden

Chain Wk
24   SG11   MENTLEY LA
Bugby's
Farm
4   The Plough
(PH)
Herringworth   Brockhold's
Hall   New Cover
Great Munden   Libury
Farm   Hall   Dane End Tributary
3   Great Munden   Stockalls
House
Brockhold's
New Clover
23   Goldsdell   Brockhold's
Common   Farm
Hornbeam
2   Common
Overley
Common   Water
King's   Camps   Twr
Hill   Farm
1   Bandy   Levens   Levens Green   Old Hall
Common   Green   Farm   Green
Fellowsfield   The Horse   PH
SG12   Common   and Groom
(PH)
22
34   A   B   35   C   D   36   E   F

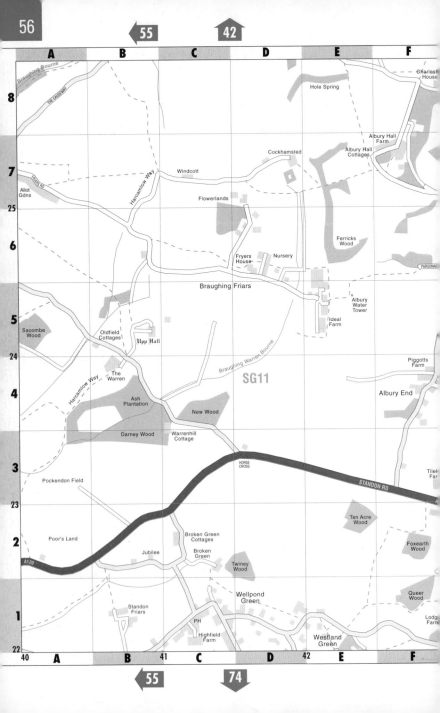

55
42

A   B   C   D   E   F

8

Braughing Bourne
THE CAUSEWAY
Hole Spring

Charles
House

7

Allot
Gdns
FRIARS RD
Harcamlow Way
Windcott
Cockhamsted
Albury Hall
Cottages
Albury Hall
Farm

25

Flowerlands

6

Fryers
House
Nursery
Ferricks
Wood

PARSONAG

Braughing Friars

Albury
Water
Tower

5

Sacombe
Wood
Oldfield
Cottages
Upp Hall
Ideal
Farm

24

Braughing Warren Bourne

SG11

Piggotts
Farm

4

Harcamlow Way
The Warren
Ash
Plantation
New Wood
Albury End

Darney Wood
Warrenhill
Cottage

3

HORSE
CROSS
STANDON RD
Tilek
Far

Pockendon Field

23

Ten Acre
Wood

2

Poor's Land
A120
Jubilee
Broken Green
Cottages
Broken
Green
Twiney
Wood
Foxearth
Wood

1

Standon
Friars
PH
Highfield
Farm
Wellpond
Green
Westland
Green
Queer
Wood
Lodg
Farm

22

40   A   B   41   C   D   42   E   F

55
74

A B C D E F

8

Gravesend

Catherine Wheel
(PH)

Patmore Heath
(Nature Reserve)

Harcamlow Way

Bogs
Cottage

Patmore
Hall

7

Hertfordshire Way

Itch
La

Bogs
Wood

CM23

High
Hall

Ypres

Mansfield
Cottages

25

Clapgate

MILL LA

Royal
Oak
(PH)

onage
arm

AGE LA

Albury
CE Sch

6

Sewage
Works

Salmon Mead
Spring

The
Common

Albury

The
Close

Ninno
Wood

Upwick
Wood

Green
Farm

Upwick
Green

5

Salmon Mead
Spring

Hoy's
Farm

Albury
Lodge

Albury Lodge
House

River Ash

SG11

Upwick
Hall

Walnuttree
Green

24

4

Folly
Gorse

Hertfordshire Way

Alburyend
Wood

3

23

STANDON RD

Little
Hadham

Church
End

Church End
Farm

CAPEL CT

Haddam
Hall

2

Little Hadham
Prim Sch

The Causeway

LLOYD TAYLOR LA

STORTFORD RD

THE SMITHY

Little Hadham
Place

Halfway
House

Stone House
Farm

CM23

1

HADHAM RD

A120

PO

Green Street
Farm

22

A B 44 C D 45 E F

A B C D E F

8

The Folly

Lincolns

Shaw
Wood

Farnham
Green

Shawwood
Cottage

7

Farnham
Hall

Thrifts

Chatter
End

Harcamlow Way

Savenend
Cottage

Savenend
Farm

Oozes
Wood

Home
Wood

Hassobury

New
Wood

25

Farnham
CE Prim Sch

6

Thrimley La

Thrimley
House

RECTORY LA
CRES

Globe
Farm

Farnham

Long Bell

Walkers

Oak
Plantation

Bourne
Bridge

Ford

Longdown
Plantation

5

SG11

Hill
Farm

Level's
Green

Earlsbury

WALNUT TREE LA

CM23

Hudshill
Plantation

24

Moorfield
Spring

Walnuttree
Cottages

Bourne Brook

4

Bailey Hills

Mast

3

Wickham
Hall

23

Foxdells
Farm

2

Bloodhounds'
Wood

Hoggate's
Wood

Blackthorn
Spring

Hadham
Park

High
Wood

Hadham
Lodge

Whitehall
Coll

1

Hertfordshire Way

Savernake

Water
Tower

Ash
Grove

Mast

Dane O'Coys
Farm

CRICKETFIELD LA

HADHAM RD
A120

A120

DANE O'COYS RD

22

46 A 47 B C 47 D 48 E F

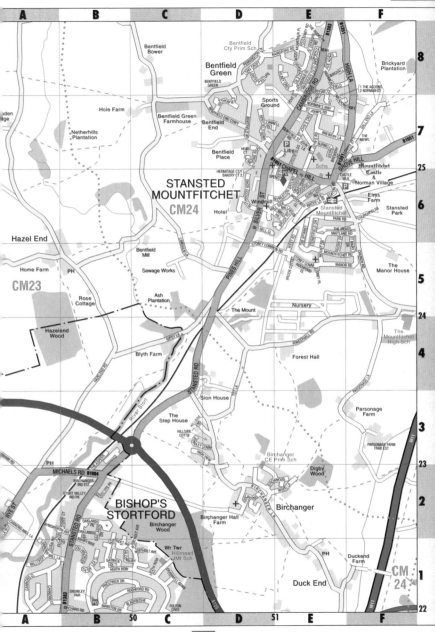

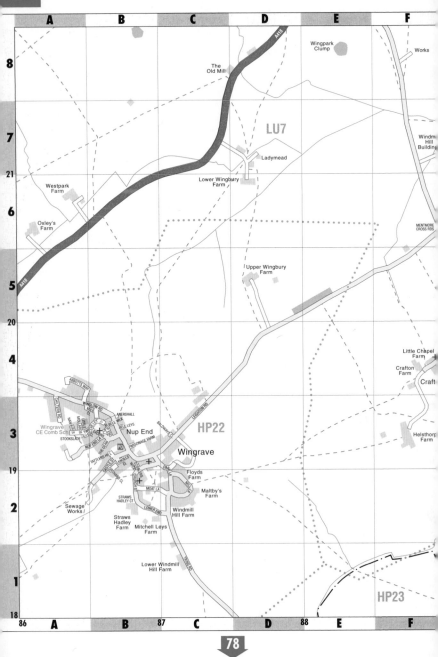

A B C D E F

8

A418

Wingpark
Clump

Works

The Old Mill

LU7

Windm
Hill
Building

7

21

Ladymead

Lower Wingbury
Farm

Westpark
Farm

6

Oxley's
Farm

MENTMORE
CROSS RDS

5

Upper Wingbury
Farm

A418

20

4

Little Chapel
Farm

Crafton
Farm

Craft

LEIGHTON RD

HP22

Helsthorp
Farm

ABBOTS RYPT

WINGSLOW RD

CHILTERN RD

ANMERSHALL

Wingrave
CE Comb Sch

BELL WLK

BELL LEYS

Nup End

BALDWAY CL

PARSONAGE FARM

3

STOOKSLADE

NUP END LA

Wingrave

19

TATTLERS HILL

Floyds
Farm

WINFLEY RD

MOAT LA

Maltby's
Farm

2

STRAWS
HADLEY CT

LOWER END

Sewage
Works

Windmill
Hill Farm

Straws
Hadley
Farm

Mitchell Leys
Farm

1

Lower Windmill
Hill Farm

ROWSHAM RD

HP23

18

86 A B 87 C D 88 E F

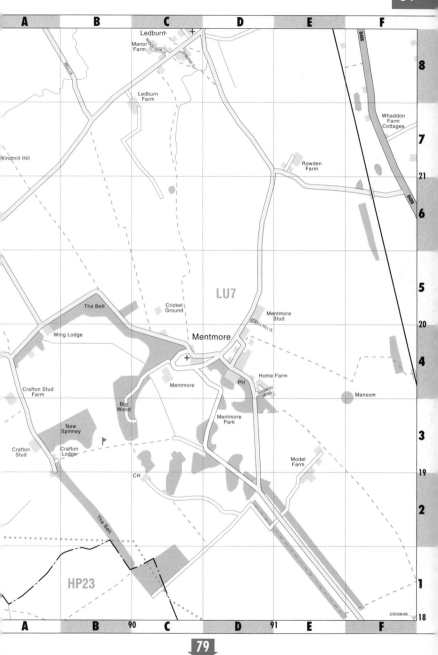

A　　**B**　　**C**　　**D**　　**E**　　**F**

8

7

21

6

5

20

4

3

19

2

1

18

Ledburn

Manor
Farm

Ledburn
Farm

Windmill Hill

Whaddon
Farm
Cottages

Rowden
Farm

LU7

Cricket
Ground

The Belt

Wing Lodge

Mentmore
Stud

Mentmore

Crafton Stud
Farm

Big
Wood

Mentmore

Home Farm

PH

Mansom

New
Spinney

Crafton
Stud

Crafton
Lodge

Mentmore
Park

Model
Farm

CH

The Belt

HP23

STATION RD

A　　**B**　90　**C**　　**D**　91　**E**　　**F**

44

LU5

LU4

LU4

Skimpot
Wood

Stanner's
Wood

Mast

Cultivation
Terraces

Foxdell
Jun Sch

COULSON CT

Work

COSGROVE WAY

Chaul End
Farm

COULSON CT

BLINDMAN'S LA

BILTON WAY

BILTON WAY

HAREFIE
CT

DALLOW RD

KENT RD

SUMMERFIELD RD

RUNLEY RD

Chaul End

Tunnels

BILLING
WORK

Zouches
Farm

Round
Wood

Mast

Twentynine
Wood

Bush
Wood

Badgerdell
Wood

CH

Blossom
Spring

Dame Ellen's
Wood

Thirty
Wood

Castlecroft
Wood

Brickkiln
Farm

LU1

Little John's
Wood

Folly
Wood

Manor
Farm

Turnpike
Farm

Bury
Farm

Cradle
Spinney

MANOR
CL

MEADOW
CROFT

PH

HEATHFIELD
CL

Willowfi
Lower S

Lodge
Farm

Gatehouse

Garden
Centre

Heathfield
Lower Sch

Five Oaks
Mid Sch

Buncer's
Wood

DUNSTABLE RD

Caddington

THE GLEN

Jockey
Farm

MILLFIELD
WAY

MANOR RD

Tipplehi
Farm

LU6

PH

Piper's
Farm

Kensworth
House

COTSWOLD

Heron
Farm

MANCROFT RD

Aley
Green

Corner
Farm

Lynch
Farm

Nurseries

Millfield
Farm

Cemy

Kensworth
Lynch

AL3

Hill Farm

04

05

06

83

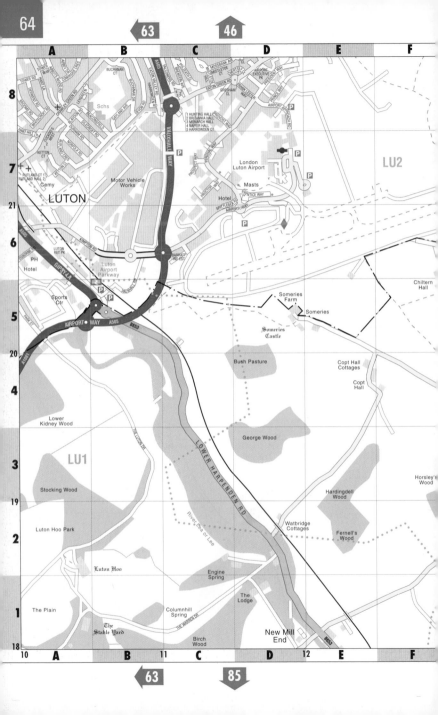

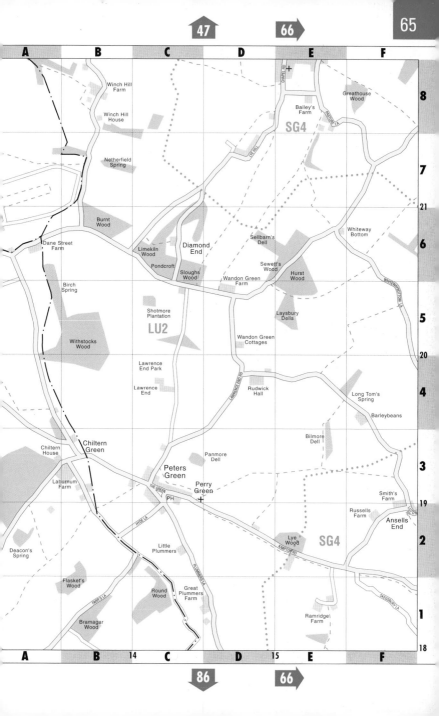

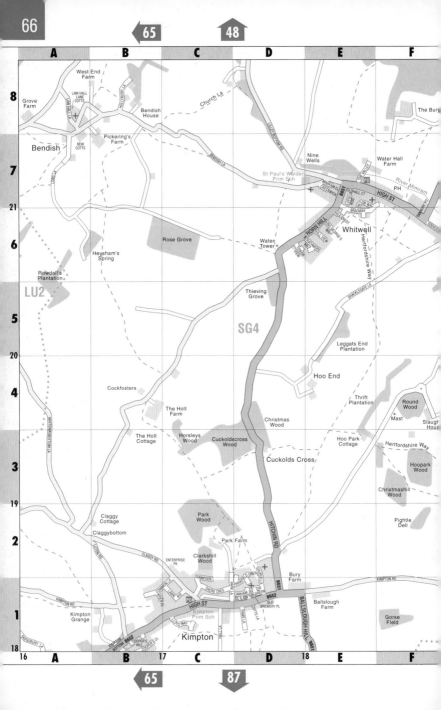

A B C D E F

8
7
21
6
5
20
4
3
19
2
1
18

Michael's
Hope

Reynolds
Wood

Peartree
Wood

Roundwood
Dell

Briary
Spring

Easthall
Farm

Claggdell
Spring

The
Fussens

Rusling
End

Graffridge
Wood

Rusling End
Farm

Warren
Wood

Rough
Bushes

Holl Lays
Wood

Winter Wood

Tower
Lodges

Crouch
Green

SG4

ose
arm

oo
otts

Pannmill
Cotts

Dumb
Hills

The
Node

Troopers
Stables

Hoo
Farm

Three Houses
Farm

Node
Wood

Nursery

Lygraves
Wood

The
Cottage

oo Park

Chalkdale
Wood

Luckswarren
Wood

River Mimram

Ealing
Lodge

Bigg's
Grove

Mansells
Farm

Mansells La

Rye-end
Cotts

High Heath
Farm

Hertfordshire Way

Rye-end
Farm

Coronation
Plantation

Hogg
Wood

The Grove

Water
Twr

The
Kennels

Kimpton
Mill

Codicote
Heath

TOWER RD

Codicote
Lodge

Kimpton Rd

Green La

Codicote

Heath La

Codicote
Lodge

PH

Codicote
CE Prim Sch

Meadow Way

High St

AL6

A B C D E F

Chain Wlk
SG2
Comb's Wood
Apsley Common
Customs Wood
Easington Common
Little Munden CE Prim Sch
Short Whiteley Common
Dane End
8

Chapel Farm
Long Spring
The Old Bourne
PAGET COTTS
Dane End House
7

Whempstead Green
Whempstead
Home Farm
PH
21

Hog's Wood
Whempstead Gate Farm
Whempstead Farm
Cottonborough Common
Claypits Wood

MILL LA
WHEMPSTEAD LA
Wicks Wood
Lodge Farm
6

Bromley Common
Bushy Leys Spring
Brookfield Common
Smart's Hill

Willeycotes Wood
Longcroft Wood
SG12
5

20

Bardolphspark Wood
Sacombe Hill Farm
Sacombe Hill
Dane End Tributary
4

Bardolphs
SACOMBE GREEN RD
Sacombe
SG14

The Spring
Heath Mount Sch
SACOMBE POUND
Sacombebury Farm
Sacombe House
19

WARE RD
Woodhall Park
Sacombe Park
The Clumps
2

River Beane
Broad Water
Home Farm
The Cuts
Ware Lodge
Sacombe Lake
1

King Edward's Gorse
A414
18

A B C D E F
32 92 72 33

← 71
↑ 54

	A	B	C	D	E	F

High Trees Farm

Hatchett Farm

BEGGARMAN'S LA

Hatchett Poultry Farm

Beggarman's Wood

8

Fullars Common

Moorfield Common

Trenchern Hills

Hill Farm

Whitehill Farm

Langton's La

Shelly's Wood

Roughground Wood

7

21

CH

Cock's Wood

Potter's Green

Rigery Farm

RIGERY LA

6

Potter's Hall Farm

Labdens Farm

Rowney Priory

ROWNEY LA

Black Grove

5

Rowney Wood

LOWGATE LA

Standon Green End Farm

Willowtree Farm

20

Knoll Farm

SG12

LOWGATE LA

Standon Green End

SG11

4

Sacombe Green

Mott's Wood

Barwick Tributar

Church Wood

Dilly Wood

The Bourne

3

Low Wood

Salmonsley Wood

LONG END RD

Home Wood

19

Home Farm

MARSHALL'S LA

Sutes

CAMBRIDGE COTTS

2

Gages Wood

Marshall's Farm PH

Pullar Memorial Juh Mix Inf Sch

High Cross

Furzeground Wood

Marshall's

SOUTH DR

NORTH DR

PASSFIELD COTTS

1

Rennesley Garden Wood

Hazelwood Farm

Mark's Wood

SG12

Highcross Hill

A10

Gravelpit Wood

18

34	A		B	35	C		D	36	E		F

← 71
↓ 93

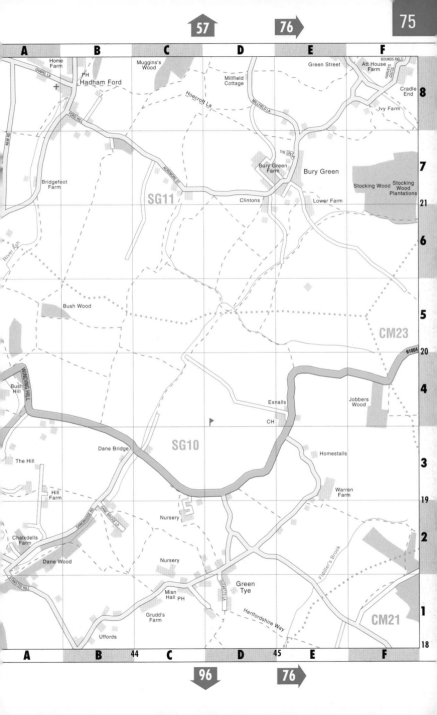

7 HOCKERILL CT
8 HARRINGTON CL
9 PRIORS
10 CLIFFORD CT
11 THOMAS HESKIN CT
12 MASTERMAN WHARF

88
1 BOYD CL
2 HEATH ROW
3 STORTFORD HALL RD
4 GROSVENOR HO
5 EATON HO
6 BELGRAVE HO

E CAUSEWAY
E OLD MALTINGS
LLER CT
MES CRES
D LION CT
KERS CT

Collins Cross
All Saints CE JMI Sch
Birchwood High Sch
Suntmererott Jun & Inf Schs
PLAW HATCH CNR
Hotel
F Ball Gd
Hotel
Birchanger Green Services
Start Hill Farm
A120 DUNMOW RD
CH
Mast
Stortford Hall Ind Pk
DUNMOW RD
Hockerill Sch
Bishop's Stortford
Hertfordshire & Essex High Sch
Hockerill
Herts & Essex High Sch
Herts & Essex Comm
CM23
Ellen Friend Ho
Thorn Grove JMI Sch
Little Beldams
Harps Farm
Grate Beldams
Great Jehkins
1 KIMBERLEY CL
2 MILL ST
3 MILLSIDE
Sewage Works
COPTHALL CL
THE POPLARS
Long Plantation
Twyford Bury Farm
THE MEWS
River Stort
TWYFORD MILL
CM22
Hall Farm
The Hall
Great Hallingbury
Ladywell Plantation
Anvil Cross
Captain's Plantation
Hallingbury Park
Latchmore Bank
LATCHMORE BANK
HALLINGBURY RD
PORT LA
Howe Green
Howe Green House Sch
Ladywell
Morleys
Normandale Kennels
HALLINGBURY CL
NEW BARN LA
BARKERS MEAD
GEORGE GREEN
PH
Woodside Green

A B C D E F

8 7 21 6 5 20 4 3 19 2 1 18

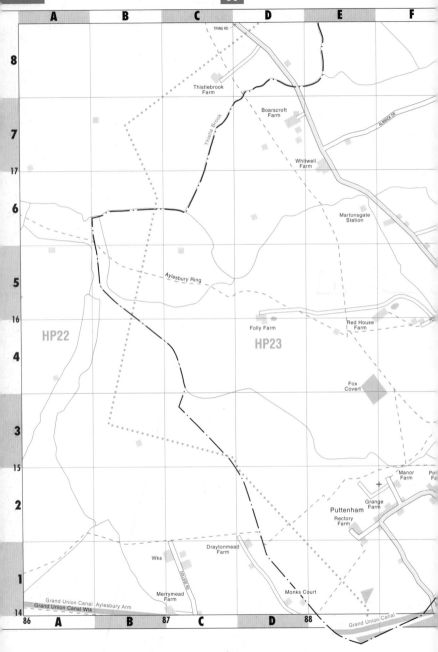

60

A   B   C   D   E   F

8

THISTLEBROOK FARM

Thistlebrook
Farm

Boarscroft
Farm

ALNWICK DR

7

Thistle Brook

17

Whitwell
Farm

6

Martonsgate
Station

Aylesbury Ring

5

16

Folly Farm

Red House
Farm

HP22

HP23

4

Fox
Covert

3

15

Manor
Farm

Pot
Fa

2

Puttenham

Grange
Farm

Rectory
Farm

Draytonmead
Farm

Wks

COLLEGE RD

1

Monks Court

Grand Union Canal Aylesbury Arm
Grand Union Canal Wlk

Merrymead
Farm

Grand Union Canal

14

86   A   B   87   C   D   88   E   F

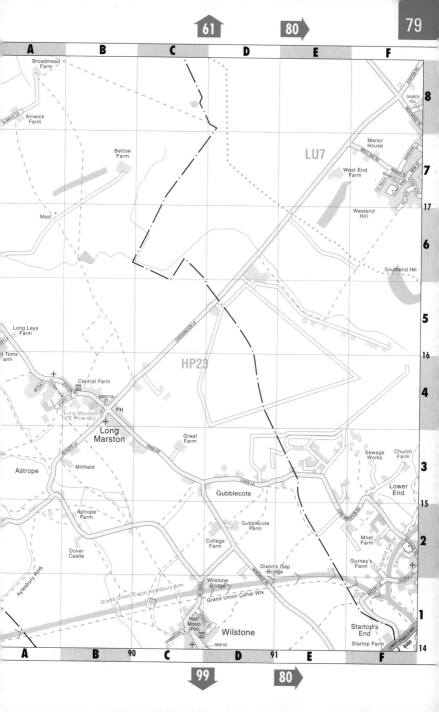

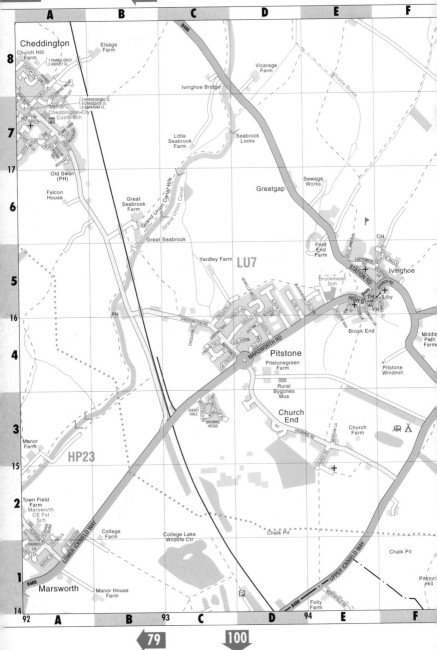

A   B   C   D   E   F

Cheddington
Church Hill Farm
Elsage Farm

1 PAINES ORCH
2 ASHLEY CL

Ivinghoe Bridge

3 HORSESHOES CL
4 CHASESIDE CL
5 BARKHAM CL

Vicarage Farm

Whistle Brook

Cheddington Cty Comb Sch

The Green

Old Swan (PH)

Falcon House

Little Seabrook Farm

Seabrook Locks

Greatgap

Sewage Works

Great Seabrook Farm

Grand Union Canal Wlk
Grand Union Canal

Great Seabrook

Yardley Farm

LU7

Ford End Farm

CH

Ivinghoe

Brookmead Sch

STATION RD

LADYSMITH RD

THE BAULK

TH
Liby
HIGH ST
YH

PH

CHEDDINGTON RD

Brook End

Middle Path Farm

Pitstone
Pitstonegreen Farm

MARSWORTH RD

Pitstone Windmill

Rural Bygones Mus

SHORT HALE

BROWNS HEDGE

Church End

VICARAGE RD

MEADOW LA

Church Farm

Manor Farm

HP23

Town Field Farm
Marsworth CE Fst Sch

LOWER ICKNIELD WAY

College Farm

College Lake Wildlife Ctr

Chalk Pit

UPPER ICKNIELD WAY

Chalk Pit

Pitston Hill

Marsworth

B489

Manor House Farm

P

NORTHFIELD RD

Folly Farm

B488

8   7   17   6   5   16   4   3   15   2   1   14

92   A   B   93   C   D   94   E   F

A B C D E F

8
7
17
6
5
16
4
3
15
2
1
14

Willow Farm

DAGNALL RD

B4506

Dell Farm

B4540

P

DUKES AVE

The Green

White Lion

ESCARPMENT AVE

CROSSWAY

P

Whipsnade Wildlife Animal Park

Chiltern Farm

MAIN RD N

DUNSTABLE RD

MISS JOANS RIDE

CUT THROAT AVE

VALLEY CT

HUMPHREY TALBOT AVE

P

Collyers

Ickfield Way Path

Bethshan Farm

Dagnall

Lower Farm

Ickfield Way Path

HAMILTON CL

PH
Dagnall Farm

B4506

CHESTNUT CL

SAINT LUCY'S

HUNTSMANS

Highbury Farm

CH

LU6

Dagnall Cty Fst Sch

MALTING LA

Dagnallhall Farm

STUDHAM LA

HP4

Cross Keys Farm

Hall

Cha Reetaa

Man's Grove

Well Farm

Sewage Works

MAIN RD S

RINGSHALL RD

Oakley Wood

ngshall pice

Meadow Farm

Goose Hill Farm

Levi Spring

Ashridge Farm

Hall Farm

Hoo Wood

Lamsey Farm

HEMEL HEMPSTEAD RD

Milebarn Farm

TRUST COTTS

BEACON RD

Ringshall

B4506

anhoe emmon

A4146

Gade Plas

99 00

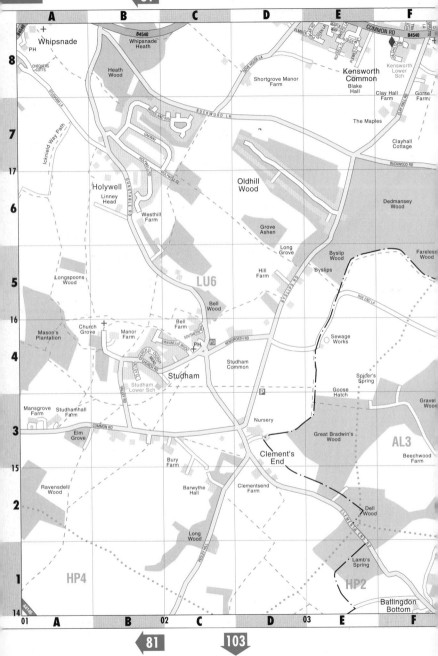

A B C D E F

8

Whipsnade

PH

CHEQUERS COTTS

Whipsnade Heath

B4540

Heath Wood

Shortgrove Manor Farm

Kensworth Common

Blake Hall

COMMON RD

B4540

Kensworth Lower Sch

Clay Hall Farm

Gorse Farm

7

ICKNIELD WAY PATH

STOCKWELL LA

WOODLAND RISE

OAKWAY

HOLYWELL RD

DUNSTABLE RD

BUCKWOOD LA

HOLYWELL CL

The Maples

Clayhall Cottage

BUCKWOOD RD

17

6

Holywell

Linney Head

Westhill Farm

Oldhill Wood

Dedmansey Wood

5

Longspoons Wood

LU6

Grove Ashen

Long Grove

Hill Farm

Byslips

Byslip Wood

Fareless Wood

ROE END LA

ST PETERS RD

16

4

Mason's Plantation

Church Grove

Manor Farm

CHURCH RD

VALLEY CL

MEAD

CHURCH RD

Bell Farm

SWANNELLS WOOD

SOUTHEND

Bell Wood

PH

PH

KENSWORTH RD

Studham Common

Sewage Works

Spicer's Spring

Goose Hatch

Gravel Wood

Studham

VALLEY RD

Studham Lower Sch

P

AL3

3

Mansgrove Farm

Studhamhall Farm

COMMON RD

Elm Grove

Nursery

P

Clement's End

Great Bradwin's Wood

Beechwood Farm

15

2

Ravensdell Wood

Bury Farm

PRIEST HILL

Barwythe Hall

Clementsend Farm

Long Wood

CLEMENTS END RD

Dell Wood

1

HP4

Lamb's Spring

HP2

Ballingdon Bottom

14

01 A 02 B C 03 D E F

A B C D E F

LYNCH HILL
B4540
PH
Works
Red Cow Farm
Hill Farm
PIPERS LA

LU6

Cell Park Farm
Foxdell Farm
Wr Twr

Kensworth Gorse
Markyatecell Park
Luton Rd
Caddington Hall

Markyate Cell

Lower Farm

Manor Farm
Tanglewood
Markyate
High Winds Farm

RUCKWOOD RD

Cemy
PARK VIEW DR

Gooseacre
Markyate JMI Sch
CAVENDISH RD
OLD VICARAGE GDNS
COWPER RD
WESLEY RD
ROMAN WAY
THE RIDINGS
PIPPS HILL
HICKS RD

ckwood Stubs

AL3

NORTH CT
PH
HIGHS RD
SCHOOL LA
LONG ROW

PARKFIELD RD
THE COPPINS
PARK CLS
THE DELL
CLEVELAND RD 1
WILLIAM ST 2
KING ST 3
THE CLOSE 4
SUMMER WLK 5
SURGUMM
FARMERS CL
MANOR CT
CHY CRW
LONGCROFT
PEEPERS CL
A5

Roe End Farm
Hertfordshire Way
Feveralls Farm
Sebright Sch
Cheverell's Green
Hertfordshire Way

Hollybush Lodge
ROE END LA
Roe End
Cheverells
PICKFORD RD

Sheepyard Dell

Cotton Spring Farm
FRIENDLESS LA

ennels Lodge
Furze Cover
Cheverell's Belt
Gillhill Plantation
Friendless Wood

Valley Cottage
Valleybottom Farm

Beechwood House
Beechwood Park Prep Sch
Valleylane Cottage
VALLEY LA

P2
Dean Wood
Babies Wood
PRODGERS LA
Hill Farm
Moonshine Wood

8
7
17
6
5
16
4
3
15
2
1
14

A B 05 C D 06 E F

A B C D E F

8
MARKYATE RD B4540
Woodside Farm and Wildfowl Park
Grove Farm
Limekiln Plantation
Birchin Grove
Chalk Wood
The New Lodge
Gibraltar Cottages

7
Top Spring
Middle Spring
Half Moon La
Pepsal End
LU1
Pepsalend Farm
Heavens Wood
Gibraltar Farm

17
Stable Spring
Sewage Works

6
Broomhill Leys Wood
Bonner's Farm
Ivy Farm
WINDMILL RD

Doone Brae Farm
Smallgrove Farm
Cockrums
Lady Bray Farm
KENNEL LA

5
Rainbow Hall Farm
Hogtrough Wood
AL5
Brickfield Farm
Eight Acre Spring
W W

16

4
A5
School House Farm
Hotel
Works
OLD WATLING ST
Highfield Farm
Chad Lane Farm
Hill & Coles Farm
AL3
Turner Hall Farm
FACTORY LA

3
River Hall
River Ver
Friar's Wash

15
Hertfordshire Way
A5

2
Millfield Cottage
MILL LA
Friendless La
PRIORY
HIGH ST
PO
SINGLETS LA
Sunny Ridge
Verlam End
DUNSTABLE RD
A5183

THORNLEY
CEMY
ROLL RD
CHURCHEND
VICARAGE GDNS
Flamstead

1
Flamstead JMI Sch
Delmerend Farm
Norringtonend
Lower Sawpit Wood
Showground

14
07 A B 08 C D 09 E F

64
86

A B C D E F

8

7

17

6

5

16

4

3

15

2

1

14

Luton Hoo
Home Farm

Saw Mill

The Gables

FARM RD

LIMETREE AVE

Tumble
Grove

LU1

Hillside

Graves
Wood

Sewage
Works

River Lea or Lee

LANGLEY CRTS

SOUTHERN RISE

B653

East
Hyde

LOWER HARPENDEN RD

MINSDEN
BRIDGE DR
CNR

PH

B653

LU2

Lee Valley
Wlk

West
Hyde

Lady Bute's
Lodge

Circus
Wood

LONDON RD

KENNEL LA

Beech
Ridge

Thrales
End

Thrales End
Farm

COOTERS END LA

Cooters Hill
Farm

Long
Spring

CHAMBERS DELL

SPRING LA

ANNABLES LA

THE COMMON

PH

Kinsbourne
Green

+

PH

+ PO

LUTON RD

KINSBOURNE

KINSBOURNE
CRES

KLONDYKE
RIDGEWAY

Kings Sch

Cooters End
Farm

AMBROSE LA

Dove House
Farm

Pollard's
Farm

AL5

KENNESBOURNE
CT

KINSBOURNE GREEN LA

TINTERN CL

CHRISTCHURCH

HEROS WAY

VALE CL

TUFFNELLS CL

RIDGE AVE

DENSBARTLEY CL

LUTON AVE

WELL CL

LIMBRICK RD

RIDGE AVE

HOMEDELL RD

BRAMBLE CL
ST NICHOLAS CT
CLOSE
TOWER CLOSE
PL
BEECH CT
BOND CT
PO

Annables
Farm

Mast

Faulkners End
Farm

Wood End
JMI Sch

WOOD END RD

SCALE DF

HOLLY GDNS

HEATHVIEW

MALCOLM CT

BOW FIELD

HARPENDEN
ROW

ST NICHOLAS
OTTERDON CL

HARPENDEN
PARK MOUNT

HARPENDEN

LAMBOURN

BOND CT

WALKDEN LA

PARK HILL

STH

Delgarth

ROUNDWOOD LA

ALCOT

Roundwood
Park Sch

Roundwood
Prim Sch

LAGATE AVE

TANGLEWOOD

BROADFIELDS

PARK AVE S

St Hilda's
Sch

THE COPSE

Northfield
Spring

LUTON RD

Harpenden
Stables

HARTWELL RD

TOWNSEND LA
TOWNSEND CL

ST ANDREW'S AVE

BADINGHAM DR

PARK AVE

DORCHESTER AVE

HARMSTEAD AVE

AL3

HARPENDEN

A B 11 C D 12 E F

106
86

87 67

A B C D E F

8

Codicote Bottom
Three Hills
POYNDERS MEADOW 1
THE OPENING 2
NEW TOWN 3
COWARDS LA
Bottom Farm
Ayot Lodge
Hollowdane Spring
Long Valley
DARK LA
ST ALBANS RD

Abbotshay
Hertfordshire Way
Brimstone Wood
SG4

7

Ayot Park
Lord Mead La
Ayot House
River Mimram
KIMPTON RD

17

BIBBS HALL LA
PH
Ayot St Lawrence
Pulmer Water

6

Ayot Farm
Shaw's Corner

Harepark Spring
Norfolk Cottages
Ryefield Farm

5

BRIDE HALL LA
HILL FARM LA
Hill Farm
Hurstling's Wood
Linces Spring

16

Bride Hall
AL6

4

Little Norfolk Wood
Round Spring
Ayot Bury

Great Norfolk Wood
Stocking Springs
CODICOTE RD
Dowdell's Wood
Ayot St Peter

3

Scratching Grove
Threegroves Wood
Fish Wood
AYOT ST PETER RD
War Meml

15

Cherrytree Spring
Warren Wood
Ayot Place
Saul's Wood

2

Coneydell Spring
Ayot Mountfitchet
Ayot Greenway

Bladder Wood
Manor Farm

Robinson's Wood
AL4
Hunter's Bridge
Bowle's Wood
WATERENDLA

1

River Lea or Lee
Ayot Greenway
Sparrowhall Bridge
AYOT LITTLE

Lea Valley Wlk
Sparrowhall Farm
James's Wood

14

19 A B 20 C D 21 E F

A   B   C   D   E   F

8

Perrywood
Farm

Chain Wlk

Hazeldell
Wood

Burgess
Corner

Widow
Bushes

Patchendon

SG3

rens
Wood

Long
Walk

Chain Wlk

Lower Blackbuck
Wood

Great Gobions
Farm

7

PERRYWOOD LA

A119

Upper Blackbuck
Wood

17

cholson's
Wood

Bramfield
Woods

Back La

Valentine
Spring

Wks

6

Barber's
Close

Chain Wlk

Bright's
Hill

Mill

A419

Open
Bailey

Basil's
Park

Greenhill

Sally Rainbow's
Dell

Winter
Dell

AL6

Symond's
Wood

Row
Wood

5

SG14

16

Greenhall
Farm

Little
Gobions

4

PH

BRAMFIELD RD

LOWER RD

Bramfield
House

BURY LA

PO

Bramfield

MAIN RD

Priest
Wood

Bramfield Park
Wood

Chain Wlk

Bramfieldbur

Bramfield Place
Farm

3

Park La

HULL GROVE RD

Sewage
Wks

BRAMFIELD LA

15

Chain Wlk

Well
House

2

Westend
Farm

PATTLE HILL

Bacon's
Green

Westend

Tattle
Hill

Gravel
Pits

HERTFORD RD

Bacon's
Farm

Oakfield
Plantation

BRAMFIELD RD

Goldings

1

14

A   B   C   D   E   F

A B C D E F

8

Burr's Green Farm

Bengeo Temple Farm

Roads Wood

HIGH RD
A119

A602

TONWELL CX

Wtr Twr

Stapleford

Clusterbolt Wood

THE ORCHARD

Tonwell

7

PH

Southend Farm

Wks

PH

CHAPPELL CT

WARE RD

Tonwell St Mary's CE Prim Sch

BARLEYCROFT

17

Hertfordshire Way

CHURCH LA

STONY HILLS

Stapleford Jun Mix Inf Sch

Stonyhills

6

PH

Dimmings

Sewage Wks

Upper Stonyhills Wood

Chapmore-end Farm

ANCHOR

Foxleys Wood

Chapmore End

Payr Ha

A119

River Beane

High Trees Farm

PH

WESTMILL RD

5

Flowersash Wood

16

Bengeo Lammas Land

SG12

Westmill Farm

Bullsmill

SACOMBE RD

POPLAR VIEW

4

SG14

Rickneys

COURTYARD MEWS

PALMER CT

GARDEN TERR

Bardon Clumps

OLIVER CT

BEETHAM CT

RIVER CT

WADESMILL RD

River Rib

3

Waterford Hall Farm

Gravel Pits

St John's Wood

Oak Wood

BRAMFIELD

15

Hertfordshire Way

HIGH RD

Eight Acre Plantation

2

Waterford

Gravel Pit

Ware Park Farm

Cowshed Corner

Waterford Marsh

Ware Park

NORTH RD

THE ORCHARD

Bardon Farm

1

A119

TIMBER ORCH

GREAT MOLEWOOD

THE WICK

COPPER CHAS

THE AVENUE

WADESMILL RD

THE VALE

1 BENGEO MEADOWS
2 TEMPLE FIELDS
3 CROUCHFIELD
4 BENGEO MEWS
5 TEMPLE CT
6 BARTLETT'S MEAD
7 SHEPARDS CT
8 BENGEO HO

Goldings

Bengeo Prim Sch

14

31

A

B

32

C

33

D

E

F

91

113

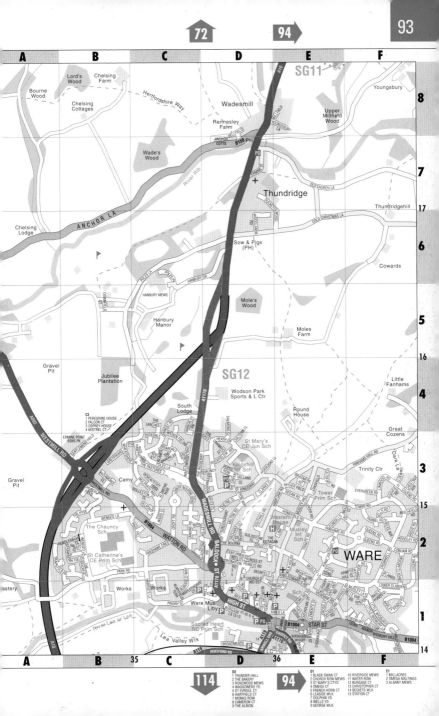

SG11

Bourne Wood

Lord's Wood   Chelsing Farm

Chelsing Cottages

Hertfordshire Way

Wadesmill

Wade's Wood

Rennesley Farm

Upper Millfield Wood

Youngsbury

ANCHOR LA

River Rib

Chelsing Lodge

B158 PH

Thundridge

OLD CHURCH LA

Thundridgehill   17

COLD CHRISTMAS LA

Sow & Pigs (PH)   6

Cowards

POLE LA   POLE LA

HANBURY DR

Hanbury Mews

DOWNFIELD

Mole's Wood

Moles Farm   5

Little Fanhams   16

Gravel Pit

Jubilee Plantation

Hanbury Manor

SG12

Wodson Park Sports & L Ctr

Great Cozens

Round House

WESTMILL RD

Gravel Pit

A602

ERMINE POINT BSNS PK

South Lodge

C3
1 PEREGRINE HOUSE
2 FALCON CT
3 OSPREY HOUSE
4 KESTREL CT

The Larches

St Mary's CE Jun Sch

Kingshill Inf Sch

Trinity Ctr   3

Cemy

The Chauncy Sch

WATTON RD

B1004

WADESMILL RD

BALDOCK ST A1170

The Pastures

Tower Prim Sch

EVERGREEN LA   15

Western House

Musley Inf Sch

WARE   2

St Catherine's CE Prim Sch

PARK RD

The Bourne

H

The Octagan

PO

Works

Works

PRIORY ST

Ware Mus Liby

HIGH ST

DEERFIELD CT

KIBES LA

CHURCH ST

STAR ST   1

Sacred Heart RC Prim Sch

River Lea or Lee

B1004

Lea Valley Wlk

BROADMEADS

Hertford Rd A119

A1170

14

A   B   35   C   D   36   E   F

D2
1 THUNDER HALL
2 THE BAKERY
3 RONEWOOD MEWS
4 WAGGONERS YD
5 ST EVROUL CT
6 HARTFIELD CT
7 MONAS ROW
8 CAMERON CT
9 THE ALBION

D1
1 BLACK SWAN CT
2 CHURCH ROW MEWS
3 ST MARY'S CTYD
4 OMEGA CT
5 FRENCH HORN CT
6 LEASIDE WLK
7 DOLPHIN YD
8 WELLS YD
9 GEORGE YD

10 RIVERSIDE MEWS
11 WATER ROW
12 BURGAGE CT
13 CHRISTOPHER CT
14 BECKETS WLK
15 STATION CT

E1
1 MILLACRES
2 OMEGA MALTINGS
3 ALBANY MEWS

| | A | B | C | D | E | F |

8

Home Farm
Hanley Spring
The Arboretum
Goss Covert
Harecroft Brow
Fabdens
Sawtrees Farm
Halfyards Common
Burleigh Common
Castlebury Farm
Nursery

River Rib

7
OLD CHURCH LA
Timber Hall
Hertfordshire Way
Baker's End

17
COLD CHRISTMAS LA
Cold Christmas
Buckney Wood

6
Swangles Farm
Nimne Wood

Ashridge Common
Legges Cottage

5
Harcamlow Way
SG12
Appleton Farm
Cook's Farm
New Hall Farm
Hogtrough La
Milletts
Babbs Green
Newhall Green

16
Noah's Ark
COONWOOD COTTS
Helh a Green
Fanhams Grange
Long La
Wareside
B

4
Fanhams Hall
THE CHASE
HILL SIDE COTTS
Reeves Green
The Lodge
White Horse (PH)

3
Morley Ponds
Wareside CE Prim Sch
Priors Wood Prim Sch
Morley Hall
Newhouse Farm
Swades Farm

15
BEACON RD
Wood La
Newhole Farm
Mardocks Mill

2
THE VINEYARD
Butlers Hall
Young Wood
Mardocks Farm

River Ash

1
Priorswood Cottages
Waterplace Farm
Ford
Harcamlow Way
Widbury House Nursery

14
B1004 WIDBURY HILL
Brokengall Hill

| 37 | A | B | 38 | C | D | 39 | E | F |

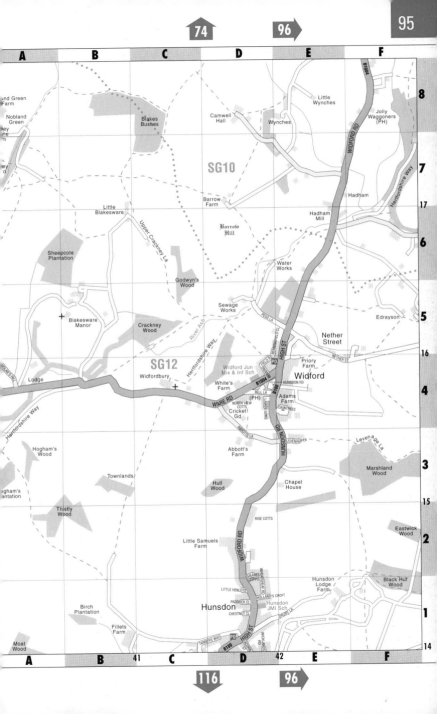

74 96

A | B | C | D | E | F

8

B1004

Little Wynches

Nobland Green Farm

Blakes Bushes

Camwell Hall

Wynches

Jolly Waggoners (PH)

WIDFORD RD

7

SG10

Hertfordshire Way

Hadham

17

Barrow Farm

Little Blakesware

Upper Crackney La

Barrow Hill

Hadham Mill

6

Sheepcote Plantation

Godwyn's Wood

Water Works

Blakesware Manor

Crackney Wood

River Ash

Sewage Works

PEGS LA

Edrayson

5

BENINGFIELD CL

Nether Street

16

SG12

Hertfordshire Way

Widfordbury

Widford Jun Mix & Inf Sch

FIELD LA

HIGH ST

Priory Farm

NETHER ST

Lodge

White's Farm

B1004

HUNSDON RD

Widford

4

WARE RD

(PH)

BELL LA

NORTH VIEW COTTS

LANES GDNS

Adams Farm

DAINTREES

HUNSDON RD

Cricket Gd

HANDS LA

Abbott's Farm

LEVENAGE LA

Levenage La

Hogham's Wood

Marshland Wood

3

Townlands

Hull Wood

Chapel House

Hogham's Plantation

Thistly Wood

15

RISE COTTS

Eastwick Wood

2

Little Samuels Farm

WIDFORD RD

CLARES SHEPPAL RD

HOLLAND'S CROFT

Hunsdon Lodge Farm

Black Hut Wood

Birch Plantation

LITTLE HENLEYS

PADDOCK CL

Hunsdon JMI Sch

DRURY LA

1

Fillets Farm

CHESTNUT LA

Hunsdon

HIGH ST

WORKHOUSE RD

Moat Wood

TANNERS WAY

B180

14

A | B | 41 | C | D | 42 | E | F

A | **B** | **C** | **D** | **E** | **F**

8

Bucklers Hall Farm

Brook La

Blount's Farm

Perry Green

The Chase Farm

Sacombs Ash

7

Hertfordshire Way

The Hoops Inn (PH)

The Bourne

Hylands Nursery

17

Warrens

SACOMBS ASH LA

The Queens Head (PH)

South-end

Old Park

Allen's Green

6

Minges

St Elizabeth's Sch & Home

Dukes Farm

SG10

Allensgreen Wood

5

Turtle Farm

Covey's La

Chandlers

NETHER ST

The Rick

Figgers Brook

Chandlers La

16

CM21

Hardings

4

Levenage Spring

Gangles

GANGLES

3

Mole Wood

Carters

Stonards

Hoskins Farm

Lawns Wood

Fryars

15

High Trees

Actons Farm

The Man of Grove

2

Maplecroft Wood

Queen's Wood

Battles Wood

Great Pennys Farm

Jeffs

Mabletts

SG12

1

Keeper's

Golden Grove

Sayes Coppice

14

CM20

43 | **A** | **B** | **44** | **C** | **D** | **45** | **E** | **F**

A   B   C   D   E   F

Chapel End

Wilstone
Great Farm

Wilstone
Green

B489

James
Farm

8

Startop's End
Resr

Manor
Farm

Wilstone
Little Farm

Cemy

Tringford

LONG FORD RD

7

Tringford
Resr

LOWER ICKNIELD WAY

P

Wilstone Resr
Nature Reserve

Tringford
Farm

13

Landing
Stage

Little Tring
Farm

Grand Union Canal Wlk

Little Tring

6

LITTLE TRING RD

Lower
Farm

Drayton
Beauchamp

HP22

Upper
Farm

Grand Union Canal Wlk

B489

HOBSONS WLK

5

HP23

The
Old Rectory

Miswell
Farm

12

Bridge
Farm

GREEN END

Miswell
House

Drayton
Bridge

Broadview
Farm

ICKNIELD WAY

Mast

Windmill

4

BUCKLAND RD

LONDON RD

THORNE WAY

WENWELL CL

WHARF
ROW

B4009

Grand Union Canal
(Wendover Arm) (disused)

Bucklandwharf

Crows Nest
(PH)

Beeches
Farm

TRING HILL

B488

B4635

Goldfield
Inf Sch

3

Aston
Clinton

UPPER ICKNIELD WAY

Lodge
Farm

GRAVEL DR

Icknield
House

AYLESBURY RD

Cemy

Sch

B4635

WESTERN RD

PARK RD

STANLEY GDNS

11

DAGGERS END LA

A41

2

Drayton
Manor

FOX LA

BUCKTON LA

Daniel's
Hole

P

Astonhill
Coppice

Buckland Hoo

Stud
Farm

West Leith
Farm

WEST LEITH

West Leith

1

Aston Hill
Farm

HASTOE HILL

10

A   B   90   C   D   91   E   F

A B C D E F

Golding's Spring

Hanging Isley

Moneybury Hill

Icknield Way Path

Aldbury Nowers

Howlett's Wood

Walk Wood

Sallow Copse

Tim's Spring

CH

Hotel

Stocks

Little Stocks

Forest Trails

Pitstone Common

The Bridgewater Monument

Hertfordshire Way

Visitor Centre

Ridgeway

Westland Farm

Aldbury Sch CE Prim Sch

PH

Old Copse

Thunderdell Cottages

Church Farm

PO

Aldbury

HP23

Aldbury Common

HP4

Gryme's Dell

Hertfordshire Way

Rail Copse

Brightwood

The Hangings

Tom's Hill

Tom's Hill House

The Scrubs

Bottom Spring

Broomfield Spring

Northchurch Common

New Ground Farm

Grand Union Canal Wlk

High Spring

Norcott Hill

New Ground

Grand Union Canal

Norcott Hall Farm

Marina

Norcott Court Farm

Hill Farm

Cow Roast

PH

Norcott Court

Tring

B4506

Station Rd

Newground Rd

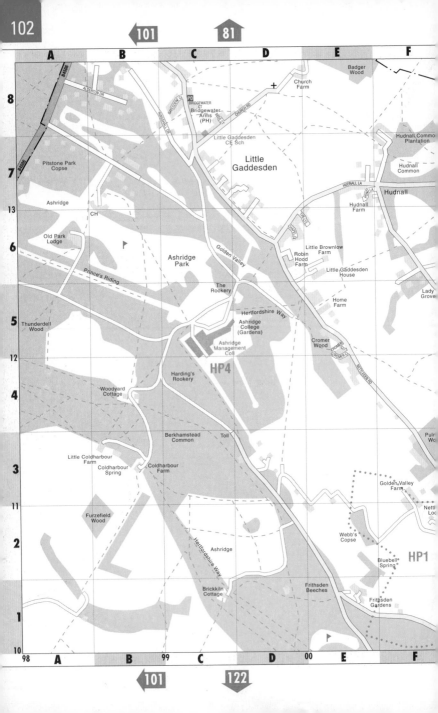

101
81

A B C D E F

8

Badger
Wood

Church
Farm

BRIDGEWATER
Bridgewater
Arms
(PH)

Little Gaddesden
CE Sch

Hudnall Common
Plantation

7

Pitstone Park
Copse

Little
Gaddesden

Hudnall
Common

HUDNALL LA

Hudnall

13

Ashridge

CH

Hudnall
Farm

6

Old Park
Lodge

Ashridge
Park

Golden Valley

Little Brownlow
Farm

Robin
Hood
Farm

Little Gaddesden
House

Prince's Riding

The
Rookery

Home
Farm

Lady
Grove

5

Thunderdell
Wood

Hertfordshire Way

Ashridge
College
(Gardens)

Cromer
Wood

12

Ashridge
Management
Coll

HP4

Harding's
Rookery

4

Woodyard
Cottage

Berkhamstead
Common

Toll

3

Little Coldharbour
Farm

Coldharbour
Spring

Coldharbour
Farm

Golden Valley
Farm

11

Furzefield
Wood

Nettl
Lod

2

Hertfordshire Way

Ashridge

Webb's
Copse

Bluebell
Spring

HP1

1

Brickkiln
Cottage

Frithsden
Beeches

Frithsden
Gardens

10

98 A B 99 C D 00 E F

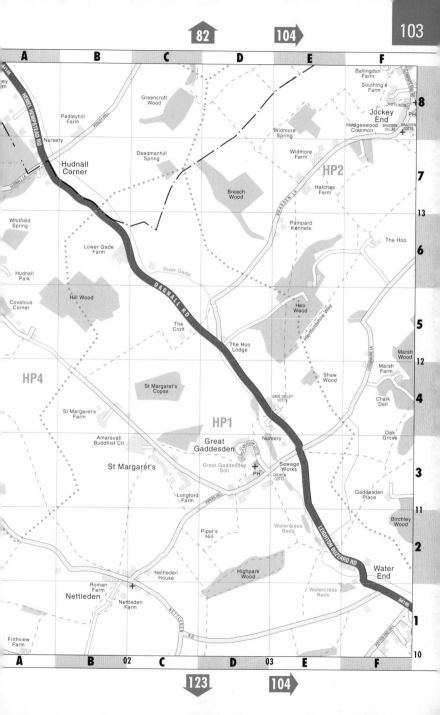

A **B** **C** **D** **E** **F**

WEST DENE

8

Dean La

Babies Wood

Little Woodend Cottages

Newland's Wood

Prior's Spring

Yewtree Spring

AL3

Scratch Wood

WOOD END LA

7

Hertfordshire Way

Six Tunnels Farm

Whitehouse Farm

Abel's Grove

Wood End Farm

PUDDEPHAT'S LA

Puddephats Farm

Green La

LEDGEMORE LA

Water Twr

13

Gaddesden Row JMI Sch

Gaddesden Row

Teakettle Wood

Upper Wood Farm

6

Gaddesden Hoo Cottages

The Lane House

GADDESDEN ROW

Round Spring Wood

Gree W

Ledgemore Farm

New Gorse

Golden Parsonage

Long Wood

5

Ye Olde Chequers (PH)

Elmtree Farm

12

Marsh Wood

Threecraft Wood

HP2

Corner Farm

GADDESDEN LA

4

Home Farm

London Wood

Hawbush Farm

3

Stable Wood

Big Wood

Thomas's Wood

LEYS GREEN LA

11

Birchley Wood

Crown & Sceptre (PH)

Briden's Camp

Millhill Farm

Millhill Gorse

Eastbrook Farm

2

Hogstrough Dell

Chalkpit Dell

Lovetts End Farm

DODDS LA

1

LEIGHTON BUZZARD RD

A4146

Red Lion (PH)

HP1

Varney's Wood

Wood Farm

Little Lovetts End Farm

ESSEX MEAD 1
ST AGNELLS LA 2
THE DEE 3
OLD MAPLE 4

MOUNT

10

04 **A** 05 **B** **C** 06 **D** **E** **F**

84
106

A B C D E F

8
7
13
6
5
12
4
3
11
2
1
10

PH
Trowley Bottom
Trowley Bottom Farm
WOOD END LA
PURDINGTON LA
Grove Farm
Green La
Nirvana
Greenlane Farm
New Wood
Hay Wood
Holtsmore End Farm
Holtsmore End

HP 2

Hertfordshire Way

GOLDEN END LA
St Agnells Farm
Wr Twr
Redding Wood
REDDING LA
DUNSTABLE RD
A5183

Nursery

Nicholls Farm
Nicholl's Great Wood
Rabbitfield Spring

Flamsteadbury Farm
Bury Cottages
Bury Wood

Church End

AL3

SAUNDERS LA

Great Revel End Farm
Woodside
Pantake Wood
Hotel
The Aubreys

Smallholding
The Beeches

Little Revel End

AUBREY LA

HEMEL HEMPSTEAD RD
B487

Nicky Way

1 ASHBY CT
2 EVERSDEN CT
3 LANGSTANTON CT
4 SEDGWICK CT
5 HADDENHAM CT

Brockswood Prim Sch

ELL'S FARM MEWS

B487

08   09

125
106

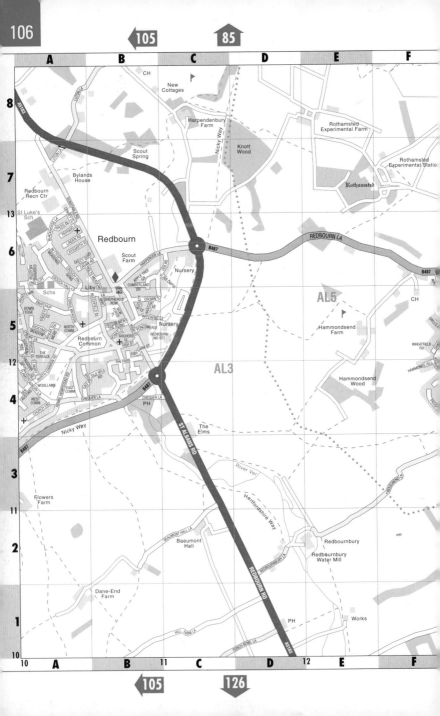

CH
New Cottages
Harpendenbury Farm
Rothamsted Experimental Farm

8

Nicky Way
Scout Spring
Knott Wood
Rothamsted Experimental Statio

Bylands House
Rothamsted

7
Redbourn Recn Ctr

13 St Luke's Sch

Redbourn
B487   REDBOURN LA
B487

6
Scout Farm
Nursery

Libv
CH

Nursery
AL5

Hammondsend Farm

5
Redbourn Common
REDBOURN IND EST

The Terrace

12
AL3

Hammondsend Wood

WOOLLAMS
WEST COMM
CHEQUER LA
PH

4
Nicky Way

WHEATFIELD RD

B487

The Elms
ST ALBANS RD

River Ver

3
Flowers Farm

Hertfordshire Way

11

BEAUMONT HALL LA
Baeumont Hall

2
Redbournbury
Redbournbury Water Mill
REDBOURN RD

Dane-End Farm

1
HILL FARM LA
PH
Works

PUNCH BOWL LA
A5183

10

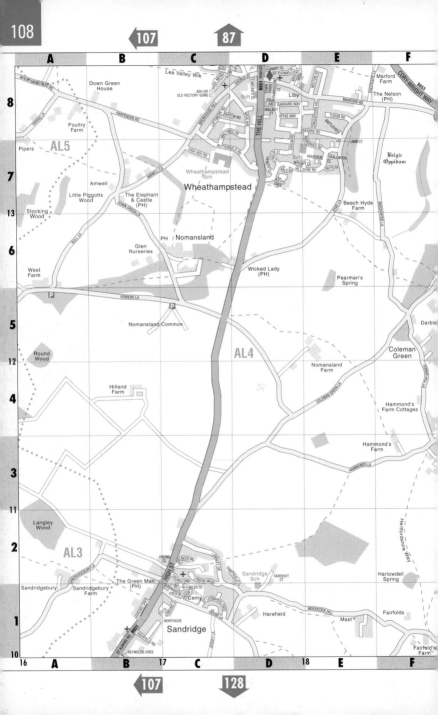

X GILLS PLUMBERS MERCHANTS

WELWYN GARDEN CITY

AL8

AL7

AL9

AL10

Sherrardspark Wood
Brock's Wood
Six Ways
Sherrardspark
Templewood JMI Sch
Oaklands Coll
Welwyn Campus
The Campus
Bridge Rd
Great North Rd
Valley Rd
Nursery
Handside
Applecroft Jun Sch
Sports Gd
Lemsford
Lemsford Springs (Nature Reserve)
Brocket Rd
New Rd
Stanborough
The Bull (PH)
Stanborough Bury
Coopers Green La
Lakeside Sch
Oaklands Coll (Lemsford Lane Campus)
Stanborough Sch
Stanborough Park
Boating Lake
Pol HQ
Stanborough Rd
Gosling Sports Park
Ski Ctr
West Burrowfield
East Burrowfield
Broadwater Rd
Twentieth Mile Bridge
Little Burrow
Welwyn Garden City
Peartree Prim Sch
Peartree
Holwell JMI Sch
Woodhall
Our Lady's JMI Sch
Chequers
Sir John Newsom Sch
Cemy
Creswick JMI Sch
Boundary House
Boundary La
Hatfield Hyde
Green Acres
Ryelands
Yachting Lake
Woodhall Farm
Lea Valley Wlk
Cheswick Plantation
Comet Way
Great North Rd
Mount Pleasant La
Hertford Rd

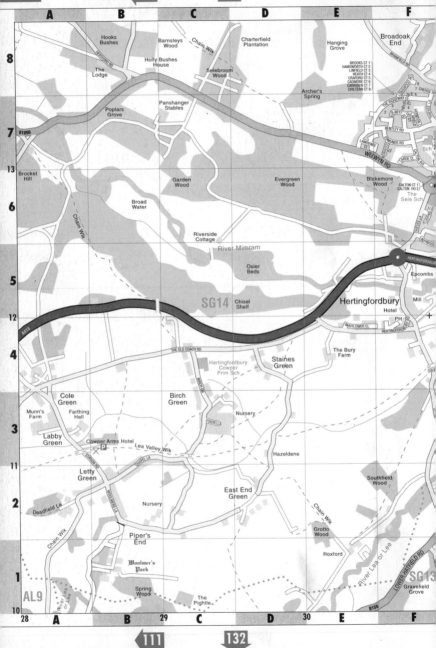

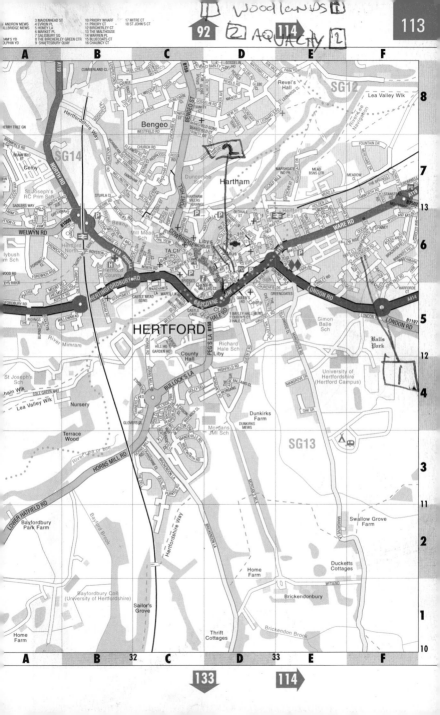

SG12

Lee Valley Wlk

New River

King's Mead

A119

8

HERTFORD RD

HILLSIDE

Hertford Regional Coll

Ware

A119 LONDON RD

CRANE MEAD

River Lee Navigation

Lee Valley Wlk

SPRING VIEW

MEADOW RD

Scott's Grotto

A119

CH

FORWAY

WARNER RD

LITTLE ACRES

BEECH MEWS

MALTINGS CT

PEERGLOW CTR

LONDON RD

7

WARE RD

TAYLOR TRAD EST

BURLEIGH RD

Wheatcroft Prim Sch

East The Pines JMI Sch

H

BIRDIE WAY

TEE SIDE

Thieves La

Presdales Sch

Pinewood Sch

Presdales

Post Wood

SG12

13

B1502

STANSTEAD RD

STOAT CL

FINCHES

Middleton Middle Sch

Amwellbury Farm

AMWELL HILL

A119

6

THE COPSE

A414

B1502

WALNUT TREE WLK

Rush Green Farm

STANSTEAD RD

Great Amwell

A414

Foxholes Farm

5

B1197

Jenningsbury Farm

DOWNFIELD RD

Leafyoak Farm

Leafyoak Wood

RYPES LA

HERTFORD RD

B15

12

JENNINGSBURY CT

WOODSTOCK CL

AMWELL PL

DOWNFIELD RD

SG13

4

VICARAGE CSWY

Hertford Heath JMI Sch

Much Wood

Chardingleye Farm

Hertford Heath

LONDON RD

RUSHEN DR

TRINITY

MOUNT PLEASANT RD

BEACON CT

OAK TREE CL

Golding's Wood

3

Great Stock Wood

WOODLAND RD

PRIORS CL

TRINITY RD

HARRINGTON CT

Springle House

11

PO

HEATHGATE

WOODS GN

WOOD GN

A119

Hailey Wood

Hailey

2

Balls Wood (Nature reserve)

THE HALL WK

COLLEGE RD

COLLEGE RD

Haileybury Coll

THE MEADOW

HAILEY LA

Hailey Farm

Hailey Hall Sch

Brides Farm

THE ROUNDINGS

ELBOW LA

High Wood

1

Hobbyhorse Wood

B1197

HERTFORD RD

Dells Wood

EN11

Roselands Prim Sch

DELLS WOOD CL

WESTBUSH CL

MORICE RD

10

HURWAYS CT
UMBERLAND CT
ESTFIELD RD
RRIS RISE
INTERSCROFT RD
LCHER RD

HODDESDON

Rye Park
Ryelands Prim Sch

EN11

CM19

Spitalbrook

Dobb's Weir
Dobb's Weir Bridge

Power Sta

Glen Faba

The Grove

Hailes Farm

Burles Farm

Netherhall (rems of)

Nazeing Mead

River Lea or Lee

River Lynch

Harcamlow Way

River Lee Navigation

Broxbourne

Lee Valley Country Park

Nurseries

Meadgate

Shottentons Farm

Keysers Estate

Works

EN10

EN9

Lower Nazeing

Brook Farm

HILLGROVE BSNS PK

B194 NAZEING RD

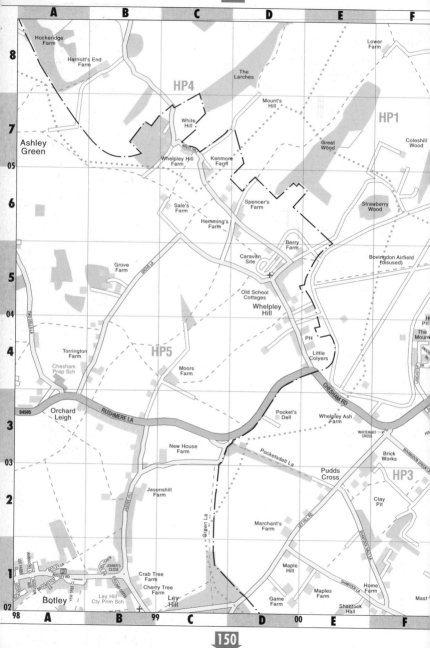

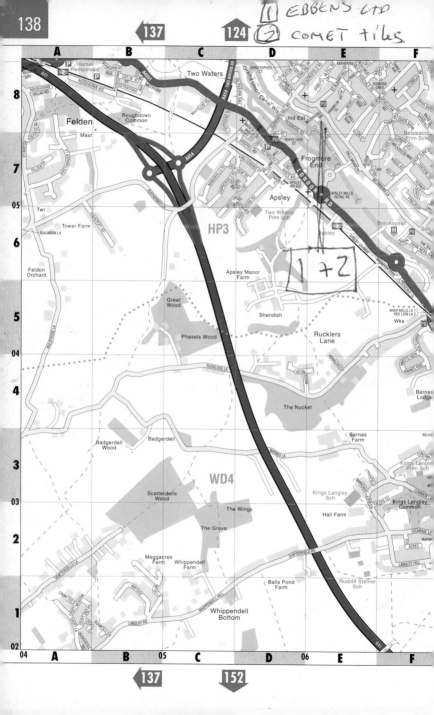

① EBBENS LTD
② COMET tiles

1 +2

159
146

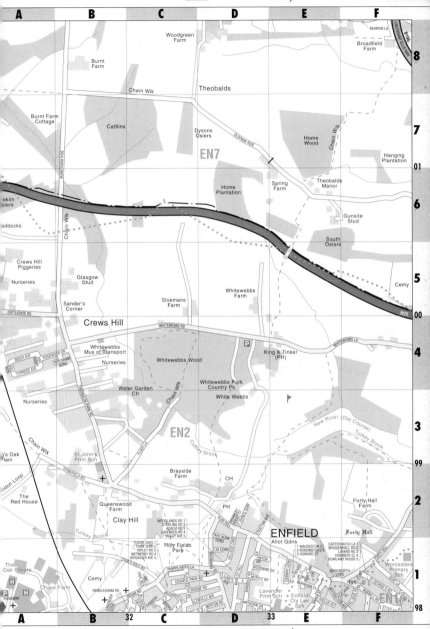

A B C D E F

8

BARROW LA

Woodgreen Farm

Broadfield Farm

Burnt Farm

Chain Wlk

Theobalds

7

Burnt Farm Cottage

Cattlins

Dysons Osiers

OLD PARK RIDE

Home Wood

Chain Wlk

Hanging Plantation

BURNT FARM RIDE

EN7

01

Home Plantation

Spring Farm

Theobalds Manor

6

ekiln osiers

Chain Wlk

addocks

Gunsite Stud

South Osiers

Crews Hill Piggeries

Nurseries

Glasgow Stud

Sloemans Farm

Whitewebbs Farm

Cemy

5

M25

00

Sander's Corner

CATTLEGATE RD

Crews Hill

WHITEWEBBS RD

WHITEWEBBS LA

4

BEECH AVE

ROSEWOOD DR

WROXHAM GDNS

CYPRESS AVE

Whitewebbs Mus of Transport

Nurseries

Whitewebbs Wood

P

King & Tinker (PH)

THEOBALDS PARK RD

Water Garden Ctr

Whitewebbs Park Country Pk

White Webbs

Chain Wlk

Nurseries

New River (Old Course)

Turkey Brook

3

EN2

FLASH LA

Cuffley Brook

's Oak lain

Chain Wlk

St John's Prim Sch

ndon Loop

STRAYFIELD RD

Brayside Farm

CH

99

The Red House

Queenswood Farm

Clay Hill

PH

2

Turkey Brook

WOODLANDS RD 1
STERLING RD 2
ACACIA RD 3
LAVENDER RD 4
VIOLET AVE 5

PARK BLOW GDNS

Forty Hall Farm

Forty Hall

ENFIELD

Allot Gdns

EN1

1 WADDESTON CT
2 KENSINGTON CT
3 HOWARD CT

CARTERHATCH LA 1
BRIDGENHALL RD 2
LAYARD RD 3
CHINNERY CL 4
DOWLAND HOUSE 5

The Oak Private

TUDOR CRES 1
YORK TERR 2
RIPLEY RD 3
WETBERRY RD 4
BRIGADIER AVE 5

Hilly Fields Park

ELM GDNS

Worcesters Primary Sch

1

H H

RIDGEWAY

P

Cemy

Chase Farm

COOK'S HOLE RD

CEDAR RD

BLOSSOM

REDDLESHAM RD

PHIPPS HATCH LA

CEDAR RD

PARK RD

BROOKE RD

GLENVILLE AVE

MERTON RD

HAWTHORN GR

ST LUKE'S

WINDMILL HILL

MYRTLE GR

WOODBINE GR

CONWAY GDNS

BURLEIGH WAY

KENILWORTH CRES

PH

ST GEORGE'S RD

Lavender Prim Sch

Enfield Cty Lwr Sch

98

A B **32** C D **33** E F

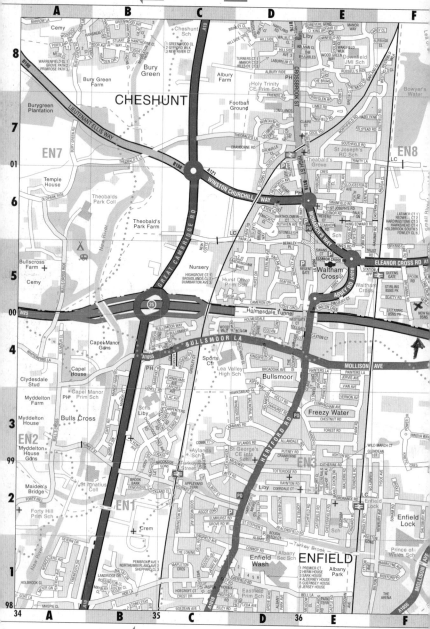

ans Mill La CM23 .....59 A1
ons Cl WD7 .....156 B4
ons Field Oaklands AL6 ..89 E8
eathampstead AL6 .....87 D1
ons Gate
neshunt EN8 .....148 F5
rrlow CM20 .....117 A2
ons Rd SG12 .....93 C2
nonsfield Ct AL6 .....89 E7
nonsfield Rd AL6 .....89 E8
opus Way HA4 .....175 A6
nelowes Ho EN5 .....171 D4
nterbury Cl Luton LU3 ...44 F4
irthwood HA6 .....174 F4
nterbury Cl AL1 .....127 F4
nterbury Ho
rehamwood WD6 .....170 A7
Watford WD1 .....167 C7
nterbury Rd
rehamwood WD6 .....170 A7
Watford WD1 .....167 B7
nterbury Way
oxley Green WD3 .....166 C6
evenage SG1 .....36 F2
e Rd AL1 .....128 B3
e Lodge SG1 .....57 E2
el Ho WD1 .....175 D6
el Manor Gdns EN7 ..162 D4
el Manor Prim Sch
1 .....162 B4
el Rd Enfield EN1 .....162 B3
tford WD1 .....167 E3
ell Ave WD3 .....164 C4
ell Rd WD3 .....164 D4
ell Way WD3 .....164 D4
ell Rd HA6 .....174 F6
elvere Wlk WD1 .....166 D8
onfield AL7 .....111 B4
ron Rd LU4 .....44 E4
tains Wlk HP4 .....122 D3
actacus Cottage View
1 .....163 A3
actacus Gn WD1 .....166 F3
avan La WD3 .....165 E2
bone Hill EN6,SG13 ...146 D5
te Cl SG14 .....112 F7
diff Cl SG2 .....69 B7
diff Gr LU1 .....63 D7
diff Pl SG2 .....2 A8
diff Rd Luton LU1 .....63 D7
tford WD1 .....167 B4
diff Way WD5 .....154 A7
digan Ct HU1 LU1 .....63 D8
digan Gdns 11 LU1 ...63 D7
digan St LU1 .....63 D7
dinal Ave WD6 .....170 B5
dinal Cl EN7 .....147 F5
dinal Ct
rehamwood WD6 .....170 B6
Luton LU2 .....45 D1
dinal Gr AL3 .....127 B1
dinal Newman
gh Sch LU2 .....31 C1
dinals Gate SG8 .....7 C6
dy Rd HP1 .....124 B3
ew Rd HA6 .....174 F4
ew Way WD1 .....175 F7
eys Croft HP4 .....122 C3
sbrook Rd AL2 .....141 B5
sbrooke Ave WD3 .167 D8
isbrooke Rd
rpenden AL5 .....86 C2
on LU4 .....44 E1
eton Rd EN8 .....148 E4
eton Rise AL6 .....89 C6
isle Ave AL3 .....127 D4
ton Bank 2 AL5 .....86 B1
ton Cl
rehamwood WD6 .....170 D5
on LU3 .....45 C2
ton Cres LU3 .....45 C2
ton Ct
Harpenden AL5 .....86 B1
tford WD1 .....167 C3
on Rd AL5 .....86 B2
man Ct HP23 .....99 F3
rnelite CM23 .....176 C2
rnelite Rd
on LU4 .....44 A3
rnelite Way HA3 .....176 C1
rnelite Wlk HP23 .....176 C2
rnelite Ct WD1 .....156 F1
naby Rd EN10 .....134 D2
narvon Rd EN5 .....171 E6
negie La SG12 .....45 A8
negie Rd AL3 .....127 D7
o La HP3 .....125 B1
ol Cl LU3 .....44 C8
te Ct LU1 .....63 E5
line Pl WD1 .....167 E3
line St LU1 .....63 D7
son Dr WD3 .....152 B3
penders Ave WD1 .175 E8
penders Ct AL5 .....85 D4
penders Park Sta
1 .....175 D7
enter Way EN6 .....159 D6
enters Rd EN1 .....162 C3
enters The CM23 ...76 B5
enters Wood Dr
3 .....164 B5
enters Yd HP23 .....100 A3
enter Cl SG14 .....112 F8
rigans CM23 .....76 E8
rington Ave WD6 .170 C4
rington Cl Barnet EN5 .171 A4
rehamwood WD6 .....170 C4

Carrington Pl HP23 .....100 C5
Carrington Sq HA3 .....176 C3
Carsdale Cl LU3 .....45 A6
Cart Path WD2 .....154 C6
Carteret Rd LU2 .....46 C1
Carterhatch La EN1 .....161 F1
Carters Cl Arlesey SG15 ...11 A7
Aston SG2 .....51 D4
Carters La SG5 .....34 A6
Carters Leys SG13 .....76 D8
Carters Mead SG1 .....11 A7
Carters Wlk SG15 .....11 A7
Cartersfield Rd EN9 ...163 C5
Carthagena Est EN9 ...135 C3
Cartwright Rd Royston SG8 ..7 D5
Stevenage SG1 .....50 D7
Carve Ley AL7 .....111 B5
Carvers Croft SG3 .....69 B2
Cary Wlk WD7 .....156 B5
Cashio La SG6 .....23 A8
Caslon Way SG1 .....51 F1
Cassandra Gate EN8 .148 F4
Cassio Rd WD1 .....167 B5
Cassiobridge Rd WD1 166 C5
Cassiobridge Terr WD1 166 D4
Cassiobury Dr WD1 .....166 F7
Cassiobury Inf Sch WD1 166 E8
Cassiobury Jun Mix Sch
WD1 .....166 E8
Cassiobury Park Ave
WD1 .....166 F6
Castano Cl WD5 .....153 E8
Castellane Cl 1 HA7 ...176 F3
Castle Cl EN8 .....163 A5
Castings Ho SG6 .....23 A7
Castle Cl Bushey WD2 ...168 B3
Hoddesdon EN11 .....115 C1
Castle Croft Rd LU3 .....63 A6
Castle Gate SG14 .....115 C5
Castle Gate Way HP4 .122 C6
Castle Hill HP4 .....122 C6
Castle Hill Ave HP4 .....122 C5
Castle Hill Cl HP4 .....122 C5
Castle Mead HP1 .....124 B1
Castle Mead Gdns SG14 113 C6
Castle Mews HP4 .....122 D4
Castle Rd Enfield EN3 .162 E2
Hoddesdon EN11 .....115 C1
St Albans AL1 .....128 B3
Castle Rise AL4 .....86 F2
Castle St
Berkhamsted HP4 .....122 C4
Bishop's Stortford CM23 ..76 F6
Hertford SG14 .....113 D5
Luton, High Town LU1 ...63 E7
Luton, New Town LU1 ...63 E7
Wingrave HP22 .....60 B3
Castle View CM23 .....77 A7
Castle Wlk CM24 .....59 E6
Castles Cl SG5 .....11 F8
Catalin Ct EN3 .....163 D6
Caterham Ct EN9 .....163 F5
Catesby Gn LU3 .....44 D5
Catham Cl AL1 .....128 B1
Cathedral Ct AL3 .....127 B1
Catherall Rd LU3 .....45 B6
Catherine Cl HP2 .....125 B8
Catherine Rd EN9 .....121 F7
Catherine St AL3 .....127 D4
Catisfield Rd EN3 .....162 E2
Catkin Cl HP1 .....124 B4
Catlin St HP3 .....138 B8
Catsbrook Rd LU3 .....45 B5
Catsbell Bottom HP3 .139 B8
Catsey La WD2 .....168 C2
Catsey Wood WD2 .....168 C2
Catterick Way WD6 .169 F8
Cattlegate Hill EN6 ...160 D7
Cattlegate Rd
Crews Hill EN7 .....161 A5
Northaw EN6 .....160 D6
Cattley Cl EN5 .....171 E5
Cattlins Cl EN7 .....147 F7
Cattsdell HP2 .....124 E5
Causeway Cl EN6 .....159 D8
Causeway Ho WD5 ...153 E8
Causeway The
1 Bishop's Stortford CM23 ..77 A7
Braughing SG9,SG11 .....42 D1
Brent Pelham SG9 .....30 B1
Buntingford SG9 .....40 F8
Furneux Pelham SG9 .....43 A4
Kneesworth SG8 .....2 A5
Potters Bar EN6 .....159 D8
Therfield SG8 .....15 F7
Cauther Ly La SG12 .....115 A5
Cavalier La SG1 .....36 B1
Cavalier Cl LU3 .....45 A5
Cavalier Ct HP4 .....122 C2
Cavan Cl AL10 .....130 A4
Cavan Dr AL3 .....106 A6
Cavell Rd EN7 .....148 A4
Cavell Wlk SG2 .....51 C5
Cavendish Cres WD6 .170 A5
Cavendish Ct WD3 .....164 B4
Cavendish Rd Barnet EN5 171 A6
Luton LU3 .....45 B2
Markyate AL3 .....83 D6
St Albans AL1 .....127 F3
Stevenage SG1 .....50 B8
Cavendish Sch The HP1 124 B4
Cavendish Way AL10 .129 F5
Cawkell Ct CM24 .....59 D7
Caxton Cl Enfield EN3 .162 E4
Luton LU4 .....44 F4
Caxton Hill SG13 .....113 F6
Caxton Rd EN11 .....115 B2

Caxton Way
Moor Park WD1 .....166 D2
Stevenage SG1 .....50 B4
Cecil Cl SG14 .....77 D7
Cecil Cres AL10 .....130 B7
Cecil Ct EN5 .....171 D6
Cecil Rd Brickendon SG13 113 C3
Cheshunt EN8 .....162 E7
Hoddesdon EN11 .....135 C8
Potters Bar EN6 .....158 B7
Cechesters Rd SG5 .....36 D1
Cecil St WD2 .....154 B1
Cedar Ave Cheshunt EN8 .162 D6
Ickleford SG5 .....21 E4
Cedar Cl Hertford SG14 .113 B6
Bishop's Stortford CM23 ..76 E8
Enfield EN2 .....161 C1
Kings Langley WD4 .....139 A2
Sawbridgeworth CM21 ...97 E1
Ware SG12 .....114 D8
Cedar Cres SG8 .....7 B6
Cedar Ct
Bishop's Stortford CM23 ...58 F1
St Albans AL3 .....128 D3
Cedar Dr HA5 .....176 A4
Cedar Gn EN11 .....135 A5
Cedar Lawn Ave EN5 .171 E4
Cedar Lodge 11 EN8 .148 D3
Cedar Park Rd EN2 .....161 C1
Cedar Pk CM23 .....76 D4
Cedar Pl HA6 .....174 C4
Cedar Rd
Berkhamsted HP4 .....122 C3
Enfield EN2 .....161 C1
Hatfield AL10 .....130 A4
Watford WD1 .....167 D3
Cedar Way HP4 .....122 D3
Cedar Wlk
Chorleywood WD3 .....164 F5
Hemel Hempstead HP3 .124 D1
Waltham Abbey EN9 .....163 D5
Welwyn Garden City AL7 111 B5
Cedar Wood Dr WD2 ...154 B4
Cedars Ave WD3 .....165 C1
Cedars Cl WD6 .....170 D8
Cedars Fst & Mid Sch
HA3 .....176 C2
Cedars The
Berkhamsted HP4 .....122 E4
1 Harpenden AL5 .....86 B1
Rickmansworth WD3 .....165 D2
St Albans AL3 .....127 C5
Stevenage SG2 .....69 B8
Cedarwood Dr AL4 .....128 C8
Celandine Dr LU3 .....45 A3
Cell Barnes Cl AL1 .....128 B1
Cell Barnes La AL1 .....128 B1
Cemetery Hill HP1 .....124 C2
Cemetery Rd CM23 .....76 F6
Cemmaes Court Rd HP1 124 C3
Cemmaes Mdw HP1 .124 C3
Centennial Ave WD6 .169 C2
Centennial Pk WD6 .....169 C2
Central App SG6 .....22 F6
Central Ave Cheshunt EN8 .162 E6
Henlow SG16 .....10 B3
Whipsnade LU6 .....81 E8
Central Dr St Albans AL4 128 C4
Welwyn Garden City AL7 110 F8
Central Prim Sch WD1 167 C5
Central Rd WD6 .....118 A4
Central Way HA6 .....174 E3
Centro HP2 .....125 C5
Century Ct WD1 .....166 C2
Century Rd
Hoddesdon EN11 .....135 A7
Ware SG12 .....93 D2
Cervantes Ct HA6 .....174 F3
Chace Ave EN6 .....159 D7
Chace The SG2 .....50 F1
Chad La AL3 .....84 C4
Chadwell SG12 .....114 C8
Chadwell Ave EN8 .....148 C3
Chadwell Cl LU2 .....45 F1
Chadwell Rd SG1 .....50 B3
Chadwell Rise SG12 .....114 C8
Chaffinch La WD1 .....166 F2
Chaffinches Gn HP3 .139 A7
Chagney Cl SG1 .....22 E6
Chalet Cl HP4 .....121 F4
Chalfont Cl HP2 .....125 B8
Chalfont Ho WD1 .....166 C2
Chalfont La
Chorleywood WD3 .....164 B4
Maple Cross WD3 .....172 D3
Chalfont Pl AL1 .....127 C2
Chalfont Rd WD3,SL9 .172 C7
Chalfont Shire Ctr HP8 .172 A7
Chalfont Wlk 4 HA5 .175 C1
Chalgrove AL7 .....111 C6
Chalk Dale AL7 .....111 B7
Chalk Cl SG2 .....23 C3
Chalk Hill Great Offley LU2 47 A5
Watford WD1 .....167 E3
Chalk Hill La LU2 .....47 A5
Chalkdell Fields AL4 .128 A7
Chalkdell Hill HP2 .....124 E3
Chalkdell Path 8 SG5 ...34 D8
Chalkdown Luton LU2 ...46 B1
Stevenage SG2 .....51 D7
Chalky Bank SG2 .....97 D3
Challinger Boys High Sch
LU4 .....44 D2
Challney Cl LU4 .....44 D2
Challney Girls High Sch
LU4 .....44 D2
Chalmers Cl WD3 .....165 F3
Chalton Rd LU4 .....44 C5
Chamberlaines AL5 .....85 A5

Chambers Gate SG1 .....50 D7
Chambers La SG5 .....21 E4
Chambers' St SG14 .....113 C6
Chambersbury La HP3 .139 A7
Chambersbury Prim Sch
HP3 .....139 B8
Champions Cl WD6 .....157 B2
Champions Gn EN11 .....115 A1
Champions Way EN11 .115 A1
Chancellor's Sch AL9 ...145 A6
Chanders Rd SG1 .....36 D1
Chancery Cl AL4 .....128 D8
Chandler's La WD3 .....152 E2
Chandlers Ct CM23 .....76 C4
Chandlers Rd AL4 .....128 C6
Chandlers Way AL1 .....113 A6
Chandos Cl HP6 .....150 C1
Chandos Rd
Borehamwood WD6 .....170 A7
Luton LU4 .....44 F1
Chandos Way
Bishop's Stortford CM23 ...76 C7
Borehamwood WD6 .....170 A6
Chantry Cl
St Albans AL1 .....127 F3
Stevenage SG1 .....50 F1
Bishop's Stortford CM23 ...76 E8
Enfield EN2 .....161 C1
Kings Langley WD4 .....139 A2
Chantry Ct AL10 .....130 A4
Chantry La Hatfield AL10 129 F4
Hatfield AL10 .....130 A4
Little Wymondley SG4 ...35 F2
London Colney AL2 .....142 D5
Chantry Mount CM23 ...76 E8
Chantry Pl HA3 .....176 B2
Chantry Rd
Bishop's Stortford CM23 ...76 E8
Harrow HA3 .....176 B2
Chantry The
6 Bishop's Stortford CM23 ..76 F8
Harlow CM20 .....118 A2
Chaomans SG6 .....22 F3
Chapel Cl
Little Gaddesden HP4 .....102 D6
Luton LU2 .....45 C8
St Albans AL1 .....141 D8
Chapel Cotts HP2 .....124 D4
Chapel Croft WD4 .....152 A8
Chapel Crofts HP4 .....121 E6
Chapel End
Buntingford SG9 .....40 E7
Hoddesdon EN11 .....135 A5
Chapel End La HP23 .....99 C8
Chapel Fields HP23 .....99 C8
Chapel Hill CM24 .....59 E6
Chapel La
Hertingfordbury SG14 .....112 B3
Little Hadham SG11 .....75 A8
Long Marston HP23 .....79 B4
Chapel Mdw HP23 .....100 B6
Chapel Pl SG5 .....11 F6
Chapel Rd
Breachwood Green SG4 ...65 E8
Flamstead AL3 .....84 B2
Chapel Row
8 Bishop's Stortford CM23 ...76 F6
Harefield UB9 .....173 C2
6 Watford WD5 .....34 F8
Chapel St
Berkhamsted HP4 .....122 D4
Hemel Hempstead HP2 .124 D4
Hinxworth SG7 .....3 D6
Luton, High Town LU1 ...63 E7
Luton, New Town LU1 ...63 E6
Tring HP23 .....99 F3
Chapel Viaduct LU1 .....63 E7
Chapel Way WD5 .....139 F4
Chapelfields SG1 .....115 D4
Chapman Rd SG1 .....36 B1
Chapmans End SG11 .....55 D3
Chapman Sch SG1 .....2 C2
Chapter House Rd LU4 ...44 A3
Chard Dr LU3 .....31 B1
Chardia Terr EN8 .....148 D1
Chardins Cl HP1 .....123 F4
Charles St
Berkhamsted HP4 .....122 B4
Hemel Hempstead HP1 .124 C2
Luton LU2 .....63 F8
Tring HP23 .....100 A3
Charlesworth Cl 4 HP3 ...76 F6
Charlock Way WD1 .....166 F3
Charlotte Cl AL4 .....128 C3
Charlton Cl EN11 .....135 A6
Charlton Mead La EN11 135 C5
Charlton Rd SG5 .....34 D5
Charlton Way EN11 .....135 B6
Charlwood Cl HA3 .....176 E4
Charlwood Rd LU4 .....44 B1
Charmbury Rise LU2 ...46 B4
Charmouth Ct AL1 .....128 A6
Charmouth Rd AL1 .....128 A5
Charndon Cl AL1 .....31 B1
Charnwood Rd EN1 .....162 B3
Charter Ho WD3 .....164 E6
Charterhouse WD1 .....167 C6
Charters Way HP4 .....176 F4
Chartridge Cl Barnet EN5 171 A4
Bushey WD2 .....168 C3
Chartridge Way HP2 .124 F5
Chartwell Cl 9 EN9 .....163 E6
Chartwell Ct CM23 .....59 D7
Chartwell Dr LU2 .....45 E3
Chartwell Rd HA6 .....174 F4
Charwood Cl WD7 .....156 E6
Charwood Rd AL7 .....123 F5
Chase Cl SG15 .....11 A8
Chase Farm Hospl EN2 .161 A1
Chase Hill Rd SG15 .....11 A7

Chase St LU1 .....63 C6
Chase The
Bishop's Stortford CM23 ...76 F6
Goff's Oak EN7 .....147 B3
Great Amwell SG12 .....115 A3
Hemel Hempstead HP2 .124 E2
Hertford SG13 .....113 F6
Oaklands AL6 .....89 B3
Radlett WD7 .....155 F4
Watford WD1 .....166 E5
Chaseside Cl LU7 .....80 A7
Chaseways CM21 .....118 C8
Chase Side SG6 .....22 D7
Chater Inf Sch WD1 .....167 A5
Chater Jun Sch WD1 .....167 B5
Chatsworth Cl
Bishop's Stortford CM23 ...76 C7
Borehamwood WD6 .....170 A6
Chatsworth Ct
St Albans AL1 .....127 F3
Stevenage SG1 .....50 F1
Chatsworth Rd LU4 .....45 B1
Chatteris Cl LU4 .....44 D4
Chatterton SG6 .....23 C5
Chatton Cl LU2 .....46 C2
Chaucer Cl HP4 .....121 F5
Chaucer Ct EN11 .....115 A1
Chaucer Ho EN5 .....171 D5
Chaucer Rd Luton LU3 ...45 C2
Royston SG8 .....7 C8
Chaucer Way Hitchin SG4 ...35 C7
Hoddesdon EN11 .....115 A1
Chaucer Wlk HP2 .....105 B1
Chauld End La LU4 .....44 E1
Chaul End Rd
Caddington LU1 .....62 D6
Luton LU4 .....44 B1
Chaulden House Gdns
HP1 .....123 F1
Chaulden Jun & Inf Schs
HP1 .....123 F2
Chaulden La HP1 .....123 E1
Chaulden Terr HP1 .....123 F2
Chauncey Ho WD1 .....166 E3
Chauncy Ave EN6 .....159 C6
Chauncy Cl SG12 .....93 D3
Chauncy Ct 18 SG14 .113 D6
Chauncy Gdns SG7 .....13 B1
Chauncy Ho SG1 .....50 E6
Chauncy Rd SG1 .....50 E6
Chauncy Sch The SG12 ...93 B2
Chaworth Gn 11 LU4 .....44 C5
Cheapside LU1 .....63 E7
Cheapside Sq 4 LU1 .....63 E7
Chedburgh AL7 .....111 D7
Cheddington
Cty Comb Sch LU7 .....80 A7
Cheddington La HP23 ...79 C5
Cheddington Rd LU7 .....80 C4
Cheffins Rd EN1 .....114 F1
Chells Ent Village SG2 ...51 C6
Chells La SG2 .....51 D7
Chells Way SG2 .....51 B6
Chelmsford Rd SG14 .113 B5
Chelsea Fields EN11 .115 B2
Chelsing Rise HP2 .....125 C2
Chelsworth Cl 11 LU2 .....46 D1
Cheltenham Ct AL1 .....128 A2
Cheltenham Ho 2 WD1 .167 C7
Chelveston AL7 .....111 D7
Chelwood Ave AL10 .130 A4
Chelwood Cl HA6 .....174 C3
Chenduit Way HA7 .....176 F5
Cheney Rd LU4 .....44 C5
Chenies Ave HP6 .....150 D1
Chenies Cty Comb Sch
WD3 .....151 B1
Chenies Ct HP2 .....125 B8
Chenies Gn CM23 .....76 D6
Chenies Manor Ho WD3 .151 A1
Chenies Rd WD3 .....164 E2
Chenies Way HD1 .....166 E2
Chennells AL10 .....129 F4
Chennells Cl SG4 .....22 B2
Chennies The AL5 .....107 C7
Chepstow AL5 .....85 D3
Chepstow Cl SG1 .....51 B8
Chequer Ct LU1 .....63 F6
Chequer La LU3 .....106 B4
Chequer St Luton LU1 ...63 F6
St Albans AL1 .....127 D3
Chequers
Bishop's Stortford CM23 ...76 C8
Hatfield AL9 .....130 D8
Welwyn Garden City AL7 110 D3
Chequers Bridge Rd SG1 .50 C6
Chequers Cl
Buntingford SG9 .....40 D8
Pitstone LU7 .....80 C4
Standon SG11 .....55 D4
Stotfold SG5 .....12 A6
Chequers Cotts
Preston SG4 .....48 D6
Whipsnade LU6 .....82 A8
Chequers Field AL7 .....110 D3
Chequers Orch AL3 .....84 C2
Chequers La
Abbots Langley WD2 .....140 C1
Pitstone LU7 .....80 C5
Preston SG4 .....48 D7
Chequers Wlk EN9 .....163 F6
Cherbank HP2 .....124 D5
Cherry Bank HP2 .....124 D5
Cherry Cl SG3 .....68 F4
Cherry Croft AL8 .....89 D2

Cherry Croft Gdns 2
HA5 .....175 F3
Cherry Ct HA5 .....175 D2
Cherry Dr SG8 .....7 E7
Cherry Gdns
Bishop's Stortford CM23 .....77 A8
Sawbridgeworth CM21 .....97 E4
Tring HP23 .....99 F3
Cherry Hill
Chiswellburn AL2 .....141 A6
Harrow HA3 .....176 E4
Rickmansworth WD3 .....165 B6
Cherry Hills WD1 .....175 D5
Cherry Hollow WD5 .....153 F8
Cherry Orch HP1 .....124 A5
Cherry Rd EN3 .....162 C1
Cherry Tree Ave AL2 .....142 D5
Cherry Tree Cl
Arlesey SG15 .....11 A4
Luton LU2 .....46 A1
Cherry Tree Gn SG4 .....112 F7
Cherry Tree La
Cholesbury HP23 .....120 A3
Chorleywood WD3 .....164 C1
Hemel Hempstead HP2 .....125 C7
Potters Bar EN6 .....159 B5
Wheathampstead AL4 .....87 A2
Cherry Tree Prim Sch
WD2 .....154 A3
Cherry Tree Rd
Hoddesdon EN11 .....135 A7
Watford WD2 .....154 A3
Cherry Tree Rise SG8 .....38 B1
Cherry Trees SG16 .....10 B3
Cherry Way AL10 .....130 A2
Cherry Wlk WD3 .....165 C7
Chertsey Cl LU2 .....64 D8
Chertsey Rise SG2 .....51 C4
Cherwell Cl WD3 .....166 A4
Chesfield Cl CM23 .....76 F5
Chesford Rd LU2 .....46 C4
Chesham Cl HA6 .....174 F4
Chesham Prep Sch HP5 .....136 A4
Chesham Rd
Berkhamsted HP4 .....122 C3
Bovingdon HP3 .....136 E3
Wigginton HP23 .....120 E7
Chesham Way WD1 .....166 F3
Cheshunt Centre The
EN8 .....148 D3
Cheshunt Folly EN8 .....148 B3
Cheshunt Sch EN8 .....148 C1
Cheshunt Sta EN8 .....148 F8
Cheshunt Wash EN8 .....148 E4
Cheslyn Cl LU2 .....46 E2
Chess Cl Latimer HP5 .....150 D3
Rickmansworth WD3 .....165 D5
Chess Hill WD3 .....165 D5
Chess La WD3 .....165 D5
Chess Vale Rise WD3 .....165 F3
Chess Way WD3 .....165 A6
Chesswood Dr WD3 .....165 D1
Chesswood Way HA5 .....175 D1
Chester Ave LU4 .....44 E3
Chester Cl Luton LU4 .....44 F2
Potters Bar EN6 .....145 B2
Chester Ho HA6 .....174 F3
Chester Pl HA6 .....174 E3
Chester Rd
Borehamwood WD6 .....170 D6
Northwood HA6 .....174 F3
Stevenage SG1 .....37 A1
Watford WD1 .....167 A5
Chesterfield Flats EN5 .....171 D4
Chesterfield
Inf & Jun Sch** EN3 .....162 E2
Chesterfield Rd
Barnet EN5 .....171 D4
Enfield EN3 .....162 E2
Chesterton Ave AL5 .....86 D1
Chestnut Ave Henlow SG16 .....10 C3
Luton LU3 .....44 C8
Northwood HA6 .....174 F2
Rickmansworth WD3 .....165 A4
Ware SG12 .....93 F3
Chestnut Cl
Bishop's Stortford CM23 .....76 E6
Dagnall HP4 .....81 C5
Hoddesdon LU2 .....95 D1
Potten End HP4 .....123 B6
Chestnut Ct 4 Hitchin SG5 .....34 D8
Watford WD1 .....166 E5
Chestnut Dr
Berkhamsted HP4 .....122 D3
Harrow HA3 .....176 F2
St Albans AL4 .....128 C5
Chestnut La Barnet N20 .....171 E1
Kneesworth SG8 .....2 B6
Chestnut Rd EN3 .....162 E3
Chestnut Rise WD2 .....168 B2
Chestnut Wlk Hitchin SG4 .....35 A4
Royston SG8 .....7 E6
Stevenage SG1 .....36 D1
Watford WD2 .....154 A2
Chestnuts The
Codicote SG4 .....67 F2
Hemel Hempstead HP3 .....137 F7
Hertford SG13 .....113 D5
Cheverells Cl AL3 .....83 D4
Cheviot Cl Bushey WD2 .....168 C3
Luton LU3 .....44 D7
Cheviot Rd LU3 .....44 D7
Cheviots Hatfield AL10 .....130 A3
Hemel Hempstead HP2 .....124 F6

Cheyne Cl Pitstone LU7 .....80 D4
Ware SG12 .....93 D3
Cheynes Inf Sch LU3 .....44 D8
Chicheley Gdns HA3 .....176 C3
Chicheley Rd HA3 .....176 C3
Chichester Way WD2 .....154 E6
Chigwell Hurst Ct HA5 .....175 D1
Chilcott Rd WD2 .....153 F3
Chilcourt SG8 .....7 C6
Childbrook Ho WD1 .....166 A3
Childs Ave UB9 .....173 C1
Childwick Ct HP3 .....139 B8
Chilham Cl HP2 .....124 E2
Chiltern Ave WD2 .....168 C3
Chiltern Cl
Borehamwood WD6 .....169 F7
Bushey WD2 .....168 B3
Goff's Oak EN7 .....147 B4
Ware SG12 .....93 D3
Chiltern Ct
10 Harpenden AL5 .....86 B1
Hertford SG14 .....112 F8
St Albans AL4 .....128 D7
Chiltern Dr WD3 .....165 A2
Chiltern Gdns LU4 .....44 F3
Chiltern Open Air
Mus HP6 .....150 A1
Chiltern Park Ave HP4 .....122 A6
Chiltern Rd Baldock SG7 .....23 C6
Hitchin SG4 .....35 A7
St Albans AL4 .....128 C7
Wingrave HP22 .....60 A3
Chiltern Rise LU1 .....63 D6
Chiltern View SG6 .....22 D5
Chiltern Way HP23 .....100 C5
Chilterns
Berkhamsted HP4 .....121 F6
Hatfield AL10 .....130 A2
Hemel Hempstead HP2 .....124 E5
Chilterns The Hitchin SG4 .....35 A6
Kensworth Common LU6 .....82 F8
Chilton Gn AL7 .....112 A1
Chilvers Bank SG7 .....23 E7
Chilwell Gdns WD1 .....175 C6
Chilworth Gate EN10 .....134 F1
Chindit Cl EN10 .....134 E3
Chinnery Cl EN1 .....161 F1
Chinnery Hill CM23 .....76 F5
Chipperfield Rd
Bovingdon HP3 .....137 C3
Hemel Hempstead HP3 .....138 C7
Kings Langley WD4 .....138 D2
Chipping Cl EN5 .....171 E6
Chippingfield CM17 .....118 C3
Chirdland Ho WD1 .....166 E3
Chishill Rd Barley SG8 .....9 A2
Great Chishill SG8 .....9 E3
Chishill Windmill SG8 .....9 C2
Chiswell Ct WD2 .....154 C1
Chiswellgreen La AL2 .....140 E6
Chittenden Cl EN9 .....115 B1
Chivenor Pl AL4 .....128 C1
Chobham St LU1 .....63 F4
Chobham Wlk 5 LU1 .....63 E6
Cholesbury La HP23 .....120 B2
Chorleywood Bottom
WD3 .....164 B4
Chorleywood Cl WD3 .....165 D2
Chorleywood Prim Sch
WD3 .....164 C3
Chorleywood Rd WD3 .....165 C4
Chorleywood Sta WD3 .....164 D5
Chouler Gdns SG1 .....36 C2
Chowns The AL5 .....107 A5
Christ Church
CE Jun Mix Sch EN5 .....171 D7
Christ Church
CE Prim Sch SG12 .....93 E1
Christ Church CE Sch
WD3 .....164 F5
Christ Church La EN5 .....171 E7
Christchurch Cl AL3 .....127 D4
Christchurch Cres WD7 .....156 A3
Christchurch Ho HP23 .....100 A3
Christchurch Rd
Hemel Hempstead HP2 .....124 D4
Tring HP23 .....99 F4
Christie Cl EN10 .....134 F3
Christie Rd SG2 .....51 D5
Christina Ct AL3 .....83 E5
Christopher Ct
Hemel Hempstead HP3 .....138 D8
St Albans AL1 .....128 B3
Christopher Pl 8 AL3 .....127 D3
Christy's Yd SG7 .....3 D6
Church Cl Codicote SG4 .....67 F2
Cuffley EN6 .....146 E2
Little Berkhamsted SG13 .....132 C4
Northwood HA6 .....174 F3
Radlett WD7 .....156 A3
Studham LU6 .....82 B4
Church Cotts
Gilston CM20 .....117 C7
Great Gaddesden HP1 .....103 D3
Church Cres
Sawbridgeworth CM21 .....97 F2
St Albans AL1 .....127 C4
Church End EN10 .....135 A3
Church End Arlesey SG15 .....11 A8
Barley SG8 .....9 A1
Braughing SG11 .....55 F7
Flamstead AL3 .....84 C2
Markyate AL3 .....83 D6
Redbourn AL3 .....106 A4
Sandridge AL4 .....108 C2
Walkern SG2 .....38 C2
Church Farm Way WD2 .....155 B1
Church Field SG12 .....93 B3

Church Field Path EN8 .....148 C2
Church Gn Benington SG2 .....52 D4
Great Wymondley SG4 .....35 G6
Harpenden AL5 .....86 A1
Church Green Row AL5 .....86 A1
Church Hill
Abbots Langley WD5 .....139 F4
Cheddington LU7 .....80 A8
Harefield UB9 .....173 C1
Hertford Heath SG13 .....114 C4
Church La Arlesey SG15 .....11 A7
Ashwell SG7 .....12 A5
Barkway SG8 .....17 C4
Berkhamsted HP4 .....122 C4
Bishop's Stortford CM23 .....76 D3
Bovingdon HP3 .....137 B4
Cheddington LU7 .....80 A8
Cheshunt EN8 .....148 C2
Colney Heath AL4 .....143 B8
Dane End SG12 .....71 F8
Graveley SG4 .....36 C4
Guilden Morden SG8 .....1 F5
Harlow HA3 .....176 F2
Hatfield AL10 .....130 C5
Hoddesdon EN10 .....134 C1
Kimpton SG4 .....66 D1
Kings Langley WD4 .....139 A2
Letchworth SG6 .....12 C1
Marsworth HP23 .....79 F1
Much Hadham SG10 .....74 F3
Northaw EN6 .....146 A1
Preston SG4 .....48 D6
Radlett WD2 .....155 B1
Reed SG8 .....16 E5
Rickmansworth WD3 .....165 B1
Royston SG8 .....7 D6
Sarratt WD3 .....152 A2
Stapleford SG14 .....92 A6
Stevenage SG1 .....50 C7
Therfield SG8 .....15 F7
Weston SG4 .....24 D1
Church Manor CM23 .....77 B8
Church Mead
Roydon CM19 .....116 B1
Studham LU6 .....82 B4
Church Meadow Cotts
HP1 .....103 D3
Church Path SG4 .....35 F3
Church Pl AL6 .....89 C5
Church Rd Flamstead AL3 .....84 B2
Great Hallingbury CM22 .....77 D3
Hemel Hempstead HP3 .....125 C2
Hertford SG14 .....113 C7
King's Walden SG4 .....47 F3
Little Berkhamsted SG13 .....132 C4
Little Gaddesden HP4 .....102 D8
Northwood HA6 .....174 F3
Pitstone, Church End LU7 .....80 D8
Pitstone, Church End LU7 .....80 F5
Potten End HP4 .....123 B6
Potters Bar EN6 .....145 B1
Slip End LU1 .....63 C2
Stansted Mountfitchet CM24 .....59 F5
Stotfold SG5 .....11 C6
Streatley LU3 .....31 A6
Studham LU6 .....82 B4
Watford WD1 .....167 B8
Welwyn Garden City AL8 .....110 D6
Church Row News 3
SG12 .....93 D1
Church St Baldock SG7 .....12 E1
Bishop's Stortford CM23 .....76 F7
Bovingdon HP3 .....137 B4
Buntingford SG9 .....40 E8
Essendon AL9 .....131 E6
Hatfield AL9 .....130 C5
Hemel Hempstead HP2 .....124 D5
Hertford SG14 .....113 D6
Luton LU2 .....63 E7
Luton, High Town LU2 .....63 F8
Rickmansworth WD3 .....165 E1
Sawbridgeworth CM21 .....97 E2
Shillington SG5 .....19 F8
St Albans AL1 .....127 D4
Waltham Abbey EN9 .....163 C6
Ware SG12 .....93 D1
Watford WD1 .....167 C5
Welwyn AL6 .....89 C5
Wheathampstead AL4 .....108 D8
Wingrave HP22 .....60 B2
Church Street Ind Est
SG12 .....93 D1
Church View
Hoddesdon EN10 .....134 F3
Long Marston HP23 .....79 A4
Church Wlk Bushey WD2 .....168 A3
Sawbridgeworth CM21 .....97 F2
Church Yd Hitchin SG5 .....34 E7
Tring HP23 .....100 A3
Churchfield Barley SG8 .....9 A1
Harlow CM20 .....118 B2
Harpenden AL5 .....107 C8
Churchfield Ho AL10 .....110 C6
Churchfield Rd AL6 .....90 C1
Churchfields
Hertford SG13 .....113 D5
Hoddesdon EN10 .....135 A3
Stansted Mountfitchet CM24 .....59 F6
Churchfields La EN10 .....135 A3
Churchfields Rd WD2 .....153 F3
Churchgate Cheshunt EN8 .....148 B1
4 Hitchin SG5 .....34 E7
Churchgate CE Prim Sch
CM17 .....118 F3
Churchgate Rd EN8 .....148 B2
Churchgate St CM17 .....118 E4

Churchill Cres AL9 .....144 C8
Churchill Rd Luton LU4 .....45 A1
St Albans AL1 .....128 A4
Churchyard Wlk 6 SG5 .....34 E7
Cicero Dr LU3 .....45 A8
Cillocks Cl EN11 .....135 A7
Claggy Rd SG4 .....66 B2
Claire Ct Bushey WD2 .....168 D1
Cheshunt EN8 .....162 D7
5 Pinner HA5 .....175 F3
Clamp Hill HA7 .....176 E5
Clappate Rd WD2 .....168 B3
Clare Cl WD6 .....169 F3
Clare Cres SG7 .....23 E6
Clare Ct Enfield EN3 .....162 E4
Northwood HA6 .....174 E5
St Albans AL1 .....127 F2
Claremont
Bricket Wood AL2 .....155 A8
Goff's Oak EN7 .....147 F2
Claremont Cres WD3 .....166 C4
Claremont Rd
Hadley Wood EN4 .....159 D2
Harrow HA3 .....176 E1
Luton LU4 .....45 B1
Clarence Cl WD2 .....168 F2
Clarence Rd
Berkhamsted HP4 .....122 C4
Harpenden AL5 .....86 A3
St Albans AL1 .....128 A4
Stansted Mountfitchet CM24 .....59 E7
Clarendon Ct 11 HP2 .....124 E4
Clarendon Cl
Harpenden AL5 .....86 B3
Moor Park HA6 .....174 F5
Clarendon Mews WD6 .....170 A6
Clarendon Par EN8 .....148 D2
Clarendon Rd
Borehamwood WD6 .....170 A6
Cheshunt EN8 .....148 D2
Harpenden AL5 .....86 B3
Luton LU2 .....45 E1
Watford WD1 .....167 B6
Clarion Cl SG5 .....33 C2
Clarion Ho SG5 .....33 C2
Clark Rd SG8 .....7 D7
Clarke Way WD2 .....154 A4
Clarke's Rd AL10 .....130 B7
Clarke's Spring HP23 .....100 F5
Clarkfield WD3 .....165 B1
Clarks Cl SG12 .....93 D3
Clarks Mead WD2 .....168 D2
Claudian Pl AL3 .....127 A1
Clarerhambury Rd EN10 .....135 A4
Claverley Gn LU2 .....46 E2
Claverton Cl HP3 .....137 A3
Clay Hall Rd LU6 .....82 F7
Clay Hill EN2 .....161 D2
Clay La WD2 .....168 D3
Claybury WD2 .....168 B2
Claybush Rd SG7 .....4 D3
Claycroft AL7 .....111 B7
Claydon Cl LU3 .....45 C7
Claydown Way LU1 .....63 B1
Claygate Ave AL5 .....85 E2
Claymore HP2 .....124 E7
Claymore Dr SG5 .....21 F5
Claymores SG1 .....50 E6
Claypods CM23 .....77 B7
Clayton Hill Ctry Pk EN9 .....149 D8
Clayton Par 7 EN8 .....148 D1
Cleall Ave EN9 .....163 C5
Cleave The AL5 .....86 D1
Clement Pl HP23 .....100 A3
Clement Rd EN8 .....148 E4
Clements End Rd LU6 .....82 E2
Clements Rd WD3 .....164 D4
Clements St SG12 .....93 E1
Clevedon Rd LU2 .....46 B2
Cleveland Cres WD6 .....170 C4
Cleveland Rd
Hemel Hempstead HP2 .....125 B5
Markyate AL3 .....83 E5
Cleveland Way HP2 .....125 B5
Clews Rd HP2 .....125 B8
Cleviscroft SG1 .....50 E4
Clewer Cres HA3 .....176 D2
Clifford Cress LU4 .....44 D5
Clifford Ct 10 CM23 .....77 A7
Clifton Cl EN8 .....148 D2
Clifton Rd Luton LU1 .....63 B8
Watford WD1 .....167 B4
St Albans AL1 .....127 E4
Clifton Way
Borehamwood WD6 .....170 A8
Ware SG12 .....93 D3
Climb The WD3 .....165 B3
Clinton Ave LU2 .....45 F3
Clinton End HP2 .....125 C3
Clitheroe Gdns WD1 .....175 D7
Clive Cl EN6 .....158 F8
Clive Ct LU2 .....45 E1
Clive Par HA6 .....174 E3
Clive Way WD2 .....167 C8
Cloister Garth
Berkhamsted HP4 .....122 C4
St Albans AL1 .....141 E7
Cloister Lawns SG6 .....22 F4
Cloister Wlk HP2 .....124 D5
Cloisters Rd
Letchworth SG6 .....23 A4
Luton LU4 .....44 B3
Cloisters The
Bushey WD2 .....168 B3
Kings Langley WD4 .....139 A2
Rickmansworth WD3 .....165 E2
3 Watford WD1 .....167 C5
Welwyn Garden City AL8 .....110 D6

Clonard Way HA5 .....17.
Close The Baldock SG7 .....2.
Brookmans Park AL9 .....144.
Bushey WD2 .....168.
Codicote SG4 .....6.
Harpenden AL5 .....85.
Hinxworth SG7 .....7.
Luton LU3 .....45.
Markyate AL3 .....83.
Potters Bar EN6 .....159.
Radlett WD7 .....155.
Rickmansworth WD3 .....165.
Royston SG8 .....7.
St Albans AL1 .....141.
Wallington SG7 .....25.
Ware SG12 .....93.
Closemead Cl HA6 .....174.
Clothall Rd Baldock SG7 .....23.
Clothall SG7 .....24.
Clovelly Way SG4 .....50.
Clover Ave CM23 .....76.
Clover Cl LU4 .....44.
Clover Field The WD2 .....167.
Clover Way HP1 .....124.
Cloverfield AL7 .....89.
Cloverland AL10 .....129.
Clump The WD3 .....165.
Clusterbolts SG13 .....92.
Clutterbucks WD3 .....152.
Clyde Rd EN11 .....135.
Clyde Sq HP2 .....124.
Clyde St SG13 .....114.
Clydesdale Cl WD6 .....170.
Clydesdale Ct LU4 .....44.
Clydesdale Path WD6 .....170.
Clydesdale Rd Luton LU4 .....44.
Royston SG8 .....7.
Clydesdale Wlk EN10 .....148.
Clyfton Cl EN10 .....148.
Clyston Rd WD1 .....166.
Coach Dr SG4 .....34.
Coach House Cloisters
SG7 .....23.
Coachman's La SG7 .....23.
Coates Dell WD2 .....154.
Coates Rd WD6 .....169.
Coates Way WD2 .....154.
Coates Way
Jun Mix Inf Sch WD2 .....154.
Cob Cl WD6 .....170.
Cob Lane Cl AL6 .....89.
Cobb Gn WD2 .....154.
Cobb Rd HP4 .....121.
Cobbett Cl EN3 .....162.
Cobbetts Ride HP23 .....99.
Cobbins The EN9 .....163.
Cobbins Way CM17 .....118.
Cobbinsbank EN9 .....163.
Cobblers Wick HP22 .....60.
Cobden Hill WD7 .....156.
Cobden St LU2 .....45.
Cobham Rd SG12 .....93.
Cobmead AL10 .....130.
Cock Gr HP23 .....121.
Cock La Brent Pelham CM11 .....30.
Hoddesdon EN11 .....134.
Cockbush Ave SG13 .....114.
Cocker Rd EN1 .....162.
Cockerhoe Endowed
Jun Mix Inf Sch LU2 .....46.
Cockfosters Rd EN4 .....159.
Cockle Way WD7 .....156.
Cockrobin La CM20 .....117.
Codicote CE Prim Sch
SG4 .....67.
Codicote Dr WD2 .....154.
Codicote Heights SG4 .....68.
Codicote Ho SG1 .....36.
Codicote Rd Ayot St
Lawrence AL4,AL6,SG4 .....88.
Welwyn AL6 .....89.
Wheathampstead AL4 .....87.
Whitwell SG4 .....66.
Codicote Row HP2 .....105.
Codmore Wood Rd HP5 .....150.
Coerdale Ct EN3 .....162.
Cohen Cl EN8 .....162.
Colborne Ho WD1 .....166.
Colbron Cl SG7 .....4.
Colburn Ave HA5 .....175.
Colchester Rd HA5 .....175.
Cold Christmas La SG12 .....93.
Coldham Gr EN3 .....162.
Coldharbour La
Bushey WD2 .....168.
Harpenden AL5 .....86.
Cole Green La
Hertingfordbury AL7 .....111.
Welwyn Garden City AL7 .....111.
Cole Green Way SG14 .....113.
Cole Rd WD1 .....167.
Colebrook Ave LU3 .....44.
Coleman Green La
Sandridge AL4 .....109.
Wheathampstead AL4 .....109.
Coleman's La EN9 .....149.
Colemans Cl SG15 .....20.
Colemans Rd SG4 .....47.
Coleridge Cl
Hammond Street EN7 .....147.
Hitchin SG4 .....33.
Coleridge Cres HP2 .....124.
Coles Hill HP1 .....124.
Colesdale EN6 .....146.
Colestrete SG1 .....50.
Colestrete Cl SG1 .....51.

eswood Rd AL5 ....107 C7
gate Ct EN5 ....171 E4
n Rd LU2 ....163 A2
grove AL8 ....110 C5
n Rd LU2 ....45 F2
indale Ave AL1 ....127 F1
lege Ave HA3 ....176 C2
.hop's Stortford CM23 ....76 D7
mstead AL3 ....84 B1
rrow HA3 ....176 E3
re SG12 ....114 D8
lege Ct Cheshunt EN8 ....148 C1
ddesdon EN11 ....134 F8
lege Hill Rd HA3 ....176 E3
lege Ho LU1 ....63 F7
lege Lake Wildlife Ctr
23 ....100 C8
lege Rd AL1 ....127 C3
oots Langley WD5 ....154 A8
ton Clinton HP22 ....78 C1
eshunt EN6 ....148 D1
re HA3 ....176 E2
rtford Heath SG13 ....114 D2
.chin SG5 ....34 F8
ddesdon EN11 ....134 F8
re HA3 ....128 B2
lege St AL1 ....127 D3
lege Way
.rthwood HA6 ....174 D4
.elwyn Garden City AL8 ....110 D7
ens Rd AL5 ....107 B5
lenswood Rd SG2 ....52 B4
lenswood Sch SG2 ....51 C4
lett Rd
.mel Hempstead HP1 ....124 C3
re SG12 ....93 D2
lett Sch The HP1 ....124 B4
.ley Land WD3 ....164 D5
lett Cl LU1 ....63 D8
lingdon St LU1 ....63 D8
lings Wells Cl LU1 ....62 E4
lingtree LU2 ....46 B4
lingwood Ct SG8 ....7 D7
lingwood Dr AL2 ....142 D6
lins Cross CM23 ....59 B1
lison Cl SG4 ....22 C2
lyer Rd AL2 ....142 D4
mer Pl HA3 ....176 D3
nbrook Dr AL2 ....142 E4
nbrook Sch WD1 ....175 C7
ne Ave
.kmansworth WD3 ....173 A8
tford WD1 ....167 C3
ne Bridge Ret Pk
D1 ....167 D4
ne Gdns AL2 ....142 E4
ne Lo WD3 ....165 A1
ne Lodge WD2 ....167 D5
ne Mead WD3 ....173 A8
ne Rd
.mel Hempstead HP2 ....124 F8
.atford WD2 ....154 E2
ne Way Ct WD2 ....154 D3
ney Heath La AL4 ....128 E2
.onial Bsns Pk WD2 ....167 E5
onial Way WD2 ....167 D8
.onsay HP3 ....125 C1
ston Cres EN7 ....147 B4
t Hatch CM20 ....117 E1
thurst Gdns EN11 ....135 D8
ts Cnr SG2 ....51 B4
ts Croft SG8 ....9 E2
ne The CM23 ....76 E4
tsfield CM24 ....59 D8
tsfoot AL7 ....111 B4
tsfoot Dr LU4 ....7 E6
tsfoot Gn LU4 ....44 A5
tsfoot La SG3 ....90 D7
tsfoot Rd SG12 ....93 E3
tsfoot The HP1 ....123 E2
.umbus Cl SG2 ....51 A7
.umbus Gdns HA6 ....175 A2
vin Gdns EN6 ....162 D4
.mmerce Way SG6 ....22 F6
.mmon Field HP23 ....100 D1
.mmon Gate Rd WD3 ....164 E4
.rpenden AL5 ....86 D5
.mmon La Ashwell SG7 ....4 B6
.mpton SG4 ....86 D5
.mbe Ho WD1 ....166 E3
.ne Rd WD1 ....166 F3
.mbewood WD2 ....154 C7
.net Cl WD1 ....153 F5
.net Rd LU1 ....129 F6
.net Way AL10,AL9 ....129 E5
.mmon The
.ipperfield WD4 ....152 B8

Common The continued
Harpenden AL5 ....85 C4
Hatfield AL10 ....130 A6
Potten End HP4 ....123 A6
Stanmore HA7 ....176 F8
Common View SG6 ....23 B8
Common Wlk SG6 ....23 B8
Common Wharf SG12 ....93 E1
Commonfields CM20 ....117 E1
Commons La HP2 ....124 E4
Commons The AL7 ....111 B3
Commonswood Sch AL7 ....111 B3
Compass Point HP4 ....121 E6
Compton Ave LU4 ....44 D4
Compton Gdns AL2 ....141 B5
Compton Pl WD1 ....175 E6
Comreton LU1 ....63 A7
Comyne Rd WD2 ....153 F3
Comyns The WD2 ....168 C1
Concorde Dr HP2 ....124 D3
Concorde St LU2 ....63 F8
Conduit La
Great Hormead SG9 ....29 B1
Hoddesdon EN11 ....135 A6
Conduit La E EN11 ....135 B6
Conemara Ct HP4 ....148 F5
Coney Cl AL10 ....130 B3
Coney Gree CM21 ....97 D3
Coneydale AL8 ....110 D8
Congreve Rd EN9 ....163 E6
Conifer Cl Goff's Oak EN7 ....147 F2
Stevenage SG2 ....51 D7
Conifer Ct 4 CM23 ....76 F8
Conifer Wlk SG2 ....51 C7
Conifers The WD1 ....154 C4
Coningesby Dr WD1 ....166 E2
Coningsby Bank AL1 ....141 D7
Coningsby Cl AL4 ....129 C7
Coningsby Ct WD7 ....156 A3
Coningsby Dr EN6 ....159 D6
Coniston Cl HP3 ....125 C2
Coniston Lodge 3 WD1 ....167 A7
Coniston Rd
Abbots Langley WD4 ....139 A4
Kings Langley WD4 ....138 F3
Luton LU3 ....44 F5
Connaught Cl HP2 ....125 A5
Connaught Gdns HP4 ....121 F7
Connaught Rd
Barnet EN5 ....171 D3
Harpenden AL5 ....86 B2
Harrow HA3 ....176 F2
Luton LU4 ....44 F1
St Albans AL1 ....127 E5
Conquest Cl SG4 ....35 A1
Constable Ct LU4 ....45 A1
Constantine Cl SG1 ....36 F1
Constantine Pl SG7 ....13 B1
Convent Cl LU4 ....34 F8
Conway Gdns EN4 ....161 C1
Conway Ho WD3 ....170 C5
Conway Rd LU4 ....45 B1
Conyers SG2 ....51 B7
Cook Rd SG2 ....51 B7
Cook's Hole Rd EN2 ....161 C1
Cooks Mead WD2 ....168 C2
Cooks Spinney CM20 ....118 A2
Cooks Vennel HP1 ....124 A5
Cooks Way Hatfield AL10 ....130 B3
Hitchin SG4 ....35 A5
Coombe Gdns HP4 ....121 F5
Coombe Hill Rd WD3 ....165 A2
Coombe Rd Bushey WD2 ....168 C2
Kelshall SG8 ....6 A1
Coombelands Rd SG8 ....2 E1
Coombes Rd AL2 ....142 A3
Coomnwood Cotts SG12 ....94 E4
Cooper's Cl SG4 ....66 B1
Cooper's Hill AL5 ....87 B8
Coopers Cl Aston SG2 ....51 D4
Bishop's Stortford CM23 ....76 F8
Coopers Cres WD7 ....170 C8
Coopers Field SG6 ....22 D7
Coopers Green La
AL4,AL8,AL10 ....109 D1
Coopers La EN6 ....145 C3
Coopers Lane Rd EN6 ....160 B6
Coopers Mdw AL3 ....106 A6
Coopers Wlk LU3 ....118 D3
Cooters End La AL5 ....85 D7
Copenhagen Cl LU3 ....44 D8
Copmans Wick WD3 ....164 D4
Coppens The SG5 ....12 A5
Copper Beech Cl HP3 ....137 F8
Copper Beeches
1 Harpenden AL5 ....86 B1
Oaklands AL5 ....89 D7
Copper Ct CM21 ....97 E2
Copperfields Luton LU4 ....44 C3
Royston SG8 ....7 C6
Copperfield La AL3 ....88 A1
Coppermill La WD3,UB9 ....172 F3
Copperwood SG13 ....113 F6
Coppice Cl Harrow HA7 ....176 F4
Hatfield AL10 ....129 F1
Coppice Mead SG5 ....11 E5
Coppice The
Harpenden AL5 ....85 F2
Hemel Hempstead HP2 ....125 B4
Watford WD1 ....167 C3
Wigginton HP23 ....100 C1
Coppings The EN11 ....115 A1
Coppins Cl HP4 ....121 F4

Coppins The Harrow HA3 ....176 E4
Markyate AL3 ....83 D5
Copse Cl HA6 ....174 C1
Copse Hill AL5 ....90 A8
Copse The
Bishop's Stortford CM23 ....77 C8
Hemel Hempstead HP1 ....123 E5
Hertford SG13 ....114 A6
Copse Way LU3 ....44 D8
Copse Wood Way HA6 ....174 C2
Copsewood Rd WD2 ....167 B8
Copthall Cl CM22 ....77 F4
Copthall Gdns CM22 ....77 F4
Copthorne Ave EN10 ....134 F3
Copthorne Cl WD3 ....165 F4
Copthorne Rd WD3 ....165 F4
Coral Gdns HP2 ....124 D3
Coral Ho CM20 ....117 A1
Corals Mead AL7 ....110 D5
Coram Cl HP4 ....122 C3
Corbridge Dr LU2 ....46 E1
Corby Cl AL7 ....141 A6
Cordell Ct EN8 ....148 C1
Cordell Cl AL3 ....141 A8
Coreys Mill La SG1 ....36 C1
Corfe Cl 4 SG2 ....124 E2
Corinium Gate AL3 ....127 A1
Corinium Gdns LU3 ....45 A5
Corn Mead AL9 ....89 C1
Corncastle Rd LU1 ....63 D6
Corncrake Cl LU2 ....46 C5
Corncroft AL10 ....130 B7
Cornel Cl LU1 ....63 A7
Cornel Ct LU1 ....45 A1
Cornelia St 5 AL5 ....86 A2
Corner Cl SG6 ....22 E6
Corner Hall HP3 ....124 D1
Corner Hall Ave HP3 ....124 D1
Corner View AL10 ....144 C7
Corner Wood AL3 ....83 D5
Cornerfield AL10 ....130 B8
Cornerfield Rd WD2 ....168 B5
Corners AL7 ....111 A7
Cornfield Cres HP4 ....121 D7
Cornfield Rd WD2 ....168 B5
Cornfields
Hemel Hempstead HP1 ....124 B2
Stevenage SG2 ....51 C7
Cornwall Cl Cheshunt EN8 ....162 E6
8 Pinner EN6 ....175 F3
Cornwall Ho CM23 ....76 E4
Cornwall Rd
Harpenden AL5 ....86 B2
Pinner HA5 ....175 F3
St Albans AL1 ....127 E1
Coronation Ave SG8 ....7 C5
Coronation Rd
Bishop's Stortford CM23 ....76 E5
Ware SG12 ....93 D2
Corton Cl SG1 ....50 B8
Cory-Wright Way AL4 ....87 E1
Cosgrove Way LU1 ....44 D1
Cosne Mews AL5 ....107 C7
Cotesmore Rd HP4 ....123 E2
Cotlandswick AL2 ....142 C5
Cotney Croft SG2 ....51 D3
Cotsmoor AL1 ....127 F3
Cotswold Cl EN8 ....148 D2
Cotswold Bsns Pk LU2 ....62 D2
Cotswold Ct LU4 ....128 C8
Cotswold Gdns LU3 ....44 F6
Cotswolds AL10 ....130 A3
Cottage Cl
Croxley Green WD3 ....165 F3
Watford WD1 ....166 F7
Cottage Gdns EN8 ....148 D2
Cottered Rd SG9 ....26 F1
Cotterells HP1 ....124 C2
Cotterells Hill HP1 ....124 C3
Cotton Dr SG13 ....114 B7
Cotton Field AL10 ....130 B7
Cotton Rd EN6 ....159 C8
Cottonmill Cres AL1 ....127 D1
Couch Cotts SG6 ....23 B2
Coulser Cl HP1 ....124 A6
Coulson Cl LU1 ....62 F8
Coulter Cl EN6 ....146 D4
Council Cotts SG7 ....12 C4
Counters CR HP1 ....124 A3
Countess Anne
CE Prim Sch AL9 ....130 C6
Countess Cl UB9 ....173 C1
Countess Ct 8 LU2 ....45 D5
Couper Ho WD1 ....166 E3
Coursers Rd AL2,AL4 ....143 C6
Court Cl CM23 ....76 E5
Courtaulds AL7 ....138 B1
Courtenay Ave HA3 ....176 C2
Courtney Gdns HA3 ....176 C2
Courtfield Cl EN10 ....135 A3
Courtfields AL5 ....86 D1
Courtlands Cl WD2 ....153 E4
Courtlands Dr WD1 ....153 E3
Courtlington AL5 ....86 D1
Courtway The WD1 ....175 E8
Courtyard Mews AL5 ....92 E4
Courtyard The AL4 ....128 F3
Courtyards The WD1 ....166 D2
Covent Garden Cl LU4 ....44 C3
Coventry Cl SG1 ....37 B1
Coverdale
Hemel Hempstead HP2 ....124 E6
Luton LU2 ....44 B6
Covert Cl HP4 ....121 D6
Covert Rd HP4 ....121 D6
Covert The HA6 ....174 C2

Cow La Bushey WD2 ....168 A3
Tring HP23 ....100 D4
Watford WD2 ....154 C3
Cowards La SG4 ....88 F8
Cowbridge SG14 ....113 C6
Cowdray Cl LU2 ....46 C3
Cowles EN7 ....147 A4
Cowley Hill WD6 ....157 B1
Cowley Hill Sch WD6 ....170 A8
Cowlins CM17 ....118 D4
Cowper CE Prim Sch AL6 ....90 E2
Cowper Cres SG14 ....92 B1
Cowper Ct Markyate AL3 ....83 C5
Watford WD2 ....154 A2
Cowper Rd
Berkhamsted HP4 ....122 B4
Harpenden AL5 ....85 B3
Hemel Hempstead HP1 ....124 B2
Markyate AL3 ....83 D5
Welwyn Garden City AL7 ....110 F4
Cowper Rise AL3 ....83 D5
Cowper St LU1 ....63 E5
Cowpers Way AL6 ....90 D5
Cowridge Cres LU2 ....64 A8
Cowslip Cl SG4 ....7 F5
Cowslip Hill SG6 ....22 E7
Cowslips AL7 ....111 C5
Cox Cl WD7 ....156 F4
Cox's Way SG5 ....11 A6
Coxfield Cl HP2 ....124 E2
Coyney Gn LU3 ....45 C1
Cozens La E EN10 ....134 F1
Cozens La W EN10 ....134 F1
Cozens Rd SG12 ....94 A2
Crab La WD2 ....155 B4
Crab Tree La SG5 ....20 D4
Crab Tree Rd SG3 ....68 F4
Crabb's La SG9 ....16 A1
Crabbes Cl SG5 ....34 E7
Crabtree Cl Bushey WD2 ....168 B4
Hemel Hempstead HP4 ....124 D1
Crabtree Ct 3 HP3 ....124 E1
Crabtree Dell SG6 ....23 B3
Crabtree Inf Sch AL5 ....86 C1
Crabtree La Harpenden AL5 ....86 C1
Hemel Hempstead HP3 ....125 B8
Crackley Mdw HP2 ....125 B8
Cradock Rd LU4 ....44 B3
Craford Cl SG14 ....112 F7
Cragg Ave WD7 ....155 F3
Cragside SG7 ....69 C7
Craig Mount WD7 ....156 B4
Craigavon Rd HP2 ....124 F7
Craigdale AL3 ....83 C5
Craigs Wlk 4 EN8 ....148 D3
Craigweil Ave WD7 ....156 B4
Crakers Mead 4 WD1 ....167 B6
Cranborne SG4 ....36 C6
Cranborne Cl
Brickendon SG13 ....113 C3
Potters Bar EN6 ....158 E8
Cranborne Cres EN3 ....158 E8
Cranborne Ct EN3 ....162 D3
Cranborne Gdns AL7 ....110 F5
Cranborne Ind Est EN6 ....144 E1
Cranborne Par AL7 ....158 C8
Cranborne Prim Sch
EN6 ....158 F8
Cranborne Rd
Cheshunt EN8 ....162 D7
Hatfield AL10 ....130 B6
Hoddesdon EN10 ....135 C7
Potters Bar EN6 ....144 E1
Cranborne Prim Sch
EN11 ....115 B2
Cranbourne Rd HA6 ....174 F1
Cranbrook Cl SG12 ....93 D3
Cranbrook Dr Luton LU3 ....44 D8
St Albans AL4 ....128 E3
Crane Mead SG12 ....114 E8
Cranefield Dr WD2 ....154 D6
Cranes Way WD6 ....170 C4
Cranfield Cres EN6 ....146 E2
Cranford Ct AL5 ....86 C1
Cranleigh Cl EN7 ....148 A3
Cranleigh Gdns LU3 ....45 D3
Cranmer Cl WD6 ....155 E5
Cranmore Cl AL4 ....127 F4
Cranwell Cl AL4 ....128 C1
Cranwell Gdns CM23 ....59 C1
Cravells Ct AL5 ....107 C7
Cravells Rd AL5 ....107 C7
Crawford Rd AL10 ....130 A7
Crawley Cl LU1 ....63 C1
Crawley Dr HP2 ....124 F7
Crawley Green Inf Sch
LU2 ....64 B8
Crawley Green Rd
Luton, Hart Hill LU2 ....64 A8
Luton, Wigmore LU2 ....46 D1
Crawley Rd LU1 ....63 D8
Crawley's La HP23 ....120 D7
Creamery Cl AL6 ....23 C3
Creasy Cl WD5 ....153 F8
Crecy Gdns AL3 ....106 A6
Creighton Ave AL1 ....141 D8
Cremer Cl LU4 ....159 C1
Crescent The
Bishop's Stortford CM23 ....77 A6
Hemel Hempstead HP2 ....124 D3
Luton LU2 ....63 F8
Crescent Rise AL3 ....83 C5
Crescent The
Abbots Langley WD5 ....139 F1

Crescent The continued
Ardeley SG2 ....38 F2
Bricket Wood AL2 ....141 A1
Caddington LU1 ....62 E3
Cottered SG9 ....39 D7
Croxley Green WD3 ....166 B3
Harlow CM17 ....118 C6
Henlow SG16 ....10 C4
Hitchin SG5 ....21 D1
Letchworth SG6 ....23 A5
Marsworth HP23 ....80 A1
Pitstone LU7 ....80 C4
Radlett WD2 ....155 B1
St Ippolyts SG4 ....35 A3
Watford WD1 ....167 C5
Welwyn AL6 ....89 C4
Crescent W EN4 ....159 C1
Cress End AL3 ....165 A1
Cresset Cl SG12 ....115 C3
Cresswick SG4 ....66 C1
Cresswick SG4 ....162 C1
Crest Pk HP2 ....125 C4
Crest The Goff's Oak EN7 ....147 B4
Luton LU3 ....45 B7
Oaklands AL6 ....89 D8
Sawbridgeworth CM21 ....97 D2
Ware SG12 ....93 D3
Cresta Cl LU5 ....44 A2
Cresta Ho 3 LU1 ....63 F7
Creswick Jun Inf Sch
AL7 ....110 D5
Crew Curve HP4 ....121 F7
Crews Hill EN2 ....160 F5
Crews Hill Sta EN2 ....160 F5
Crib St SG12 ....93 D2
Cricketer's Rd SG15 ....11 A4
Cricketers Cl AL3 ....127 E4
Cricketfield La CM23 ....76 E8
Cringle Ct SG6 ....142 C4
Crispin Field LU7 ....180 C4
Croasdaile Rd CM24 ....59 E8
Croasdale Cl CM24 ....59 E8
Crocus Field EN5 ....171 F3
Croft Cl EN Harpenden AL5 ....86 A3
Croft Ct 4 Harpenden AL5 ....86 A3
Hitchin SG5 ....34 E7
Croft End Rd WD3 ....138 A1
Croft Field
Chipperfield WD4 ....138 A1
Hatfield AL10 ....130 A6
Croft La Chipperfield WD4 ....138 A1
Letchworth SG6 ....12 B1
Croft Lodge LU2 ....46 B3
Ware SG12 ....93 C2
Croft The Barnet EN5 ....171 C5
Chiswellgreen AL2 ....141 A6
Hoddesdon EN10 ....148 E8
Wareside SG12 ....94 E4
Welwyn Garden City AL7 ....110 F3
Croft Wlk EN10 ....148 E8
Crofters CM21 ....97 E3
Crofters Path CM21 ....97 E3
Crofters Rd HA6 ....174 E6
Crofts Path HP3 ....125 B1
Crofts The
Hemel Hempstead HP3 ....125 B2
Stevenage SG5 ....11 F6
Croftwell AL5 ....107 F8
Cromer Cl HP4 ....102 E5
Cromer Rd WD2 ....154 C1
Cromer Way
Luton, Stopsley Common LU2 ....45 E6
Luton, Warden Hill LU2 ....45 D7
Cromer Windmill SG2 ....38 C6
Crompton Rd SG1 ....50 A6
Cromwell Ave AL7 ....148 B1
Cromwell Cl
Bishop's Stortford CM23 ....76 B7
St Albans AL4 ....128 D8
Cromwell Gn SG6 ....23 B8
Cromwell Hill LU2 ....45 D1
Cromwell Rd
Borehamwood WD6 ....169 E8
Cheshunt EN7 ....148 B3
Hertford SG13 ....114 A7
Letchworth SG6 ....23 B8
Luton LU3 ....45 D1
Stevenage SG2 ....51 C5
Ware SG12 ....93 F2
Cromwell Way SG5 ....20 D4
Crooked Mile EN9 ....163 C7
Crooked Way EN9 ....135 E1
Crookhams AL7 ....90 A1
Crop Comm AL10 ....130 B7
Crosby Cl Luton LU4 ....45 A2
St Albans AL4 ....142 C8
Cross La Harpenden AL5 ....107 C5
Hertford SG14 ....113 B6
Cross Oak Rd HP4 ....122 A4
Cross Rd Cheshunt EN8 ....162 E6
Hertford SG14 ....113 C7
Watford WD1 ....167 E3
Cross St Letchworth SG6 ....22 F7
Ware SG12 ....93 F1
2 St Albans AL3 ....127 D3
Ware SG12 ....93 F1
Watford WD1 ....167 C6
Cross Way AL5 ....86 C5
Cross Way The
Harrow HA3 ....176 E1
Luton LU1 ....63 C5

Crossbrook AL10 . . . . .129 E4
Crossbrook St EN8 . . . . . .162 D8
Crossett Gn HP3 . . . . .125 C1
Crossfell Rd HP3 . . . . .125 C2
Crossfield Cl HP4 . . . . .121 F4
Crossfield Rd EN11 . . . . . . .135 B8
Crossfields AL3 . . . . .141 B8
Crossgates SG1 . . . . .50 E5
Crosslands LU1 . . . . .62 E3
Crossleys SG6 . . . . .11 F2
Crossmead WD1 . . . . .167 B3
Crossoaks La Ridge EN6 . . .157 F5
　Shenley EN6 . . . . .157 D5
Crosspath The WD7 . . . . . .156 A4
Crosspaths AL5 . . . . .85 C4
Crossway Pinner HA5 . . . . .175 E1
　Welwyn Garden City AL8 . . .89 C2
Crossways Barley SG8 . . . . .8 F1
　Berkhamsted HP4 . . . . . . .121 F3
　Hemel Hempstead HP3 . . .125 B3
Crouch Ct CM20 . . . . .117 C3
Crouch Hall Gdns AL3 . . . .106 A6
Crouch Hall La AL3 . . . . . . .106 A6
Crouch La EN7 . . . . .147 C4
Crouchfield
　Hemel Hempstead HP1 . . .124 B2
　Hertford SG14 . . . . .92 C1
Crouchfield La SG14 . . . . . . .92 E4
Crow Furlong SG5 . . . . .34 D7
Crowborough Path WD3 . . .175 D6
Crowland Rd LU2 . . . . .46 C5
Crown Cl CM22 . . . . .98 E1
Crown La SG8 . . . . .16 F5
Crown Lodge SG15 . . . . .11 A4
Crown Rd WD6 . . . . .170 B8
Crown Rise WD2 . . . . .154 D5
Crown Rose Ct HP23 . . . . . .100 A3
Crown St AL3 . . . . .106 B5
Crown Terr CM23 . . . . .77 A7
Crownfield EN10 . . . . .135 A2
Croxdale Rd WD6 . . . . .170 A7
Croxley Ctr WD1 . . . . .166 D4
Croxley Sta WD3 . . . . .166 B3
Croxley View WD1 . . . . . . .166 E3
Croxton Cl 3 LU3 . . . . .45 A7
Crozier Ave CM23 . . . . .76 C8
Crunnel's Gn SG4 . . . . .48 E5
Crusader Way WD1 . . . . . . .166 F3
Cubbington Cl LU3 . . . . .45 A7
Cubitt Cl SG4 . . . . .35 C7
Cubitts Cl AL6 . . . . .89 F3
Cublands SG13 . . . . .114 B6
Cuckmans Dr AL2 . . . . .141 A6
Cuckoo's Nest LU2 . . . . .64 A7
Cucumber La AL9 . . . . .132 A1
Cuffley Ave WD2 . . . . .154 D5
Cuffley Cl LU3 . . . . .44 F8
Cuffley Ct HP2 . . . . .125 C8
Cuffley Hill EN7 . . . . .147 B2
Cuffley Sch EN6 . . . . .146 F1
Cuffley Sta EN6 . . . . .146 F2
Cullera Cl HA6 . . . . .174 E4
Cullings Ct EN9 . . . . .163 F6
Culver Cl SG10 . . . . .74 F1
Culver Lo AL1 . . . . .127 E5
Culver Rd AL1 . . . . .127 E5
Culverden Rd WD1 . . . . . . .175 B7
Culverhouse Rd LU3 . . . . . . .45 C3
Culworth Ct LU1 . . . . .62 E3
Cumberland Cl
　Hemel Hempstead WD5 . . .139 D7
　Hertford SG14 . . . . .113 C8
Cumberland Ct
　4 Hoddesdon EN11 . . . . .135 A7
　St Albans AL3 . . . . .127 E4
Cumberland Dr AL3 . . . . . .106 B6
Cumberland St LU1 . . . . .63 E6
Cumberlow Pl HP2 . . . . . . .125 C2
Cumcum Hill AL9 . . . . .131 E3
Cundalls Rd SG12 . . . . .93 E2
Cunningham Ave
　Enfield EN3 . . . . .162 E3
　St Albans AL1 . . . . .127 F3
Cunningham Ct EN8 . . . . . .148 E3
Cunningham Hill Inf Sch
　AL1 . . . . .128 A1
Cunningham Hill
　Jun Mix Sch AL1 . . . . . . .128 A1
Cunningham Hill Rd AL1 . .128 A1
Cunningham Rd EN8 . . . . .148 E4
Cupid Green La
　Great Gaddesden HP2 . . . .104 E3
　Hemel Hempstead HP2 . . .105 A1
Curlew Cl
　Berkhamsted HP4 . . . . . . .122 C3
　Letchworth SG6 . . . . .11 E1
Curlew Ct EN10 . . . . .148 F8
Curlew Rd LU2 . . . . .46 C5
Curlew St SG13 . . . . .113 E6
Curteys CM17 . . . . .118 D5
Curtis Cl WD3 . . . . .165 A1
Curtis Rd HP3 . . . . .125 D2
Curtis Way HP4 . . . . .122 D3
Curzon Gate Ct 1 WD1 . . .167 A8
Curzon Rd LU3 . . . . .45 C1
Cussans Ho WD1 . . . . .166 E3
Cussons Ct EN7 . . . . .148 A2
Cut Throat Ave HP4,LU6 . . . .81 E7
Cutenhoe Rd LU1 . . . . .63 E4
Cutforth Rd CM21 . . . . .97 E3
Cuthbert Cl EN7 . . . . .147 F2
Cutlers Gn LU2 . . . . .46 F2
Cutmore Dr AL4 . . . . .129 B1
Cutts La SG4 . . . . .66 D1
Cuttsfield Terr HP1 . . . . . . .123 F2

Cuttys La SG1 . . . . .50 E5
Cwmbran Ct HP2 . . . . .124 F7
Cygnet Cl
　Borehamwood WD6 . . . . .170 C8
　Northwood HA6 . . . . .174 C4
Cygnet Ct 11 CM23 . . . . .76 F6
Cylers Thicket AL6 . . . . .89 C6
Cymbeline Ct AL3 . . . . .127 C4
Cypress Ave
　Crews Hill EN2 . . . . .161 A4
　Welwyn Garden City AL7 . .111 C5
Cypress Cl EN9 . . . . .163 D5
Cypress Rd HA3 . . . . .176 D1
Cypress Wlk WD2 . . . . .154 B4
Cyrils Way AL1 . . . . .141 D8

D

Dacorum Coll of F Ed
　HP1 . . . . .124 C4
Dacorum Way HP1 . . . . . . .124 C3
Dacre Bldgs EN8 . . . . .148 F2
Dacre Cres SG4 . . . . .66 C1
Dacre Gdns WD6 . . . . .170 D4
Dacre Gn SG8 . . . . .9 F6
Dacre Rd SG5 . . . . .35 A8
Dagger La WD6 . . . . .169 B4
Daggs Dell Rd HP1 . . . . . . .123 E5
Dagnall Cty Fst Sch HP4 . . . .81 C5
Dagnall Rd
　Great Gaddesden HP1 . . . .103 C5
　Whipsnade HP4,LU6 . . . . . .81 D8
Dagnalls SG6 . . . . .22 F2
Dahlia Cl
　Hammond Street EN7 . . . .147 C6
　Luton LU4 . . . . .46 B4
Daintrees SG12 . . . . .95 E4
Daintry Lodge HA6 . . . . . . .174 F3
Dairy Cotts SG5 . . . . .19 B2
Dairy Mews WD1 . . . . .167 A4
Dairyglen Ave EN8 . . . . . . .162 E7
Daisy Ct SG6 . . . . .23 A8
Dalby Cl LU4 . . . . .44 B3
Dale Ave AL4 . . . . .87 B5
Dale Cl Hitchin SG4 . . . . . . .34 F4
　Pinner HA5 . . . . .175 B2
Dale Ct CM21 . . . . .97 D1
Dale Rd LU1 . . . . .63 C7
Dale The Letchworth SG6 . . .22 F5
　Waltham Abbey EN9 . . . . .163 D5
Dales Path WD6 . . . . .170 D4
Dales Rd WD6 . . . . .170 D4
Daleside Dr EN6 . . . . .158 E6
Dalewood Harpenden AL5 . . .86 D1
　Welwyn Garden City AL7 . . .111 D5
Dalkeith Rd AL5 . . . . .86 C1
Dallow Inf Sch LU1 . . . . .63 C8
Dallow Jun Sch LU1 . . . . . . .63 C8
Dallow Rd LU1 . . . . .63 B8
Dallow Road Jun & Inf Sch
　LU1 .63 C8
Dalroad Ind Est LU1 . . . . . . .63 B8
Dalton Cl LU3 . . . . .31 B1
Dalton Gdns CM23 . . . . .76 E4
Dalton St AL3 . . . . .127 D4
Dalton Way Watford WD1 . .167 D4
　Whitwell SG4 . . . . .66 E7
Daltry Cl SG1 . . . . .36 C2
Daltry Rd SG1 . . . . .36 C2
Damask Ct CM23 Tring HP23 .100 C4
　Weston SG4 . . . . .37 B8
Damask Gn HP1 . . . . .123 E2
Damask Green Rd SG4 . . . . .37 B8
Dame Alice Owen's Sch
　EN6 . . . . .158 E6
Dammersey Cl AL3 . . . . .83 F4
Damson Way AL4 . . . . .128 C5
Dancers End La HP23 . . . . . .99 C2
Dancers Hill Rd EN5 . . . . . .158 D3
Dancote SG3 . . . . .69 A5
Dane Acres CM23 . . . . .76 D8
Dane Bridge La SG10 . . . . . .75 B2
Dane Cl Harpenden AL5 . . . .86 C4
　Stotfold SG5 . . . . .11 F8
Dane End Ho SG1 . . . . .36 C1
Dane End La SG4 . . . . .69 A6
Dane End Rd SG11 . . . . .72 E3
Dane Ho CM23 . . . . .76 D8
Dane O'Coys Rd CM23 . . . . .58 E1
Dane Pk CM23 . . . . .76 D8
Dane Rd LU3 . . . . .45 D2
Dane St CM23 . . . . .77 A7
Danebridge Rd SG10 . . . . . .75 B2
Danefield Rd SG5 . . . . .20 C4
Danemead EN11 . . . . .115 A1
Danes The AL2 . . . . .141 C3
Danesbury La AL6 . . . . .89 D8
Danesbury Park Caravan
　Site AL6 . . . . .89 D8
Danesbury Park Rd AL6 . . . .89 D8
Danesbury Pk
　Hertford SG14 . . . . .113 D7
　Welwyn AL6 . . . . .89 C7
Danescroft SG6 . . . . .12 A1
Danesgate SG1 . . . . .50 D4
Danestrete SG1 . . . . .50 D5
Daniells AL7 . . . . .111 A7
Danvers Croft HP23 . . . . . .100 C5
Danvers Dr LU3 . . . . .31 C1
Danziger Way WD6 . . . . . . .170 C8
Darby Dr
　Waltham Abbey EN9 . . . . .163 C6
　Welwyn AL6 . . . . .68 E3
Darcy Cl EN8 . . . . .162 E8
Dark La Cheshunt EN7 . . . .148 A1
　Codicote SG4 . . . . .88 E8
　Harpenden AL5 . . . . .107 D7

Dark La continued
　Sandon SG9 . . . . .15 B1
　Wingrave HP22 . . . . .60 C3
Darkes La EN6 . . . . .159 A4
Darlands Dr EN5 . . . . .171 D4
Darley Rd LU2,SG4 . . . . .47 C2
Darnhills WD7 . . . . .155 F4
Darnicle Hill EN7 . . . . .147 A6
Darr's La HP4 . . . . .121 D6
Darrington Rd WD6 . . . . . .169 E8
Darwin Cl
　Hemel Hempstead HP2 . . .105 B1
　St Albans AL3 . . . . .127 E7
Darwin Gdns WD1 . . . . . . .175 C5
Darwin Rd SG2 . . . . .51 B6
Dashes The CM20 . . . . .117 E1
Datchet Ct HP2 . . . . .125 B8
Datchworth
　Jun Mix Inf Sch SG3 . . . . .69 D3
Datchworth Turn HP2 . . . . .125 C3
Dauphin Ct 5 LU2 . . . . .45 D1
Davenham Ave HA6 . . . . . .174 F5
Daventer Dr HA7 . . . . .176 F3
Davies Ct SG13 . . . . .113 E6
Davis Cres SG5 . . . . .20 C4
Davis Ct AL1 . . . . .127 E3
Davis' Row SG15 . . . . .11 A4
Dawson Cl EN8 . . . . .148 D3
Dawson Dr EN8 . . . . .148 D3
Dawys Cl AL4 . . . . .108 E7
Dawes La WD3 . . . . .151 F3
Dawley AL7 . . . . .89 F1
Dawley Rd HP2 . . . . .125 A7
Dawlish Cl SG2 . . . . .69 D7
Dawlish Rd LU4 . . . . .44 F3
Dawson Cl SG16 . . . . .10 C5
Day's Cl SG8 . . . . .7 C5
Dayemead AL7 . . . . .111 B3
Days Cl AL10 . . . . .129 F5
Days Mead AL10 . . . . .129 F5
De Haviland Cl AL10 . . . . . .129 F6
De Havilland Dr WD7 . . . . .156 E7
De Havilland Way WD5 . . .153 F7
De Tany Ct AL1 . . . . .127 D2
De Vere Wlk WD1 . . . . .166 E7
Deacon Cl AL1 . . . . .141 D7
Deacon's Hill Rd WD6 . . . .170 A4
Deacons Cl
　Borehamwood WD6 . . . . .170 A5
　Pinner HA5 . . . . .175 B1
Deacons Ct 6 LU2 . . . . .63 D8
Deacons Hill WD1 . . . . .167 C3
Deacons Hts WD6 . . . . .170 A3
Deacons Way SG5 . . . . .21 D1
Deaconsfield Rd HP3 . . . . . .138 E8
Dead Woman's La SG4 . . . . .48 C7
Deadman's Ash La WD3 . . .152 B3
Deakin Cl WD1 . . . . .166 E2
Dean Cl WD2 . . . . .154 D6
Dean Field WD3 . . . . .137 A4
Dean Moore Ct AL1 . . . . . .127 D2
Dean The HP22 . . . . .60 B3
Dean's Gdns AL4 . . . . .128 A7
Deans Cl
　Abbots Langley WD5 . . . . .153 D7
　Tring HP23 . . . . .100 A4
Deans Furlong HP23 . . . . . .100 A4
Deans Mdw HP4 . . . . .81 C5
Deanscroft SG3 . . . . .68 F5
Deansway HP3 . . . . .138 D8
Deard's End La SG3 . . . . .68 F6
Deards Wood SG3 . . . . .68 F5
Debenham Ct EN5 . . . . .171 C4
Debenham Rd EN7 . . . . . . .148 B4
Dee The HP2 . . . . .124 F8
Deep Denes LU2 . . . . .46 A2
Deepdene EN6 . . . . .158 D8
Deeping Cl SG3 . . . . .68 F4
Deer Cl SG13 . . . . .113 F6
Deerfield Cl SG12 . . . . .93 D2
Deerings The AL5 . . . . .107 A4
Deerswood Ave AL10 . . . . .130 B3
Deeves Hall La EN6 . . . . . . .157 E6
Deimos Dr HP2 . . . . .125 A6
Delahay Rise EN4 . . . . .122 B6
Delamare Rd EN8 . . . . .148 E1
Delamere Rd WD6 . . . . .170 B8
Delfcroft SG12 . . . . .93 C2
Delfield Gdns LU1 . . . . .62 E4
Delius Cl WD6 . . . . .169 C3
Dell Cl AL5 . . . . .86 B3
Dell La Bishop's Stortford,
　Hockerill CM23 . . . . .77 A7
　Bishop's Stortford,
　Latchmore Bank CM22 . . .77 B1
　Spellbrook CM22 . . . . .98 A8
Dell Mdw HP3 . . . . .138 E7
Dell Rd Berkhamsted HP4 . .121 D7
　Enfield EN3 . . . . .162 C1
　Watford WD2 . . . . .154 A2
Dell Rise AL2 . . . . .141 B5
Dell Side WD2 . . . . .154 A2
Dell Springs SG9 . . . . .40 E8
Dell The Baldock SG7 . . . . . .23 E6
　Brickendon SG13 . . . . .113 C3
　Caddington LU1 . . . . .62 D2
　Luton LU2 . . . . .46 F1
　Markyate AL3 . . . . .83 D5
　Moor Park HA6 . . . . .174 E8
　Pinner HA5 . . . . .175 D1
　Radlett WD7 . . . . .156 A4
　Royston SG8 . . . . .7 D7
　St Albans AL1 . . . . .128 A4
　Stevenage SG1 . . . . .50 E5
　Welwyn AL6 . . . . .90 A4
Dellcott Cl LU2 . . . . .46 B4
Dellcott Cl AL8 . . . . .110 C7

Dellcroft Way AL5 . . . . .107 A5
Dellcut Rd HP2 . . . . .125 A5
Dellfield
　Berkhamsted HP4 . . . . . . .122 A6
　St Albans AL1 . . . . .127 F2
　Thundridge SG12 . . . . .93 D8
Dellfield Ave HP4 . . . . .122 A6
Dellfield Cl Radlett WD7 . . .155 F4
　Watford WD1 . . . . .167 A7
Dellfield Ct Harlow CM17 . .118 C4
　Luton LU2 . . . . .46 D2
Dellfield Rd AL10 . . . . .130 A5
Dellmeadow WD5 . . . . .139 E1
Dellors Cl EN5 . . . . .171 D4
Dells The
　11 Bishop's Stortford CM23 . .76 F7
　Hemel Hempstead HP3 . . .125 B2
Dells Wood Cl EN11 . . . . . .114 F1
Dellsome La
　Colney Heath AL4,AL9,AL10 .143 F8
　Welham Green AL9 . . . . . .144 B8
Dellswood Cl SG13 . . . . . . .113 E5
Dellwood WD3 . . . . .165 B1
Delmar Ave HP2 . . . . .125 A6
Delmer Ct WD6 . . . . .156 F1
Delmerend La AL3 . . . . .84 C1
Delphine Cl LU1 . . . . .63 B6
Delta Gain WD1 . . . . .175 D7
Demontfort Rise SG12 . . . . . .93 C3
Denbigh Cl 2 HP2 . . . . .124 E2
Denbigh High Sch LU3 . . . . .45 B2
Denbigh Inf Sch LU3 . . . . . . .45 B2
Denbigh Jun Sch LU3 . . . . . .45 B2
Denbigh Rd LU3 . . . . .45 B2
Denby SG6 . . . . .23 A4
Dencora Way LU3 . . . . .44 B8
Dendridge Cl EN1 . . . . .162 B2
Dene La SG2 . . . . .51 E2
Dene Rd HA6 . . . . .174 D4
Denes The HP3 . . . . .138 F7
Deerwood Cl WD3 . . . . .153 F2
Denham Cl
　Hemel Hempstead HP2 . . .125 A8
　Luton LU3 . . . . .44 E8
Denham La AL9 . . . . .172 A2
Denham Way WD3 . . . . . . .170 C8
Denham Way
　(North Orbital Rd)
　WD3 . . . . .172 C4
Denmark Ct LU3 . . . . .44 E8
Denmark St HP2 . . . . .167 B7
Dennis Cl HP22 . . . . .99 A4
Dennis Ct AL3 . . . . .127 D4
Denny Gate EN8 . . . . .163 D5
Denny Ct CM23 . . . . .59 B7
Denny Gate EN8 . . . . .148 F4
Denny's La HP4 . . . . .121 F3
Densley Cl AL3 . . . . .110 D8
Denton Cl Barnet EN5 . . . . .171 C4
　Luton LU4 . . . . .44 B3
Denton Ho WD1 . . . . .175 C7
Denton Rd SG1 . . . . .50 E4
Dents Cl SG3 . . . . .23 C3
Derby Ave HA3 . . . . .176 D2
Derby Ho AL5 . . . . .175 D1
Derby Rd Hoddesdon EN11 . .135 D4
　Luton LU4 . . . . .44 D2
　Watford WD1 . . . . .167 C5
Derby Way SG1 . . . . .50 B6
Derwent Ave Luton LU3 . . . .45 B7
　Pinner HA5 . . . . .176 C4
Derwent Lower Sch SG16 . .10 B5
Derwent Rd
　Harpenden AL5 . . . . .85 C4
　Hemel Hempstead HP3 . . .125 C2
　Henlow SG16 . . . . .10 B4
　Luton LU3 . . . . .45 B8
　Luton LU2 . . . . .46 A8
Des Fuller Ct 3 LU1 . . . . . . .63 F6
Desborough Cl SG14 . . . . . . .92 C1
Desborough Dr AL6 . . . . . . .90 D5
Desborough Rd SG4 . . . . . . .35 C8
Desmond Rd WD2 . . . . .153 F3
Devereux Dr AL3 . . . . .127 A1
Devereux Dr WD1 . . . . .153 E1
Devoils La 9 CM23 . . . . .76 F7
Devon Ct AL1 . . . . .127 E2
Devon Rd Luton LU2 . . . . . . .64 B8
　Watford WD2 . . . . .167 D8
Devonshire Cl SG2 . . . . .69 A8
Devonshire Rd
　5 Harpenden AL5 . . . . .86 B1
　Pinner HA5 . . . . .175 D2
Dewars Cl AL6 . . . . .89 C6
Dewes Green Rd CM23 . . . .30 F1
Dewgrass Gr EN8 . . . . .162 D4
Dewhurst Rd EN8 . . . . .148 B3
Dewhurst St Mary CE
　Prim Sch EN8 . . . . .148 C2
Dewpond Cl SG1 . . . . .50 C8
Dewsbury Rd LU3 . . . . .45 C6
Dexter Cl Luton LU3 . . . . . . .31 B1
　St Albans AL1 . . . . .128 A2
Dexter Rd Barnet EN5 . . . . .171 D3
　Harefield UB9 . . . . .173 C1
Diamond Ind Ctr SG6 . . . . . .23 C7
Diamond Rd WD2 . . . . .154 A1
Dickens Cl AL3 . . . . .127 D4
Dickens Ct WD7 . . . . .156 A5
Dicker Mill SG13 . . . . .113 D7
Dicket Mead AL6 . . . . .89 C5
Dickins Ct EN7 . . . . .148 A5
Dickinson Ave WD3 . . . . . . .166 A3
Dickinson Sq WD3 . . . . .166 A3
Dickson EN7 . . . . .147 F4
Dig Dag Hill EN7 . . . . .147 F4
Digswell Cl WD6 . . . . .157 A1
Digswell Ct AL8 . . . . .110 E8
Digswell Hill AL6 . . . . .89 B2

Digswell House Mews
　AL8 .89 E7
Digswell La AL7 . . . . .89 F6
Digswell Park Rd
　Welwyn Garden City AL8 . . .89 E7
　Welwyn Garden City AL8 . . .89 D7
Digswell Rd AL8 . . . . .89 E7
Digswell Rise AL8 . . . . .110 E8
Dimmocks La WD3 . . . . . . .152 B5
Dimsdale Cres CM23 . . . . . . .77 A6
Dimsdale St SG14 . . . . .113 C6
Dinant Link Rd EN11 . . . . . .135 A7
Dingle Cl EN5 . . . . .170 E8
Dinmore HP3 . . . . .136 F8
Ditchfield Rd EN11 . . . . . . .115 B1
Ditchling Cl LU2 . . . . .46 A2
Ditchmore La SG1 . . . . .50 D7
Ditton Gn LU2 . . . . .46 F2
Divine Saviour
　RC Prim Sch WD1 . . . . . . .153 F1
Divot Pl SG13 . . . . .114 A5
Dixies Cl SG7 . . . . .4 C4
Dixon Pl SG9 . . . . .40 D5
Dixons Hill Cl AL9 . . . . .144 A5
Dixons Hill Rd AL9 . . . . . . .144 A6
Dobb's Weir Rd EN11 . . . . .135 E1
Docklands SG5 . . . . .20 D3
Doctor's Commons Rd
　HP4 . . . . .122 A3
Dodds La HP1 . . . . .104 C1
Dodwood AL7 . . . . .111 C6
Dog Kennel La
　Chorleywood WD3 . . . . . .164 D6
　Hatfield AL10 . . . . .130 C6
　Royston SG8 . . . . .7 E6
Doggetts Way AL1 . . . . .127 E2
Dognell Gn AL8 . . . . .110 B6
Dolesbury Dr AL6 . . . . .89 E5
Dollis Brook Wlk EN5 . . . . .171 E4
Dollis Valley Way EN5 . . . . .171 E3
Dolphin Ct HA3 . . . . .176 F1
Dolphin Sq HP23 . . . . .100 C4
Dolphin Way CM23 . . . . .77 A8
Dolphin Yd
　7 Hertford SG14 . . . . .113 D6
　St Albans AL1 . . . . .127 D3
　7 Ware SG12 . . . . .93 F1
Dominic Ct EN9 . . . . .163 E6
Doncaster Cl SG1 . . . . .51 A8
Doncaster Gn WD1 . . . . . . .175 B6
Donkey La HP23 . . . . .99 F5
Donne Cl SG8 . . . . .7 E5
Dorant Ho AL3 . . . . .107 A8
Dorchester Ave EN11 . . . . .135 C4
Dorchester Ct
　Croxley Green WD3 . . . . . .166 C5
　St Albans AL1 . . . . .128 B5
　Watford WD1 . . . . .167 C6
Dordans Rd LU4 . . . . .44 A5
Dorel Cl LU2 . . . . .45 F1
Dormans Cl HA6 . . . . .174 C2
Dormer Ct EN5 . . . . .171 D4
Dormie Cl AL3 . . . . .127 A2
Dornan Ct LU1 . . . . .63 C6
Dorrien's Croft HP4 . . . . . .121 F7
Dorrington Cl LU3 . . . . .45 A5
Dorrofield Cl WD3 . . . . .166 F5
Dorset Cl HP4 . . . . .121 F7
Dorset Ct 4 LU1 . . . . .63 C7
Dorset Ho WD6 . . . . .76 C3
Douglas Ave WD2 . . . . .154 C8
Douglas Cl SG1 . . . . .51 B5
Douglas Ho EN8 . . . . .148 F3
Douglas Rd Harpenden AL5 . .85 F3
　Luton LU4 . . . . .45 A3
Douglas Way AL7 . . . . .111 E5
Dove Cl
　Bishop's Stortford CM23 . . .76 F8
　Stansted Mountfitchet CM24 . .59 D7
Dove Ct AL10 . . . . .130 C2
Dove House La LU6 . . . . .82 F8
Dove La EN6 . . . . .159 F7
Dove Pk
　Chorleywood WD3 . . . . . .164 D6
　Pinner HA5 . . . . .176 F1
Dovedale Luton LU2 . . . . . . .46 A4
　Stevenage SG2 . . . . .51 D5
　Ware SG12 . . . . .93 E2
Dovedale Cl EN9 . . . . .163 E6
Dovehouse Croft CM20 . . . .118 A1
Dovehouse Hill LU2 . . . . .46 C1
Dover Cl LU3 . . . . .45 A5
Dover Way WD3 . . . . .166 F5
Doverfield EN7 . . . . .147 F2
Dower Ct 1 SG4 . . . . .34 F5
Dowland Ho EN11 . . . . .161 F8
Dowling Ct HP3 . . . . .138 D7
Down Edge AL3 . . . . .83 D5
Down Green La AL4 . . . . . . .108 D8
Downalong WD2 . . . . .168 A8
Downage AL3 . . . . .152 B3
Downer Dr WD3 . . . . .152 B3
Downes Rd AL4 . . . . .128 A7
Downfield Cl SG13 . . . . .114 A6
Downfield Ct SG12 . . . . .93 E2
Downfield Jun Mix Inf Sch
　HP4 . . . . .122 B5
Downfield Rd
　Cheshunt EN8 . . . . .162 D5
　Hertford Heath SG13 . . . .114 B4
Downhall Ley SG9 . . . . .40 D6
Downings Wood WD3 . . . . .172 B5
Downlands Baldock SG7 . . . .23 E6
　Luton LU3 . . . . .45 B7
　Royston SG8 . . . . .7 E5
　Stevenage SG2 . . . . .51 D5
　Waltham Abbey EN9 . . . . .163 D5

er Hall LU2 64 C8
er Rd LU1 63 D7
sbury Rd LU4 44 D5
bury Ave AL2 142 C5
bury La AL1 142 A7
ot Pl WD1 167 B7
ot Rd WD1 167 B7
ot St WD1 167 B7
ot Wood Inf Sch 154 A1
ot Wood Jun Sch 154 A1
ot Wood Rd WD1 153 F1
by Rd LU1 63 B7
Cl
hamwood WD6 169 F5
enage SG2 51 B6
am Green AL9 144 D8
Gn HP3 138 F6
Mills CE Prim Sch 138 F6
Mills La HP3 138 F5
Rd SG8 7 D5
aniel Wlk HP23 100 A5
ans Cl AL6 89 C6
and Cl LU2 46 E1
ng Cty Prim Sch 149 E8
ing New Rd EN10 135 B2
ng Rd EN9 135 D1
ngbury Cl EN9 135 D1
ngbury Par EN9 135 D1
n Cl SG1 37 C3
Cl HA6 175 A2
Ct Hertford SG14 113 C6
ham Abbey EN9 163 F6
St WD1 167 C4
le Cl WD6 170 C8
on Rd AL4 108 E8
ham Rd LU4 44 B6
Way WD3 164 F2
Gwynn Cl WD7 156 E7
n Ave AL1 142 B8
n Rd
op's Stortford CM23 77 A5
all HP4 81 C5
n St SG14 113 B7
Rd SG16 10 B4
ne Ct WD6 170 A6
ne Dr HP2 124 E5
ne Gate SG2 51 D8
n Rd WD2 154 C2
er St SG12 95 E4
erby Cl HP23 100 C6
ercott Cl LU2 46 C1
erfield Ct SG12 115 D3
erfield La SG12 115 E3
erfield Rd AL5 107 B4
erhall Rd CM19 135 F5
erstones SG5 11 F7
erway AL3 141 A8
y Dell SG6 23 B3
swell Cross CM20 117 E2
swell Orch CM20 117 D1
swell Rd CM20 117 F3
swell Twr CM20 117 D1
ecroft
el Hempstead HP1 124 B2
wyn Garden City AL7 111 B7
eden Rd
Gaddesden HP4 102 E4
eden HP1 103 C1
n End HP4 123 B8
l's Gn SG6 22 F6
ls Rd SG6 22 F6
Cl HA6 174 D5
Gr WD2 167 B8
e Cl EN6 158 F8
e Rd LU3 45 A5
e Road Pas LU3 45 A5
e's Ct SG6 23 B7
Barn La CM22 77 D1
Barnes Ave AL1 142 A8
Barns La SG10 74 E4
Bedford Rd LU3 45 D3
Briars Prim Sch 130 A5
Cl SG3 68 F6
Cotts
kmans Park AL9 144 D3
hunt EN8 162 C5
well SG4 66 A7
Ct SG3 69 A2
England Cl SG4 34 F4
England St AL3 127 C3
Farm La HA6 174 E2
Ford Bsns Pk EN8 162 F5
Ford Rd EN8 162 F5
Forge Pl AL3 106 B5
Greens Ave AL3 127 D7
House Pk AL1 142 B7
nn Rd SG7 3 D5
Kent Rd AL1 127 D3
Mill Terr HP23 100 B6
Par WD3 164 C5
Park Dr HP2 125 B3
Park La SG2 51 F2
Park Rd
field UB9 173 C2
gate Street SG13 146 D7
Pl AL6 89 B4
Rd Berkhamsted HP4 122 D6
hamsted,
church HP4 121 F7
erfield WD4 137 F1
ey Green WD3 166 A4
e WD6 169 D3
Chishill SG8 9 D6

New Rd *continued*
Harlow CM17 118 D4
Hatfield AL8 110 A3
Hertford SG14 113 D8
Hoddesdon EN10 135 A4
Little Hadham SG11 75 A7
Lower Stondon SG17 10 A8
Radlett WD7 155 E2
Radlett, Letchmore
Heath WD7 168 E8
Ridge EN6 158 A6
Sarratt WD3 151 F1
Shenley WD7 157 A5
Tring HP23 100 B6
Ware SG12 93 D1
Watford WD1 167 C5
Welwyn AL6 89 F3
Woolmer Green SG3 69 B3
New River Ave SG12 115 B4
New River Cl EN11 135 B7
New River Ct EN7 162 B8
New River Trad Est EN8 148 D5
New St Berkhamsted HP4 122 D4
Cheddington LU7 79 F7
Luton LU1 63 E6
Sawbridgeworth CM21 97 E3
Slip End LU1 63 C1
Watford WD1 167 C5
New Town SG4 67 F1
New Town Rd 9 LU1 63 E6
New Town St LU1 63 E6
New Wood AL7 111 C7
Newark Cl SG8 7 C8
Newark Gn WD6 170 D6
Newark Rd LU4 45 A2
Newberries Ave WD7 156 B4
Newberries Prim Sch
WD7 156 C4
Newbiggin Path WD1 175 C6
Newbold Rd LU3 45 B7
Newbolt SG8 7 D8
Newbolt Rd HA7 176 F5
Newbury Ave EN3 162 F2
Newbury Cl
Bishop's Stortford CM23 76 E8
Luton LU4 44 E2
Stevenage SG1 36 D1
Newcastle Cl SG1 36 F2
Newcombe Rd LU1 63 C7
Newcome Path WD7 157 A5
Newcome Rd WD7 157 A5
Newdigate Gn UB9 173 D2
Newdigate Rd UB9 173 C2
Newdigate Rd E UB9 173 D2
Newell La SG2 38 D7
Newell Rd HP3 138 E8
Newell Rise HP3 138 E8
Newells SG6 23 D4
Newells Hedge LU7 80 D5
Newfield La HP2 124 F3
Newfield Way AL4 128 D1
Newfields AL8 110 B5
Newford Cl HP2 125 B4
Newgate SG2 51 A4
Newgate Cl AL4 128 D6
Newgate St SG13 146 D7
Newgate Street Village
SG13 146 E6
Newgatestreet Rd EN7 147 B4
Newground Rd HP23 101 B3
Newhall Cl HP3 137 A4
Newhall Ct EN9 163 F6
Newhouse Cres WD2 154 B6
Newhouse Rd HP3 137 A4
Newland Cl Pinner HA5 175 F4
St Albans AL1 142 A8
Newlands Hatfield AL9 130 C7
Letchworth SG6 23 A3
Newlands Ave WD7 155 F5
Newlands Cl E SG4 34 F4
Newlands Cl W SG4 34 F4
Newlands La SG4 34 F4
Newlands Pl EN5 171 D4
Newlands Rd
Hemel Hempstead HP1 123 E3
Luton LU1 63 C3
Newlands Way EN6 145 B1
Newlands Wlk WD2 154 D6
Newlyn Cl
Bricket Wood AL2 140 E1
Stevenage SG1 50 A6
Newlyn Rd EN5 171 F5
Newman Ave SG8 7 F6
Newmans Ct SG14 70 D3
Newmans Dr AL5 85 F2
Newmarket Ct AL3 127 C4
Newmarket Rd Royston SG8 7 E6
Royston SG8 7 F6
Newnham Cl LU2 46 D1
Newnham Par 5 EN8 148 D1
Newnham Rd SG7 12 E6
Newnham Way SG7 4 B2
Newport Cl EN3 162 E2
Newport Mead WD1 175 D6
Newports CM21 97 C1
Newquay Gdns WD1 175 B8
Newstead AL10 129 F2
Newstead Ho UB9 173 C1
Newteswell Dr EN9 163 D7
Newton Cl Harpenden AL5 107 D6
Hoddesdon EN11 115 B2
Newton Cres WD6 170 C5
Newton Dr CM21 97 D1
Newton Rd Harrow HA3 176 E1
Stevenage SG2 51 B6
Newtondale LU4 44 C5
Newtons Way SG4 34 F6
Newtown Rd CM23 76 F6

Niagara Cl EN8 148 D2
Nicholas Breakspear
RC Sch AL4 128 E2
Nicholas Cl St Albans AL3 127 D7
Watford WD2 154 B2
Nicholas La SG14 113 D6
Nicholas Pl SG1 36 D1
Nicholas Rd WD6 169 F4
Nicholas Way
Hemel Hempstead HP2 124 F5
Northwood HA6 174 C2
Nicholls Cl AL3 105 F5
Nichols Cl LU2 46 C2
Nicholson Court Ind Ctr
EN11 135 B6
Nicholson Dr WD2 176 C8
Nicola Cl HA3 176 D1
Nicoll Way WD6 170 D5
Nidderdale HP2 124 F6
Nightingale Ave SG8 2 A5
Nightingale Cl Luton LU2 46 C6
Radlett WD7 155 F3
Watford WD5 154 A8
Nightingale Ct
Hertford SG14 113 C6
Hitchin SG5 35 A8
Luton LU3 63 C8
Rickmansworth WD3 165 C2
Nightingale La AL1,AL4 142 C7
Nightingale Lodge HP4 122 B4
Nightingale Pl WD3 165 D2
Nightingale Rd
Bushey WD2 168 A4
Hammond Street EN7 147 C6
Hitchin SG5 34 F8
Rickmansworth WD3 165 C2
Nightingale Terr SG15 11 A3
Nightingale Way SG7 23 F6
Nightingale Wlk
Hemel Hempstead HP2 105 C1
Stevenage SG2 51 C5
Nightingales EN9 163 E5
Nimbus Way SG4 35 C7
Nimmo Dr WD2 168 D2
Nimrod Cl AL4 128 C5
Ninefields EN9 163 F6
Ninesprings Way SG4 35 B6
Ninefield Ct LU2 46 C3
Ninian Rd HP2 124 E8
Ninning's La AL6 68 D2
Ninth Ave LU3 44 D7
Niton Cl EN5 171 D3
Niven Cl WD6 170 C8
Nobel Sch SG2 51 C7
Nobel Villas EN9 163 D5
Nobles The CM23 76 D6
Nodes Dr SG2 51 A1
Noke La AL2 140 E4
Noke Shot AL5 86 C4
Noke Side AL2 141 A4
Noke The SG2 69 B8
Nokes The HP1 124 A5
Nokeside SG2 69 B8
Nook The SG12 115 B4
Norbury Ave WD1 167 C7
Norfolk Ave WD2 154 C1
Norfolk Ct 4 EN5 171 E5
Norfolk Gdns WD6 170 D5
Norfolk Rd Buntingford SG9 40 E8
Luton LU2 64 A7
Rickmansworth WD3 165 E1
Norfolk Way CM23 76 F5
Normady Ct HP1 124 D4
Norman Ave CM23 76 D6
Norman Cl EN9 163 D6
Norman Cres HA5 175 C2
Norman Ct
Potters Bar EN6 145 C1
Stansted Mountfitchet CM24 59 E8
Stevenage SG1 36 F1
Norman Rd Luton LU3 45 B2
Welwyn AL6 89 B3
Norman's La SG8 7 D5
Norman's Way CM24 59 E7
Normandy Ave EN5 171 F5
Normandy Dr HP4 122 B6
Normandy Rd AL3 127 D4
Normandy Way EN11 135 D8
Normans Cl SG6 11 F1
Normans La AL6 68 E2
Normansfield Cl WD2 168 B2
Norris Cl CM23 77 C7
Norris Gr EN10 134 E3
Norris La EN11 135 A7
Norris Rd EN11 135 A6
Norris Rise EN11 134 F7
North App Moor Park HA6 174 C8
Watford WD2 154 A5
North Ave
Letchworth SG6 23 B8
Shenley WD7 156 E7
North Barn EN10 135 B1
North Cl Barnet EN5 171 C4
Chiswellgreen AL2 141 B6
Royston SG8 7 C7
North Comm AL3 106 A5
North Common Rd AL3 106 A4
North Ct AL3 83 E5
North Dr St Albans AL4 128 E5
Thundridge SG11 72 E1
North Drift Way LU1 63 B6
North Gate CM20 117 C1
North Hertfordshire Coll
SG6 22 F5
North Hertfordshire Coll
(Hitchin Ctr) SG4 35 B8
North Hertfordshire Coll
(Stevenage Ctr) SG1 50 D4

North Herts Ed Support Ctr
SG6 22 D3
North Hill WD3 164 E8
North Luton Ind Est LU4 44 B7
North Orbital Rd
Bricket Wood AL2 140 E2
Chiswellgreen AL2 141 B5
Colney Heath AL4 129 C2
London Colney AL1,AL2,AL4 142 D6
Park Street AL2 141 E6
Watford WD2 154 D7
North Orbital Trad Est
AL1 142 A7
North Pl Harlow CM20 118 B5
Hitchin SG5 21 D1
Waltham Abbey EN9 163 B6
North Rd Baldock SG7 12 E2
Berkhamsted HP4 122 B4
Cheshunt EN8 162 E6
Chorleywood WD3 164 D4
Hertford SG14 113 A7
Hertford SG14 113 C6
Hoddesdon EN11 135 A7
Stevenage SG1 36 C2
North Ride AL6 89 C6
North Riding AL2 141 A1
North Road Ave SG14 113 A7
North Road Gdns SG14 113 B6
North St
4 Bishop's Stortford CM23 76 F7
Lower Nazeing EN9 135 E1
Luton, Hart Hill LU2 45 E1
Luton, High Town LU2 63 E8
North Terr 5 CM23 76 F8
North View Cotts SG12 95 D4
North Western Ave
Abbots Langley WD2 153 D4
Stanmore WD6 169 A2
Watford WD2 154 C3
Northaw CE Sch EN6 146 A1
Northaw Cl HP2 125 B8
Northaw Pk EN6 159 F7
Northaw Rd E EN6 146 E1
Northaw Rd W EN6 160 C8
Northbridge Rd HP4 122 A6
Northbridge Way HP1 124 A3
Northbrook Dr HA6 174 E3
Northbrook Rd EN5 171 E3
Northcliffe Dr N20 171 F1
Northcote 1 HA5 175 C1
Northcotts AL9 130 C6
Northcourt WD3 165 A1
Northdown Rd AL10 130 A2
Northend HP3 125 C1
Northern Ave SG16 10 C3
Northern Ho SG4 35 B7
Northfield Braughing SG11 55 F7
Hatfield AL10 130 B8
Standon SG11 55 E2
Northfield Gdns WD2 154 C2
Northfield Rd
Aldbury HP23 100 F7
Borehamwood WD6 170 B8
Cheshunt EN8 162 E7
Guilden Morden SG7 1 C2
Harpenden AL5 86 C4
Sawbridgeworth CM21 97 E4
Northfields SG6 11 F1
Northfields Inf Sch SG6 11 F1
Northgate HA6 174 C3
Northgate End CM23 76 F8
Northgate Ho EN8 148 D2
Northgate Jun Mix Inf Sch
CM23 76 E8
Northgate Path WD6 169 F8
Northlands EN6 159 D8
Northolt Ave CM23 59 B1
Northridge Way HP1 124 A3
Northside AL4 108 B1
Northumberland Ave
EN1 162 B1
Northview Rd LU2 45 F2
Northway
Rickmansworth WD3 165 D2
1 Welwyn Garden City AL7 89 F1
Northwell Dr LU3 44 F7
Northwick Rd WD1 175 C6
Northwood AL7 111 D6
Northwood Cl EN7 147 F4
Northwood Coll HA6 174 D3
Northwood Comp Sch
HA6 175 B2
Northwood Hills Cir
HA6 175 A2
Northwood Hills Sta
HA6 175 A1
Northwood & Pinner
District Hospl HA6 175 A2
Northwood Prep Boys Sch
WD3 174 C8
Northwood Rd UB9 173 E3
Northwood Sta HA6 174 E3
Northwood Way
Harefield UB9 173 D2
Northwood HA6 175 A3
Norton Bury La SG6 12 C2
Norton Cl WD6 170 A8
Norton Cres SG7 23 E8
Norton Gn SG1 50 B3
Norton Green Rd SG1 50 C4
Norton Mill La SG6 12 D3
Norton Rd Letchworth SG6 12 C2
Luton LU3 44 F4
Stevenage SG1 50 D4
Stotfold SG5 12 A4
Norton Road Prim Sch
LU3 44 F4
Norton Sch SG6 23 A8

Norton Way N SG6 23 A7
Norton Way S SG6 23 A5
Nortonstreet La SG4 67 B7
Norvic Rd HP23 80 A1
Norwich Cl SG1 37 B1
Norwich Way WD3 166 B5
Norwood Cl SG14 112 F7
Norwood Rd EN8 148 E1
Nottingham Cl WD2 154 A6
Nottingham Rd WD3 164 C1
Novello Way WD6 170 D8
Nugent's Pk HA5 175 F2
Nugents Ct HA5 175 E2
Nun's Cl SG5 34 E7
Nunfield WD4 152 B8
Nunnery Cl AL1 127 E1
Nunnery La LU3 45 B5
Nunnery Stables AL1 127 D1
Nuns La AL1 141 E8
Nunsbury Dr EN10 148 E6
Nunsbury Drive Cotts
EN10 148 E6
Nup End Cl HP22 60 B3
Nup End La HP22 60 B3
Nupton Dr EN5 171 C3
Nurseries Rd AL4 108 E7
Nursery Cl
Bishop's Stortford CM23 76 F6
Stevenage SG2 69 A8
Nursery Cotts SG1 50 A6
Nursery Fields CM21 97 D2
Nursery Gdns
Goff's Oak EN7 147 D3
Tring HP23 100 B4
Ware SG12 93 E1
Welwyn Garden City AL7 89 E1
Nursery Hill AL7 89 E1
Nursery Par LU3 44 E5
Nursery Rd
Bishop's Stortford CM23 76 F6
Cheshunt EN10 148 F6
Hoddesdon EN11 115 B1
Lower Nazeing EN9 135 D2
Luton LU3 44 F5
Nut Gr AL8 89 D1
Nut Slip SG9 40 E6
Nutcroft SG3 69 D2
Nutfield AL7 90 A1
Nuthampstead Rd SG8 17 E2
Nutleigh Gr SG5 21 D1
Nuttfield Cl WD3 166 B3
Nye Way HP3 137 A3
Nymans Cl LU2 46 D3

O

Oak Ave Bricket Wood AL2 141 A1
Enfield EN2 160 F1
Oak Cl
Hemel Hempstead HP3 138 F7
Waltham Abbey EN9 163 D5
Oak Ct HA6 174 D4
Oak Dr Berkhamsted HP4 122 D3
Sawbridgeworth CM21 118 C8
Oak End SG9 40 D7
Oak Farm WD6 170 C4
Oak Glade HA6 174 B2
Oak Gn WD5 153 E7
Oak Gr Hatfield AL10 129 F5
Hertford SG13 113 E4
Oak Green Way WD5 153 E7
Oak Hall CM23 76 E8
Oak La Cholesbury HP23 120 B2
Cuffley EN6 146 F3
Graveley SG4 36 C4
Oak Piece AL6 89 E7
Oak Piece Ct AL6 89 E7
Oak Rd Luton LU4 63 C8
Woolmer Green SG3 69 B1
Oak St
Bishop's Stortford CM23 76 F6
Hemel Hempstead HP3 138 F7
Oak Tree Cl
Abbots Langley WD5 153 D7
Benington SG2 52 F4
Hatfield AL10 130 A6
Hertford Heath SG13 114 C3
Oak Tree Ct Elstree WD6 169 D3
Oaklands AL6 89 E8
Oak Way AL5 107 A5
Oak Wood HP4 121 F3
Oakbank WD7 156 B3
Oakcroft Cl HA5 175 B1
Oakdale AL8 89 D1
Oakdale Ave HA6 175 A1
Oakdale Cl WD1 175 C6
Oakdale Rd WD1 175 C6
Oakdene EN8 148 E1
Oakdene Cl HA5 175 F3
Oakdene Rd
Hemel Hempstead HP3 138 F7
Watford WD2 154 B3
Oakdene Way AL1 128 C3
Oaken Gr AL7 110 E3
Oakfield WD3 165 A2
Oakfield Ave SG4 35 B5
Oakfield Cl EN6 158 F8
Oakfield Rd AL5 107 A5
Oakfields SG2 51 C1
Oakfields Ave SG3 69 A6
Oakfields Cl SG2 51 C1
Oakfields Rd SG3 69 A6
Oakhill SG6 23 D4
Oakhill Ave HA5 175 E1

Oakhill Cl WD3 ....172 E6
Oakhill Dr AL6 ....89 A6
Oakhill Rd WD3 ....172 D6
Oakhurst Ave AL5 ....107 A5
Oakhurst Pl WD1 ....166 C6
Oakhurst Rd EN3 ....162 D3
Oakington AL7 ....111 D6
Oakland's Coll AL4 ....128 D1
Oaklands HP4 ....122 A4
Oaklands Ave
  Brookmans Park AL9 ......144 E4
  Watford WD1 ....167 B1
Oaklands Cl CM23 ....59 B2
Oaklands Coll AL1 ....127 E3
Oaklands Coll Boreham
  Wood Campus WD6 ....170 C7
Oaklands Coll
  (Lemsford Lane Campus)
  AL8 ....110 B4
Oaklands Coll (Welwyn
  Garden City Campus)
  AL8 ....110 D7
Oaklands Ct WD1 ....167 A8
Oaklands Dr CM23 ....59 B2
Oaklands Gate HA6 ....174 E4
Oaklands La Barnet EN5 ...117 B5
  St Albans AL4 ....128 F5
Oaklands Pk CM23 ....59 B2
Oaklands Rd Barnet EN5 ...171 F2
  Hammond Street EN7 ......147 E5
Oaklands Rise AL5 ....89 F7
Oaklands Sch AL6 ....89 E7
Oaklawn HP23 ....100 A3
Oaklea AL6 ....89 E7
Oaklea Cl AL6 ....89 E8
Oaklea Wood AL6 ....89 E7
Oakleigh Dr WD3 ....166 C3
Oakleigh Rd HA5 ....175 F4
Oakley Cl LU4 ....44 D4
Oakley Ct SG8 ....7 D7
Oakley Rd Harpenden AL5 ..107 D7
  Luton LU4 ....44 E3
Oakmeade Barnet EN5 ......171 D5
  Pinner HA5 ....176 A4
Oakmere Ave EN6 ....159 C6
Oakmere Cl EN6 ....159 D8
Oakmere La EN6 ....159 C7
Oakmere Prim Sch EN6 ....159 D7
Oakridge AL2 ....140 F2
Oakridge Ave WD7 ....155 E6
Oakridge La WD2 ....155 E5
Oakroyd Ave EN6 ....158 F6
Oakroyd Cl EN6 ....158 F6
Oaks Ave Litchin SG4 ....94 F7
  Radlett WD7 ....155 F4
Oaks Cross SG2 ....51 B1
Oaks Ret Pk CM20 ....117 F3
Oaks The
  Berkhamsted HP4 ....122 A4
  Slip End LU1 ....63 C1
  Watford WD1 ....167 C1
Oaktree Cl CM23 ....76 F7
Oaktree Garth AL7 ....110 E5
Oakview Cl Cheshunt EN7 ..148 B3
  Harpenden AL5 ....106 F5
Oakway LU4 ....82 B7
Oakwell Cl SG2 ....69 D7
Oakwell Dr EN6 ....160 B7
Oakwood Ave WD6 ....170 B5
Oakwood Cl SG2 ....51 C2
Oakwood Dr Luton LU3 .....44 C8
  St Albans AL4 ....128 C4
Oakwood Est CM20 ....118 B4
Oakwood Prim Sch AL4 ....128 C4
Oakwood Rd
  Bricket Wood AL2 ....140 F2
  Pinner HA5 ....175 B1
Oban Terr LU1 ....63 B8
Oberon Cl WD6 ....170 C8
Obrey Way CM23 ....76 E3
Occupation Rd WD1 ....167 B4
Octagan The SG12 ....93 D2
Octavia Ct WD2 ....167 C7
Oddy Hill Tring HP23 .....100 C3
  Wigginton HP23 ....100 C2
Odessey Rd WD6 ....170 B8
Offa Rd AL1 ....127 C3
Offas Way AL4 ....108 D8
Offerton Ho WD1 ....175 C7
Offley Cross SG5 ....34 B5
Offley Endowed Prim Sch
  SG5 ....33 C3
Offley Hill SG5 ....36 C3
Offley Rd SG5 ....34 B6
Ogard Rd EN11 ....135 C8
Okeford Cl HP23 ....99 F4
Okeford Dr HP23 ....99 F4
Okeley La HP23 ....99 E3
Old Bakery SG5 ....34 E7
Old Barn La WD3 ....166 E6
Old Bedford Rd Luton LU2 ..45 E4
  Luton, Warden Hill LU2 ...45 D6
Old Bell Cl CM24 ....59 D6
Old Bourne Way SG1 ....37 A3
Old Brewery Cl SG1 ....11 F7
Old Brewery PY SG4 ....66 D1
Old Chantry La SG4 ....35 F2
Old Charlton Rd SG5 ....34 E6
Old Church La SG12 ....93 E7

Old Common The SG9 ....43 B4
Old Crabtree La HP2 ......124 E2
Old Cross SG14 ....113 C6
Old Dean HP3 ....137 A4
Old Dr The AL3 ....110 B5
Old Farm LU7 ....80 D4
Old Fishery La
  Hemel Hempstead HP1 ....123 F1
  Hemel Hempstead HP1 ....137 F8
Old Fold Cl EN5 ....171 E8
Old Fold La EN5 ....171 E8
Old Fold View EN5 ....171 C6
Old Forge Cl
  Abbots Langley WD5 ......154 A6
  Welwyn Garden City AL7 ...89 C2
Old Forge Rd EN1 ....161 F1
Old French Horn La
  AL10 ....130 B6
Old Gannon Cl HA6 ....174 C5
Old Garden Ct AL3 ....127 C3
Old Hale Way SG5 ....34 E7
Old Hall Cl HA5 ....175 E2
Old Hall Dr HA5 ....175 E2
Old Harpenden Rd AL3 ....127 E6
Old Hat Factory The ■
  LU2 ....45 D1
Old Herns La AL5 ....111 C8
Old Hertford Rd AL9 ......130 C7
Old Highway EN11 ....135 C8
Old House Ct HP2 ....124 F3
Old House La
  Lower Nazeing EN9 ....149 F8
  Sarratt WD4 ....152 F4
Old Knebworth La
  SG3,SG2 ....68 D8
Old La SG3 ....69 B5
Old Leys AL10 ....130 A2
Old London Rd
  Hertford SG13 ....113 C6
  St Albans AL1 ....127 E2
Old Maltings The ☑ CM23 ..77 A7
Old Maple HP2 ....104 F1
Old Meadow Cl HP4 ....122 A2
Old Mill La HP4 ....122 D4
Old Mill La CM22 ....98 B6
Old Mill Rd WD4 ....153 C5
Old Nazeing Rd EN10 .....135 C1
Old North Rd
  Kneesworth SG8 ....2 B4
  Royston SG8 ....7 C8
Old Oak AL1 ....141 E8
Old Oak Cl SG15 ....11 A8
Old Oak Gdns HP4 ....121 E7
Old Oaks EN9 ....163 E7
Old Orch Luton LU1 ....63 D5
  Park Street AL2 ....141 D5
Old Orchard Cl EN4 ......159 D1
Old Orchard Mews HP4 ...122 C3
Old Park Rd SG5 ....34 E7
Old Parkbury La AL2 ......141 F1
Old Parkway Sch AL8 .....110 C5
Old Priory Pk AL1 ....127 E2
Old Rd CM17 ....118 D5
Old Rectory Cl AL5 ....86 A2
Old Rectory Dr AL10 ......130 B5
Old Rectory Gdns AL4 ....108 D8
Old Redding HA3 ....176 F6
Old River La CM23 ....76 F7
Old School Cl SG4 ....67 F1
Old School Gn SG2 ....92 C1
Old School Orch SG14 .....70 E3
Old School Wlk Arlesey SG15 11 A4
  Slip End LU1 ....63 C1
Old Shire La
  Chalfont St Peter WD3 ...172 B6
  Chorleywood WD3 ....164 A2
Old Sopwell Gdns AL1 .....127 E1
Old Uxbridge Rd WD3 .....172 E3
Old Vicarage Gdns AL3 .....83 D6
Old Walled Garden The
  SG1 ....36 C1
Old Watford Rd AL2 ......140 E2
Old Watling St AL3 ....84 B3
Old's App WD1 ....166 C1
Old's Cl WD1 ....166 B1
Olden Mead SG6 ....23 B3
Oldfield Cl EN8 ....148 E3
Oldfield Ct AL1 ....127 E3
Oldfield Dr EN8 ....148 E3
Oldfield Farm Rd
  Hemel Hempstead HP1 ....123 D8
  London Colney AL2 ....142 D6
Oldfield Rise SG4 ....66 E7
Oldhall St SG14 ....113 D6
Oldhouse Croft CM20 .....117 E2
Oldings Cnr AL9 ....130 B1
Oldpark Ride EN7 ....146 E2
Oldwood AL6 ....89 D7
Olive Taylor Ct HP2 ......124 F7
Oliver Cl
  Hemel Hempstead HP3 ....138 E7
  Park Street AL2 ....141 D4
Oliver Ct SG12 ....92 E4
Oliver Rd HP3 ....138 F7
Oliver Rise HP3 ....138 E7
Oliver's La SG5 ....11 F7
Oliver's Cl HP4 ....123 C7
Olivia Gdns UB9 ....173 A8
Olleberrie La WD3 ....151 D7
Olwen Mews HA5 ....175 D1
Olyard Ct LU1 ....63 B6
Olympus Rd SG16 ....10 B4
Omega Ct ☑ SG12 ....93 D1

Omega Maltings ☑ SG12 ...93 E1
On–The–Hill WD1 ....175 E8
Onslow Cl AL10 ....130 B5
Onslow Rd LU4 ....44 A8
Onslow St Audrey's Sch
  AL10 ....130 B5
Opening The SG4 ....88 F8
Openshaw Way SG6 ....23 A6
Oram Pl HP3 ....138 D8
Orbital Cres WD2 ....153 F4
Orchard Ave
  Berkhamsted HP4 ....122 A4
  Harpenden AL5 ....85 F1
  Watford WD2 ....154 B8
Orchard Cl
  Borehamwood WD6 ....169 F6
  Bushey WD2 ....168 D1
  Chorleywood WD3 ....164 D5
  Cuffley EN6 ....146 E3
  Hemel Hempstead HP2 ....124 F5
  Kneesworth SG8 ....2 A5
  Letchworth SG6 ....155 E3
  Little Berkhamsted SG13 ..132 C4
  Radlett WD7 ....155 E3
  St Albans AL1 ....127 F2
  St Ippolyts SG4 ....34 F3
  Stanstead Abbotts SG12 ..115 C4
  Ware SG12 ....93 D2
  Watford WD1 ....166 F7
  Wigginton HP23 ....60 B3
Orchard Cres SG1 ....50 C7
Orchard Croft CM20 ......118 A2
Orchard Ct HP9 ....137 A4
Orchard Dr
  Chiswellgreen AL2 ....141 B5
  Chorleywood WD3 ....164 D5
  Watford WD1 ....166 F7
Orchard Gdns EN9 ....163 C5
Orchard House La AL1 ....127 D2
Orchard Lea CM21 ....97 C1
Orchard Mead AL10 ......129 F5
Orchard On The Green
  The WD3 ....165 F4
Orchard Prim Sch WD2 ...153 F3
Orchard Rd Baldock SG7 ...12 E1
  Barnet EN5 ....171 F5
  Bishop's Stortford CM23 ..59 B1
  Hitchin SG4 ....82 B1
  Royston SG8 ....7 B7
  Stevenage SG1 ....44 A1
  Tewin AL6 ....90 C5
  Welwyn AL6 ....89 C5
Orchard Sq EN10 ....148 F7
Orchard St
  Hemel Hempstead HP3 ....138 D8
  St Albans AL1 ....127 C2
Orchard The Baldock SG7 ...23 F8
  Codicote SG4 ....67 F1
  Hertford SG14 ....92 C1
  Kings Langley WD4 ....139 A2
  Tonwell SG12 ....92 E7
  Welwyn Garden City AL8 ..110 D8
Orchard Way
  Bovingdon HP3 ....137 A3
  Breachwood Green SG4 ....47 E1
  Brookmans Park EN6 ......145 B2
  Goff's Oak EN7 ....147 B3
  Knebworth SG3 ....68 C5
  Letchworth SG6 ....22 F8
  Lower Stondon SG16 ......10 B3
  Luton LU4 ....44 C4
  Pitstone LU7 ....80 E5
  Rickmansworth WD3 .....165 A2
  Royston SG8 ....7 C8
Orchards The
  Sawbridgeworth CM21 .....97 E3
  Slip End LU1 ....63 C2
  Tring HP23 ....99 F3
Orchid Ho AL1 ....127 F3
Ordelmere SG6 ....11 F1
Ordnance Rd EN3 ....162 E2
Oregon Way LU3 ....45 A8
Organ Hall Rd WD6 ......169 E8
Orient Cl AL1 ....127 E2
Orient Ctr The WD2 ......154 D2
Oriole Cl WD5 ....154 A6
Oriole Way CM23 ....76 C6
Orion Way HA6 ....175 A6
Orkney Ho WD1 ....166 F3
Orlando Cl SG4 ....35 A6
Ormesby Dr EN6 ....158 D7
Ormonde Rd HA6 ....174 D6
Ormsby Cl LU1 ....63 E5
Ormskirk Rd WD1 ....175 D5
Oronsay HP3 ....124 E8
Orphanage Rd WD1 ......167 C7
Orpington Cl LU4 ....44 A3
Orton Cl AL4 ....128 A7
Orwell Cl ☑ WD2 ....167 D7
Orwell View SG7 ....13 B1
Osborn Way AL8 ....110 D6
Osborne Cl ☑ LU1 ....63 F6
Osborne Gdns EN6 ....145 B1
Osborne Rd Cheshunt EN8 .148 E4
  Hoddesdon EN10 ....135 A4
  Luton LU1 ....63 F6
  Potters Bar EN6 ....145 B1
Osborne Way HP23 ....100 D1
Osborne Ave WD4 ....138 F3
Osbourne Gdns ⑤ CM23 ..76 E5
Osmington Pl HP23 ....99 F4
Osprey Cl SG8 ....7 B6
Osprey Gdns SG2 ....51 D2
Osprey Ho ⑤ SG2 ....93 C3
Osprey Wlk LU4 ....44 A5
Oster St AL3 ....127 C4
Osterley Cl SG2 ....69 C7

Ostler Cl CM23 ....76 C4
Oswald Rd AL1 ....127 E2
Otley Way WD1 ....175 C7
Otter Gdns AL10 ....130 B3
Otterden Cl LU2 ....46 D2
Otterspool La WD2 ....154 E1
Otterspool Way WD2 .....154 F1
Otterton Cl AL5 ....85 F3
Ottoman Terr WD1 ....167 C6
Otway Cl EN5 ....89 C4
Otway Gdns WD2 ....168 E2
Otways Cl EN6 ....159 B6
Oude La SG10 ....74 F2
Oughton Cl SG5 ....34 C8
Oughton Head Way SG5 ...34 C8
Oughtonhead
  Jun & Inf Schs SG5 ......21 C1
Oughtonhead Jun Sch
  SG5 ....34 C8
Oughtonhead La SG5 ......34 C8
Oulton Cres LU6 ....158 D7
Oulton Rd AL5 ....86 C3
Oulton Rise AL5 ....86 C3
Oulton Way WD1 ....175 F6
Oundle Ave WD2 ....168 C3
Oundle Ct SG2 ....69 C8
Oundle Path SG2 ....69 C8
Oundle The SG2 ....69 C8
Our Lady's Jun Mix Inf Sch
  AL7 ....110 A1
Our Lady's RC Jun Mix Inf
  Sch SG5 ....21 E2
Ousden Cl EN8 ....148 E1
Ousden Dr EN8 ....148 E1
Ouseley Cl LU4 ....44 D3
Oval The Cheshunt EN10 ..148 E7
  Henlow SG16 ....10 C4
  Stevenage SG1 ....37 A1
Overfeild Rd LU2 ....46 A1
Overlord Cl EN10 ....134 E3
Overstone Rd
  Harpenden AL5 ....86 C1
  Luton LU4 ....44 D2
Overstream WD3 ....165 B5
Overtrees AL5 ....85 F3
Oving Cl LU2 ....46 D2
Owen Dr SG8 ....2 C1
Owen Jones Cl SG16 ....10 C5
Owens Way WD3 ....166 A5
Owles La SG9 ....41 A6
Ox La AL5 ....86 B3
Oxcroft CM23 ....76 F4
Oxen Rd LU2 ....45 F1
Oxendon Dr EN11 ....135 A5
Oxfield Cl HP4 ....122 A3
Oxford Ave AL1 ....128 C2
Oxford Cl Cheshunt EN8 ..148 D2
  Kneesworth SG8 ....2 A5
  Moor Park HA6 ....174 D6
Oxford Rd
  Breachwood Green SG4 ....47 E1
  ☑ Luton LU1 ....63 E6
Oxford St WD1 ....167 B4
Oxhey Ave WD1 ....167 B7
Oxhey Dr WD1 ....175 B7
Oxhey Inf Sch WD2 ......167 E4
Oxhey La Pinner HA5 .....176 A5
  Watford WD1 ....175 F7
Oxhey Rd WD1 ....167 D2
Oxhey Wood Prim Sch
  WD1 ....175 C7
Oxleas Dr AL10 ....130 B4
Oxleys Rd SG2 ....51 B3
Oxleys The CM17 ....118 E4
Oysterfields AL3 ....127 C4

P

Pacatian Way SG1 ....51 C8
Packhorse Cl AL4 ....128 C6
Packhorse La EN6 ....157 D8
Paddock Cl EN11 ....134 F7
Paddock Cl Hunsdon SG12 ..95 D1
  Letchworth SG6 ....23 A5
  Watford WD1 ....167 C3
Paddock Rd SG9 ....40 E8
Paddock The
  Bishop's Stortford CM23 ..59 D8
  Hatfield AL10 ....130 A6
  Henlow SG16 ....35 A5
  Hoddesdon EN10 ....135 A3
  Kimpton SG4 ....47 D6
  Knebworth SG3 ....68 C5
  Standon SG11 ....56 A1
Paddocks Cl SG2 ....51 B4
Paddocks The
  Chorleywood WD3 ....164 F5
  Hertford Heath SG13 .....114 B3
  Kimpton SG4 ....47 D6
  Welwyn Garden City AL7 ..111 B7
Padgate Ho WD1 ....175 C7
Page Cl SG7 ....23 F6
Page Hill SG12 ....93 C2
Page Rd SG13 ....114 A6
Pageant Rd AL1 ....127 D2
Pages Cl CM23 ....76 D5
Pages Croft HP4 ....122 A6
Paget Cl SG12 ....71 F7
Paignton Cl LU4 ....44 A3
Paine's La HA5 ....175 E1
Paines Orch LU7 ....80 A8
Painters La EN3 ....162 E4
Palace Cl WD3 ....139 A1
Palace Gdns
  Bishop's Stortford CM23 ..76 C5
  Royston SG8 ....7 C6

Palfrey Cl AL3 1
Pallas Rd AL3 1
Palmar Cl CM23 1
Palmer C SG14 1
Palmer Ct SG12 1
Palmer Ave WD2 1
Palmer Rd SG14 1
Palmer Gdns EN5 1
Palmer Rd SG14 1
Palmers La ☑ CM23 1
Palmers Rd WD6 1
Palmers Way EN8 1
Palmerston Cl AL8 1
Palmerston Ct SG2 1
Pamela Ave HP3 1
Pams La SG4 1
Pancake La HP2 1
Pankhurst Cres SG2 1
Pankhurst Pl WD2 1
Panshanger Dr AL7 1
Panshanger Prim Sch
  AL7 1
Pantiles The WD2 1
Panxworth Rd AL3 1
Paper Mill La SG12 1
Parade The Hatfield AL10 ..1
  Letchworth SG6 1
  Luton LU3 1
  South Oxhey WD1 1
South Oxhey, Carpenders
  Park WD1 1
Paradise AL3 1
Paradise HP2 1
Paradise Cl EN7 1
Paradise Ct HP2 1
Paradise Wildlife Park
  EN10 1
Paramount Ind Est WD2 ...1
Parish Cl WD2 1
Parishes Mead SG2 1
Park Ave
  Bishop's Stortford CM23 ..1
  Bushey WD2 1
  Luton LU3 1
  Potters Bar EN6 1
  Radlett WD7 1
  Rickmansworth WD3 1
  St Albans AL1 1
  Watford WD1 1
Park Ave N AL5 1
Park Ave S AL5 1
Park Avenue Trad Est
  WD2 1
Park Cl Harlow CM20 1
  Letchworth SG6 1
  Luton LU2 1
Park Ct Harlow CM20 1
Park Dr Baldock SG7 1
  Potters Bar EN6 1
  Standon SG11 1
  Stanmore HA3 1
Park Farm Cl SG16 1
Park Farm Ind Est
  Buntingford SG9 1
  Nuthampstead SG8 1
Park Farm Ind Pk SG8 1
Park Farm La SG8 1
Park Gate SG7 1
Park Hill Harlow CM17 1
  Harpenden AL5 1
  Park Ho Berkhamsted HP4 ..1
  Welwyn Garden City AL8 ..1
Park Ind Est AL2 1
Park La
  Bishop's Stortford CM23 ..1
  Cheshunt EN7 1
  Colney Heath AL4 1
  Hammond Street EN7 1
  Harefield UB9 1
  Harlow CM20 1
  Hemel Hempstead HP2 1
  Hoddesdon EN10 1
  Kimpton SG4 1
  Knebworth SG3 1
  Standon SG11 1
Park Lane Paradise EN7 ...1
Park Lodge WD2 1
Park Mansions HA6 1
Park Mdw AL9 1
Park Mead CM20 1
Park Mews AL9 1
Park Mount AL5 1
Park Nook Gdns EN4 1
Park Pl Harefield UB9 1
  Stevenage SG1 1
Park Place
  Chambers SG1 1
Park Rd Barnet EN5 1
  Bushey WD2 1
  Cheshunt EN8 1
  Enfield EN3 1
  Hemel Hempstead HP1 1
  Hertford SG13 1
  Hoddesdon EN11 1
  Northaw EN6 1
  Radlett WD7 1

Rd continued
Rickmansworth WD3 ......165 E2
West Mountfitchet CM24 ...59 E6
Par ....HP23 ....100 A3
Tring SG12 ....93 B2
Watford WD1 ....187 B8
Rise
Harpenden HP4 ....121 E6
Royston 85 E3
Ware HA3 ....176 E2
Rise Cl AL5 ....85 E3
Sq LU1 ....63 E7
St Baldock SG7 ....23 E8
Harpenden HP4 ....122 B5
Field AL9 ....130 C6
Luton SG4 ....34 E6
ton LU1 ....32 F6
Luton LU2 ....141 D5
field HP23 ....100 A3
St W LU1 ....63 E7
Street La AL2 ....141 C3
Street Sch AL2 ....141 D4
Terr Enfield EN3 ....162 E1
don LU1 ....63 F6
Ha Hadham SG10 ....74 F3
The Redbourn AL3 ....106 B5
Ilbans AL1 ....128 A5
Viaduct LU1 ....63 F6
View
har Hormead SG9 ....42 A7
Field AL9 ....130 C7
desdon EN11 ....135 A5
ther HA5 ....176 F6
ters Bar EN6 ....159 C6
enage SG2 ....51 B1
s **View Cl** Luton LU3 ....44 D6
lbans AL1 ....128 A2
s **View Ct** HP4 ....122 B4
s **View Dr** AL3 ....83 D6
s **View Rd**
rkhamsted HP4 ....122 B4
her HA5 ....175 B3
s Way Hitchin SG5 ....34 E6
amsted WD23 ....165 C1
er Ave SG14 ....113 D8
er Cl SG6 ....22 E4
er St WD2 ....167 B8
er's **Field** SG2 ....51 C4
field
tters Bar EN6 ....159 C7
atford WD1 ....167 C3
lands AL1 ....89 C5
yddial SG9 ....27 D2
kside **Comb Sch**
D6 ....156 F1
rk WD1 ....166 F7
tch Rd HA6 ....174 F5
kview Ho WD1 ....167 D3
rkway
axbridgeworth CM21 ....97 F1
evenage SG2 ....51 A1
elwyn Garden City AL8 ....110 C6
rkway Cl AL8 ....110 C6
rkway Ct AL1 ....142 B8
rkway Gdns AL8 ....110 C6
rkwood Cl EN10 ....134 D4
rkwood Dr HP1 ....123 F3
rliament Sq SG14 ....113 D6
armiter's Sch WD2 ....154 C8
rndon Mill La CM20 ....117 B3
rnel Rd SG12 ....93 F2
rnell Cl HA8 ....139 F1
rr Cres HP2 ....125 B8
rrott's La HP23 ....120 A4
rrotts Cl WD3 ....166 A4
rrotts Field EN11 ....135 B7
rson's Cl AL3 ....84 B1
rsonage Cl
abbots Langley WD5 ....139 E1
Tring HP23 ....100 A4
rsonage Farm
Nelham Green WD3 ....139 D5
Wingrave HP22 ....60 B3
rsonage Farm Trad
Est CM24 ....59 F3
rsonage La Albury SG11 ......57 A6
Bishop's Stortford CM23 .....59 C1
Spellbrook CM21 ....97 D6
West Mountfitchet CM24 .....59 F4
Welham Green AL9 ....144 B8
rsonage Pl HP23 ....100 A4
rsonage Rd
Rickmansworth WD3 ....165 D2

Parsonage Rd continued
Welham Green AL9 ....144 B8
Parsons Green Est SG1 ......37 C2
Parthia Cl 7 E6
Partridge Cl Barnet EN5 ...171 C3
Bushey WD2 ....168 C1
Luton LU4 ....44 A5
Partridge Hill AL2 ....45 A1
Partridge Rd AL3 ....127 D7
Parva Cl AL5 ....107 D6
Parvills EN9 ....163 D7
Parys Rd LU3 ....45 B6
Pascal Way SG6 ....23 B8
Pasfield EN9 ....163 D6
Passfield Cotts SG1 ....72 F1
Passingham Ave SG4 ....35 A6
Paston Rd HP2 ....124 E5
Pasture Cl WD2 ....168 C2
Pasture La SG4 ....65 E8
Pasture Rd SG6 ....22 E3
Pastures LU4 ....44 A3
Pastures The Barnet N20 ...171 F1
Chiswellgreen AL2 ....141 A7
Hatfield AL10 ....130 B4
Hemel Hempstead HP1 ....123 E4
Stevenage SG2 ....51 D8
Ware SG12 ....93 C3
Watford WD1 ....167 C2
Welwyn Garden City AL7 .....111 B4
Pastures Way LU4 ....44 A4
Pat Larner Ho AL1 ....127 D2
Paternoster Ct EN9 ....163 F6
Paternoster Hill EN9 ......163 F7
Pathway The Radlett WD7 ...155 F3
Watford WD1 ....167 D1
Patmore Cl CM23 ....76 C8
Patmore Heath
(Nature Reserve) SG11 ...57 D8
Patmore Link Rd HP4 ....125 C2
Patmore Rd EN9 ....163 E5
Patricia Gdns CM23 ....76 E5
Patrick Gr EN9 ....163 B6
Paul's Grn EN8 ....162 E6
Pauls La EN11 ....135 A6
Paxton Rd
Berkhamsted HP4 ....122 D4
St Albans AL1 ....127 E2
Payne End SG9 ....15 B3
Payne's Pk SG5 ....34 E7
Paynes Cl SG6 ....12 A1
Paynes La EN9 ....149 C7
Paynesfield Rd WD2 ....168 F2
Pea La HP4 ....121 C7
Peabody Ct EN3 ....163 A2
Peace Cl EN7 ....148 B2
Peace Dr WD1 ....167 A6
Peace Gr AL4 ....90 A7
Peace Prospect WD1 ....167 A6
Peach Cl LU1 ....64 B5
Peacock Wlk WD5 ....154 A8
Peacocks Cl HP4 ....121 F6
Peakes La EN7 ....147 F4
Peakes Pl AL1 ....127 F3
Peakes Way EN7 ....147 F4
Pear Tree Cl SG16 ....10 B3
Pear Tree Dell SG6 ....23 B3
Pear Tree Wlk EN7 ....147 E5
Pearl Ct EN1 ....135 A6
Pearman Dr SG12 ....117 F2
Pearsall Cl SG6 ....23 B5
Pearson Ave SG13 ....113 C4
Pearson Cl SG13 ....113 C4
Peartree Cl
Hemel Hempstead HP1 ....124 A4
Welwyn Garden City AL7 ....110 C6
Peartree Ct Watford WD4 ...154 D3
Welwyn Garden City AL7 ....110 C5
Peartree Farm AL7 ....110 C6
Peartree La AL7 ....110 C6
Peartree Prim Sch AL7 ....110 C5
Peartree Rd
Hemel Hempstead HP1 ....124 A4
Welwyn Garden City AL7 ....110 C4
Peartree Spring Inf Sch
SG2 ....51 B3
Peartree Spring Jun Sch
SG2 ....51 B3
Peartree Way SG2 ....51 A3
Peascroft Rd HP3 ....125 B1
Peasecroft SG9 ....39 D7
Peasmead SG9 ....40 E6
Pebbles The SG2 ....12 C4
Peck's Hill EN9 ....135 C2
Peckworth Ind Est SG16 ....10 A4
Pedlars La SG8 ....15 C5
Pedley Hill HP4,LU6 ....82 C1
Peel Cres SG14 ....113 C8
Peel Pl [7] LU1 ....63 D7
Peel St [6] LU1 ....63 D7
Peerglow Ctr SG12 ....114 B8
Peerglow Ind Est WD1 ......166 B1
Peg's La SG13 ....113 D5
Pegmire La WD2 ....168 C8
Pegs La SG12 ....95 D5
Pegsdon Cl LU3 ....45 B7
Pegsdon Way SG5 ....7 E6
Pelham Ct
Hemel Hempstead HP2 ....125 C3
Welwyn Garden City AL7 ....111 C5
Pelham Rd WD3 ....154 D4
Pelhams The WD2 ....154 E6
Pelican Way SG6 ....11 F1
Pemberton Cl AL1 ....141 D8
Pembridge Chase HP3 ....137 A4
Pembridge La EN10 ....133 E2
Pembridge Rd HP3 ....137 A4
Pembroke Ave
Enfield EN1 ....162 B1

Pembroke Ave continued
.............................44 F3
Pembroke Cl EN10 ....148 E8
Pembroke Dr EN7 ....147 B2
Pembroke Rd Baldock SG7 ....23 F8
Moor Park HA6 ....174 C7
Pemsel Ct HP3 ....124 E1
Penda Cl LU3 ....44 F7
Pendennis Ct AL5 ....107 D7
Penfold Cl SG7 ....24 A7
Penfold Trad Est WD2 ....142 F8
Pengelly Cl EN7 ....148 B1
Penhill LU3 ....44 E6
Penhill Ct LU3 ....44 E6
Penman Cl AL2 ....141 A4
Penn Cl WD3 ....164 A5
Penn Ho Moor Park HA6 ......174 C7
South Oxhey WD1 ....175 C7
Penn Pl WD3 ....165 D2
Penn Rd
Chiswellgreen AL2 ....141 C4
Rickmansworth WD3 ....165 A1
Stevenage SG1 ....50 E4
Penn Way
Chorleywood WD3 ....164 D3
Letchworth SG6 ....23 C8
Pennard Ho WD1 ....175 D7
Penne Cl WD7 ....156 A5
Pennine Ave LU3 ....44 D8
Pennine Way HP2 ....125 A7
Penny Croft AL5 ....107 A4
Penny Ct WD1 ....167 B7
Pennyfathers La AL6 ....90 B4
Pennymead CM20 ....118 A1
Penrose Ave WD1 ....175 E8
Penrose Ct HP2 ....124 E7
Penscroft Gdns WD6 ....170 D5
Penshurst CM17 ....118 C3
Penshurst Cl AL5 ....85 D4
Penshurst Rd EN6 ....159 D7
Pentland HP2 ....124 E7
Pentland Rd WD2 ....168 C3
Pentley Cl AL8 ....89 D1
Penton Dr EN8 ....148 D2
Pentrich Ave EN1 ....162 A1
Penzance Cl UB9 ....173 C3
Peplins Cl AL3 ....144 E5
Peplins Way AL3 ....144 E5
Peppard Cl AL3 ....106 A6
Pepper Ct SG2 ....23 F8
Pepper Hill SG12 ....114 F4
Peppercorn Wlk SG4 ....35 B7
Peppett's Grn WD1 ....120 D1
Pepsal End SG2 ....69 B8
Pepsal End Rd LU1 ....84 C7
Pepys Cres EN5 ....171 C4
Pepys Way SG7 ....23 E8
Perchero Dr LU4 ....44 A3
Percheron Rd WD6 ....170 D3
Percival Ct EN8 ....148 E1
Percival Way LU2 ....64 C7
Percy Rd WD1 ....167 B5
Peregrine Cl
Bishop's Stortford CM23 .....76 D6
Watford WD1 ....154 E5
Peregrine Ho [1] SG12 ....93 C3
Peregrine Rd LU4 ....44 A2
Perham Way AL2 ....142 D6
Perivale Gdns WD1 ....154 B5
Periwinkle Cl SG6 ....17 C5
Periwinkle La SG5 ....21 F1
Permain Cl WD7 ....156 A6
Perowne Way SG1 ....55 E3
Perram Ct EN10 ....148 E5
Perriors Cl EN7 ....148 A4
Perry Dr SG8 ....7 E7
Perry Grn HP2 ....105 A1
Perry Hill EN9 ....148 B2
Perry Mead WD2 ....168 C3
Perrymead LU2 ....46 F2
Perrysfield Rd EN8 ....148 E5
Perrywood AL8 ....110 C6
Perrywood La SG14 ....91 B7
Pescot Hill HP1 ....124 B5
Petard Cl LU4 ....44 A2
Peter Kirk Sch CM24 ....59 F6
Peter's Pl HP4 ....121 E6
Peterlee Ct [2] HP2 ....124 E7
Peters Ave AL2 ....142 C5
Peters Way SG3 ....68 F6
Peters Wood Hill SG12 .....114 F7
Petersfield AL3 ....127 E7
Pettys Cl EN8 ....148 D3
Petunia Ct LU3 ....45 C1
Petworth Cl SG2 ....69 C7
Pevensey Cl LU2 ....46 B4
Pewterers Ave CM23 ....76 C4
Pheasant Cl
Berkhamsted HP4 ....122 C3
Tring HP23 ....100 B6
Pheasants Way WD3 ....155 E3
Phillimore Cl WD7 ....155 E3
Phillimore Pl WD7 ....155 E3
Phillipers WD2 ....154 E6
Phillips Ave SG8 ....7 C8
Phipps Hatch La EN2 ....161 C1
Phoenix Cl HA6 ....174 F6
Phoenix Ct EN1 ....162 A3
Phyllis Courtnage Ho
HP2 ....124 D5
Piccotts End HP1 ....124 C7
Piccotts End La HP2 ....124 D7
Piccotts End Rd HP1 ....124 C8
Pick Hill EN9 ....163 C6
Pickets Cl WD23 ....168 E1
Picketts AL8 ....89 D1
Pickford Hill AL5 ....86 C3

Pickford Rd AL3 ....83 C3
Picknage Cnr SG8 ....9 A2
Picknage Rd SG8 ....9 A2
Pie Cnr AL3 ....84 B1
Pie Gdn AL3 ....84 B1
Pierian Spring HP1 ....124 B5
Pietley Hill AL3 ....84 A1
Pig La CM22 ....77 A3
Pigeonwick AL5 ....86 B3
Piggotts La LU4 ....44 F6
Piggotts Way CM23 ....76 E5
Piggottshill La AL5 ....107 D8
Pightle Cl SG8 ....7 D7
Pike End SG1 ....50 D6
Pilgrim Cl
Chiswellgreen AL2 ....141 C4
Watford WD2 ....154 D6
Pilgrims Row SG9 ....40 F3
Pilgrims Way SG1 ....37 B2
Piltdown Rd WD1 ....175 D6
Pin Green Ind Est SG1 ......37 C2
Pin Green Jun Mix Inf Sch
SG1 ....50 F6
Pinchfield WD3 ....172 D5
Pindar Rd EN11 ....135 C7
Pine La [2] Berkhamsted HP4 ...122 B4
Cheshunt EN8 ....148 D3
Northwood HA6 ....174 E4
Pine Crest AL6 ....89 E8
Pine Gr Barnet N20 ....171 F1
Bishop's Stortford CM23 ...77 B6
Bricket Wood AL2 ....140 F1
Brookmans Park AL9 ....145 B6
Bushey WD2 ....167 F8
Pine Ridge AL1 ....142 A8
Pine Tree Cl HP1 ....124 B4
Pine Wlk HP4 ....121 D7
Pinecroft HP3 ....138 F7
Pinecroft Cres EN5 ....171 E5
Pinehill Hospl SG4 ....35 A7
Pinehurst Cl WD5 ....153 A7
Pinelands CM23 ....58 F1
Pineridge Ct EN5 ....171 D5
Pines Ave EN1 ....162 B3
Pines Hill CM24 ....59 D5
Pines Jun Mix Inf Sch The
SG13 ....114 B7
Pines The
Borehamwood WD6 ....169 F7
Hemel Hempstead HP3 ....137 F7
Pinetree Ho SG14 ....154 E3
Pinewood Ave LU4 ....110 E4
Pinewood Ave AL4 ....176 B4
Pinewood Cl
Borehamwood WD6 ....170 D7
Pinner HA5 ....176 B4
St Albans AL4 ....128 C8
Watford WD1 ....167 A8
Pinewood Dr EN6 ....158 F8
Pinewood Gdns
Hemel Hempstead HP1 ....124 B3
[6] Hemel Hempstead HP2 ...124 E7
Welwyn Garden City AL7 ....111 D7
Pinewoods [4] SG2 ....50 F1
Pinfold Rd WD2 ....167 F7
Pinford Dell LU2 ....46 D1
Pinnacles EN9 ....161 B8
Pinnate Pl AL7 ....110 E2
Pinner Grn HA5 ....175 C1
Pinner Hill HA5 ....175 B3
Pinner Hill Rd HA5 ....175 C1
Pinner Park Ave HA2 ....176 C1
Pinner Park Gdns HA2 ......176 C1
Pinner Rd Northwood HA6 ...175 A1
Watford WD1 ....167 C2
Pinner Wood
Fst & Mid Schs** HA5 ....175 C2
Pinnocks Cl SG7 ....23 E8
Pinnocks La SG7 ....23 F8
Pinto Cl WD6 ....170 D3
Pioneer Way WD1 ....166 F3
Pipers Ave AL5 ....107 D7
Pipers Cl AL3 ....106 A6
Pipers Hill HP1 ....103 D3
Pipers La
Caddington AL3,LU1 ....62 F1
Wheathampstead AL5 ....107 F7
**Pippens AL8 ....89 E1
Pippin Cl WD7 ....156 E6
Pirton Cl
Hemel Hempstead HP2 ....124 F4
Hitchin SG5 ....34 D6
St Albans AL4 ....128 C7
Pirton Cross SG5 ....44 D7
Pirton Hill Inf Sch LU4 .....44 B6
Pirton Hill Jun Sch LU4 .....44 B6
Pirton Jun Mix Inf Sch
SG5 ....20 D4
Pirton Rd Hitchin SG5 ....34 C6
Holwell SG5 ....21 A7
Luton LU4 ....44 D5
Pishiobury Dr SG12 ....118 D1
Pitsfield AL8 ....89 C1
Pitsford Terr LU2 ....46 A1
Pitstone Cl AL4 ....128 C8
Pitstone Windmill LU7 ....80 F4
Pitt Ct SG2 ....51 B1
Pitt Dr AL4 ....142 C8
Pittman's Field CM20 ......117 F1
Pix Ct SG15 ....11 A8
Pix Farm La HP1 ....123 C2
Pix Rd Letchworth SG6 ....11 E5
Stotfold SG5 ....11 E5
Pixies Hill Cres HP1 ....124 A2
Pixies Hill
Jun Mix Inf Sch HP1 ....123 F2
Pixies Hill Rd HP1 ....123 F2
Pixmore Ave SG6 ....23 B6

Pixmore Ind Est SG6 ....23 A6
Pixmore Jun Sch SG6 ....23 A5
Pixmore Way SG6 ....23 A5
Plaistow Way SG8 ....9 E2
Plaiters Cl HP23 ....100 B4
Plaitford Cl WD3 ....172 D4
Plantagenet Pl EN9 ....163 B6
Plantation Rd LU3 ....44 D7
Plantation Wlk HP1 ....124 A6
Plash Dr SG1 ....50 C5
Plashes Cl SG11 ....55 D7
Plashets CM22 ....98 D1
Platt Cl LU4 ....44 D4
Plaw Hatch Cl CM23 ....77 B8
Plaw Hatch Cnr CM23 ....77 D8
Playford Sq LU4 ....44 D5
Pleasance The AL5 ....85 D4
Pleasant Pl WD3 ....172 E3
Pleasant Rd CM23 ....76 E8
Pleasant Rise AL9 ....130 C8
Plewes Cl LU6 ....82 E8
Plough Hill EN6 ....146 F2
Plough La Harefield UB9 ....173 C4
King's Walden SG4 ....48 A5
Potten End HP4 ....123 B7
Sarratt WD3 ....151 F6
Ploughmans Cl CM23 ....76 C5
Ploughmans End AL7 ....111 C5
Plover Cl HP4 ....122 C3
Plum Tree Rd SG16 ....10 B2
Plummers La LU2 ....65 C2
Plumpton Cl LU2 ....46 B3
Plumpton Rd EN11 ....135 C8
Pluto Rise HP2 ....124 F5
Plymouth Cl LU2 ....46 B1
Poets Cl HP1 ....124 B4
Poets Ct AL5 ....86 B1
Poets Gate EN7 ....147 E3
Poets Gn LU4 ....44 A2
Polayn Garth AL8 ....110 C7
Polegate LU2 ....46 D2
Polehanger La HP1 ....123 E5
Polhill WD3 ....151 E6
Poles La Thundridge SG12 ....93 C6
Ware SG12 ....93 C3
Poles Pk SG12 ....93 C6
Police Row SG8 ....15 F7
Police Station La WD2 ......168 B2
Pollard Gdns SG1 ....50 F8
Pollards WD3 ....172 D5
Pollards Ct AL1 ....147 C2
Pollards Way SG5 ....20 D4
Pollicott Cl AL4 ....128 C8
Pollywick Rd HP23 ....100 D1
Polzeath Cl LU2 ....64 C8
Pomeroy Cres WD2 ....154 B3
Pomeroy Gr LU2 ....45 E6
Pomfret Ave LU2 ....46 F2
Pond Cl Harefield UB9 ......173 C1
Luton LU4 ....44 B5
Stevenage SG2 ....50 C7
Tring HP23 ....100 A4
Pond Croft Hatfield AL10 ...129 F5
Welwyn Garden City AL7 ...110 E8
Pond Field AL7 ....90 A1
Pond La Baldock SG7 ....23 E8
Little Gaddesden HP4 ......102 E7
Pond Lodge SG4 ....67 F1
Pond Rd HP3 ....139 A6
Pondcroft Rd SG4 ....69 A4
Pondfield Cres AL4 ....128 B7
Pondside SG4 ....36 C4
Pondsmeade AL3 ....106 B5
Pondwick Rd AL5 ....86 C4
Pondwicks Cl AL1 ....127 C2
Pondwicks Rd LU1 ....63 F7
Ponsbourne Park Cotts
SG13 ....146 B3
Ponsbourne St Mary's
CE Sch SG13 ....146 E7
Pooleys La AL9 ....144 C8
Pope Paul RC Prim Sch
EN6 ....158 F6
Pope's Rd WD5 ....153 E8
Popes Cl AL2 ....45 D1
Popes La WD2 ....154 B1
Popes Row SG12 ....93 D3
Popis Gdns SG12 ....93 E2
Poplar Ave Hatfield AL4 ....129 D5
Luton LU3 ....45 C8
Poplar Cl Hitchin SG4 ....35 B6
Pinner HA5 ....175 D2
Royston SG8 ....7 E7
Thundridge SG11 ....72 F2
Poplar Dr SG8 ....7 E8
Poplar Rd LU6 ....82 E8
Poplar Shaw EN9 ....163 F6
Poplar Way SG14 ....92 E4
**Poplars AL7 ....111 B7
Poplars Cl Hatfield AL10 ...129 D5
Luton LU2 ....46 B3
Watford WD2 ....154 B7
Poplars The Arlesey SG15 ...11 A8
Great Hallingbury CM22 ....77 F4
Hammond Street EN7 ....147 E5
Luton LU4 ....44 B3
Ickleford SG5 ....21 F5
St Albans AL1 ....142 B7
Popple Way SG1 ....50 E6
Poppy Cl EN7 ....123 E4
Poppy Mead SG1 ....50 F4
Poppy Wlk EN7 ....147 D3
Poppyfields AL7 ....111 C5
Porlock Dr LU2 ....46 C1

Port Hill SG14 113 C7
Port La CM22 77 B2
Port Vale SG14 113 C6
Porters Cl SG9 40 E8
Porters Hill AL5 86 C4
Porters Park Dr WD7 156 E7
Porters Wood AL3 127 F7
Portland Ct LU4 45 A1
Portland Dr
Cheshunt EN7 162 A8
Enfield EN2 161 E1
Portland Hts HA6 174 F6
Portland Ind Est SG15 11 A3
Portland Pl
17 Bishop's Stortford CM23 76 F7
Hertford Heath SG13 114 C4
Portland Rd
Bishop's Stortford CM23 76 F7
Luton LU4 45 A1
Portland St AL3 127 C4
Portman Cl Hitchin SG5 21 D2
St Albans AL4 128 C7
Portman Ho AL3 127 D6
Portmill La SG5 34 F7
Post Office Cotts CM22 98 C8
Post Office Rd CM20 117 D1
Post Office Row SG4 24 B1
Post Wood Rd SG12 114 E7
Postfield AL7 90 A1
Postwood Gn SG13 114 C3
Potash La HP23 79 A5
Potten End CE First Sch
HP4 123 B6
Potten End Hill HP1 123 E8
Potter St
Bishop's Stortford CM23 76 F7
Pinner HA5 175 B2
Potter Street Hill HA5 175 B3
Potters Bar Hospl EN6 159 C5
Potters Bar Sta EN6 158 F7
Potters Field AL3 127 E7
Potters Heights Cl HA5 175 B3
Potters La
Borehamwood WD6 170 C8
Stevenage SG1 50 B4
Potters Mews WD6 169 D3
Potterscrouch La
AL2,AL3 140 E7
Pottersheath Rd AL6 68 D1
Pottery Cl LU3 44 F7
Potton Rd SG8 1 F6
Pouchen End La HP1 123 D3
Poulteney Rd CM24 59 E8
Poultney Cl WD7 156 F7
Pound Ave SG1 50 D6
Pound Cl
Lower Nazeing EN9 149 E8
Sandridge AL4 108 C2
Pound Field WD2 153 F4
Pound Gn SG8 1 F5
Pound La WD7 156 F6
Poundwell AL7 111 A5
Powdermill La EN9 163 B6
Powdermill Mews EN9 163 B6
Powdermill Way EN9 163 B6
Power Ct LU1 63 F7
Power Dr EN3 162 F3
Powis Ct Bushey WD2 168 D1
Potters Bar EN6 159 C5
Powys Ct WD6 170 D6
Poynders Hill HP2 125 C3
Poynders Mdw SG4 88 F8
Poynings Cl AL5 107 F8
Poynters Rd LU5 44 A1
Prae Cl AL3 127 B3
Prae Wood Prim Sch
AL3 127 A1
Praetorian Ct AL1 141 C8
Prebendal Dr LU1 63 B2
Precinct The EN10 134 F3
Premier Ct EN3 162 D1
Prentice Way LU2 64 D7
Prescott Rd EN8 148 E4
Presdales Dr SG12 114 E8
Presdales Sch SG12 114 D7
Presentation Ct LU1 63 F6
President Way LU2 64 D8
Prestatyn Cl SG1 50 B8
Preston Gdns
Enfield EN3 162 E2
Luton LU2 45 F2
Preston Path LU2 45 F2
Preston Prim Sch SG4 48 D6
Preston Rd Preston SG4 48 E7
St Ippolyts SG4 34 F1
Prestwick Cl LU2 45 E5
Prestwick Dr CM23 59 B1
Prestwick Rd WD1 175 D6
Pretoria Rd WD1 167 A5
Pretty Cnr HA6 175 A5
Priestleys LU1 63 A7
Primary Way SG15 11 A4
Primett Rd SG1 50 C7
Primley La CM22 98 C1
Primrose Cl Arlesey SG15 11 A4
Bishop's Stortford CM23 76 C6
Hatfield AL10 130 B4
Primrose Cotts WD7 156 A4
Primrose Ct SG1 50 D7
Primrose Dr SG13 114 B6
Primrose Gdns WD2 168 B2
Primrose Hill WD4 139 B3
Primrose Hill Rd SG1 50 D7
Primrose La SG15 11 A4
Primrose Path EN7 162 A8
Primrose View SG8 7 F5
Prince Andrew's Cl SG8 7 D5
Prince Edward St HP4 122 C4
Prince of Wales
Inf & Jun Sch EN3 162 F2
Prince Pk HP1 124 A2
Prince St WD1 167 C6
Prince Way LU2 64 D8
Prince's St SG5 11 F7
Princes Ave
Enfield EN3 162 E4
Watford WD1 167 A5
Princes Cl HP4 122 A6
Princes Ct CM23 76 C7
Princes Gate
Bishop's Stortford CM23 76 C7
Harlow CM20 117 E3
Princes Mews SG8 7 C6
Princes Pl 15 LU2 45 D1
Princes St SG12 93 D2
Princess Alexandra Hospl
CM20 117 C1
Princess Diana Dr AL4 128 D2
Princess Helena Coll SG4 48 E6
Princess St LU1 63 D7
Printers Way CM20 118 A5
Priors 9 CM23 77 A7
Priors Cl SG13 114 B3
Priors Ct CM22 98 A2
Priors Hill SG5 20 C4
Priors Wood Prim Sch
SG12 94 A3
Priors Wood Rd SG13 114 C3
Priory Ave CM17 118 C5
Priory Cl Barnet N20 171 F2
Cheshunt EN10 148 E7
Hoddesdon EN11 135 A5
Royston SG8 7 E6
Stanmore HA7 176 F7
Priory Ct
Berkhamsted HP4 122 C4
Bishop's Stortford CM23 76 F7
Bushey WD2 168 C1
11 Hertford SG14 113 D6
Hitchin SG4 34 F5
St Albans AL1 127 E2
Priory Dell SG1 50 F5
Priory Dr Stanmore HA7 176 F7
Stansted Mountfitchet CM24 59 E5
Priory End SG4 34 F5
Priory Gate EN8 148 F4
Priory Gdns
Berkhamsted HP4 122 C4
Luton LU2 45 D4
Priory La
Great Wymondley SG4 35 F4
Royston SG8 7 D6
Priory Lo WD3 165 D2
Priory Orch AL3 84 B2
Priory Sch The SG5 21 E2
Priory St Hertford SG14 113 D6
Ware SG12 93 C1
Priory View Bushey WD2 168 E2
Little Wymondley SG4 35 E4
Priory Way SG4 34 F4
Priory Wharf 10 SG14 113 D6
Priory Wlk AL1 141 E8
Proctor Way LU2 64 C7
Proctors Way CM23 77 A4
Progress Way LU4 44 B7
Progression Ctr HP2 125 A6
Prospect La AL5 107 A4
Prospect Pl AL6 89 C5
Prospect Rd
Cheshunt EN8 148 C2
St Albans AL1 127 D1
Prospect Way LU2 64 C7
Protea Way SG6 23 B6
Providence Gr SG1 50 E8
Providence Way SG7 23 F7
Provost Way LU2 64 C8
Prowse Ave WD2 176 C8
Pryor Cl WD5 153 F7
Pryor Rd SG7 23 F6
Pryor Way SG6 23 D5
Pryors Cl CM23 77 A6
Pryors Ct SG7 12 F1
Puddephat's La AL3 104 D7
Pudding La Barley SG8 9 A1
Hemel Hempstead HP1 124 A5
Puddingstone Dr AL4 128 C1
Pudgell The SG8 9 E2
Pulham Ave EN10 134 E3
Pullar Memorial
Jun Mix Inf Sch SG11 72 E2
Puller Rd Barnet EN5 171 E7
Hemel Hempstead HP1 124 A2
Pulleys Cl HP1 123 F4
Pulleys La HP1 123 F4
Pullman Dr SG4 35 B7
Pulter's Way SG4 35 A6
Pump Hill SG9 30 A2
Punch Bowl La AL3 126 B8
Purbeck Ho 8 WD1 166 F3
Purbrock Ave WD2 154 C3
Purcell Cl Datchworth AL6 90 E6
Radlett WD6 169 D8
Purcell Ct SG1 50 C8
Purcell Sch of Music
WD2 168 A7
Purkiss Rd SG13 113 C3
Purley Ctr LU3 44 E7
Purlings Rd WD2 168 B4
Pursley Gdns WD6 157 A1
Purway Cl LU3 44 E7
Purwell La SG4 35 C8
Purwell Prim Sch SG4 35 D8
Putney Rd EN3 162 D3
Puttenham Cl WD1 175 D8
Putteridge High Sch LU2 46 C5
Putteridge Inf Sch LU2 46 C5
Putteridge Jun Sch LU2 46 C5
Putteridge Par LU2 46 B4
Putteridge Rd LU2 46 C4
Putteridge Recn Ctr LU2 46 C5
Putterills The AL5 86 A1
Putters Croft HP2 124 F8
Puttocks Cl AL9 144 C8
Puttocks Dr AL9 144 C8
Pye Cnr CM20 117 D5
Pyghtle Ct LU1 63 A7
Pyghtle The
Buntingford SG9 40 D7
Luton LU1 63 A7
Pyms Cl SG6 23 B8
Pynchbek CM23 76 E3
Pynchon Paddocks
CM22 98 D7
Pynefield Ho WD3 164 F2
Pytchley Cl LU2 45 E5

Q

Quadrangle The AL8 110 C7
Quadrant The
Letchworth SG6 22 F6
Royston SG8 7 C8
St Albans AL4 128 B6
Stevenage SG1 50 D4
Quaker La EN9 163 C5
Quaker Rd SG12 93 E3
Quakers La EN6 159 B8
Quantock Cl Luton LU3 45 B8
St Albans AL4 128 C7
Quantock Rise LU3 31 B1
Quantocks HP2 124 F6
Quartermass Cl HP1 124 A4
Quartermass Rd HP1 124 A4
Queen Anne's Cl SG5 11 F5
Queen Elizabeth Ct EN5 171 F5
Queen Elizabeth II Hospl
AL7 111 A2
Queen Elizabeth's
Boys Sch EN5 171 D6
Queen Elizabeth's
Girls Sch EN5 171 F5
Queen Hoo La AL6 90 F6
Queen Mary's Ave WD1 166 E5
Queen St
Chipperfield WD4 152 A7
Hitchin SG4,SG5 34 F7
Pitstone LU7 80 D4
St Albans AL3 127 C3
Stotfold SG5 12 A6
Tring HP23 100 A3
Queen Victoria
Memorial Hospl AL6 89 B4
Queen's Cl CM21 97 F4
Queen's Ct Aspenden SG9 40 D5
Hertford SG13 113 D5
St Albans AL1 128 B3
Queen's Dr EN8 163 A5
Queen's Dr The WD3 165 A3
Queen's Pl WD1 167 C6
Queen's Rd Cheshunt EN8 162 E6
Harpenden AL5 107 B7
Hertford SG13 113 D5
Watford WD1 167 C6
Queen's Sq The HP2 124 F4
Queens Ave WD1 166 F5
Queens Cl 4 Luton LU1 63 E6
Stansted Mountfitchet CM24 59 E8
Queens Cres
Bishop's Stortford CM23 76 E5
St Albans AL4 128 B6
Queens Ct 14 Luton LU2 45 D1
Watford WD1 167 C6
Queens Dr WD5 153 F7
Queens Head Wlk
EN10 148 E8
Queens Rd Barnet EN5 171 D6
Berkhamsted HP4 122 A5
Royston SG8 7 D7
Ware SG12 93 F2
Queens' Sch WD2 168 A6
Queens Way
Cheshunt EN8 162 F5
Shenley WD7 156 E7
Queensgate EN8 162 F5
Queensgate Ctr CM20 117 F4
Queensway
1 Hatfield AL10 130 A6
Hemel Hempstead
HP1,HP2 124 E4
Royston SG8 7 D7
Stevenage SG1 50 D5
Queenswood Cres WD2 154 A6
Queenswood Dr SG4 22 C1
Queenswood Sch AL9 145 D3
Quendell Wlk HP2 124 E3
Quendon Dr EN9 163 D6
Quickbeams AL7 90 A1
Quickley La WD3 164 C4
Quickley Rise WD3 164 C3
Quickly Brow WD3 164 B3
Quickmoor La WD4 152 C6
Quickwood LU3 45 A7
Quickwood Cl WD3 165 A3
Quills SG6 23 D4
Quilter Cl LU3 44 F4
Quinces Croft HP1 124 A5
Quincey Rd SG12 93 C4
Quinn Ct SG11 55 F7
Quinn Way SG6 23 C5
Quinta Dr EN5 171 C4

R

Raans Rd HP6 150 A1
Raban Cl SG2 51 C1
Raban Ct SG7 12 F1
Rabley Heath Rd AL6 68 B2
Rackman Dr LU3 45 C5
Radburn Prim Sch SG6 23 C5
Radburn Way SG6 23 C4
Radcliffe Rd SG5 35 A8
Radlett Inf Sch WD7 156 B3
Radlett La WD7 156 E6
Radlett Park Rd WD7 156 A4
Radlett Rd
London Colney AL2 141 E2
Watford WD1,WD2 167 D7
Radlett Sta WD7 156 A4
Radnor Ct HA3 176 F2
Radstone Pl LU2 46 E1
Radwell La SG7 12 C4
Raebarn Gdns EN5 171 B4
Raffin Cl SG3 69 E3
Raffin Green La SG3 69 F4
Raffin Pk SG3 69 E3
Ragged Hall La AL2 140 E7
Raglan Ave EN8 162 D5
Raglan Gdns WD1 167 B1
Raglan Ho HP4 122 A4
Rags La EN7 147 E4
Railway Pl SG13 113 E6
Railway Rd EN8 162 F6
Railway St SG13,SG14 113 D6
Railway Terr WD4 139 A4
Rainbow Cl AL3 105 F6
Rainbow Ct WD1 167 C3
Rainer Cl EN8 148 D2
Rainsford Rd CM24 59 E8
Raleigh Cres SG2 51 B8
Raleigh Gr LU4 44 D1
Rally The SG15 11 A7
Ralph Sadleir Sch SG11 55 E3
Ralston Way WD1 175 D8
Ram Gorse CM20 117 B2
Ramblers Way AL7 111 C5
Rambling Way HP4 123 C6
Ramerick Gdns SG15 11 A2
Ramney Dr EN3 162 E2
Ramparts The AL3 127 B2
Ramridge Inf Sch LU2 46 B2
Ramridge Jun Sch LU2 46 B2
Ramridge Rd LU2 46 A2
Ramryge Ct AL1 127 D1
Ramsay Cl EN10 134 E2
Ramsbury Rd AL1 127 E2
Ramsdell SG1 50 F5
Ramsey Cl
Brookmans Park AL9 145 D4
St Albans AL1 128 A1
Ramsey Lodge Ct AL1 127 E4
Ramson Rise HP1 123 E2
Rand's Cl SG5 21 B7
Rand's Cotts SG5 21 B7
Rand's Mdw SG5 21 B7
Randalls Ride HP2 124 E5
Randalls Wlk AL2 140 F1
Randals Hill SG2 51 C3
Randolph Ct HA5 176 A3
Randon Cl HA2 176 B1
Ranelagh Rd HP2 125 B3
Ranleigh Wlk AL5 107 D6
Ranock Cl LU3 44 D8
Ranskill Rd WD6 170 A8
Ransom Cl SG4 34 F4
Ransome Cl WD1 167 C2
Rant Mdw
Hemel Hempstead HP3 125 A1
Hemel Hempstead HP3 125 A2
Ranulf Cl CM17 118 C6
Ranworth Ave
Hoddesdon EN11 115 B2
Stevenage SG2 69 C7
Ranworth Cl 2 HP3 124 D1
Raphael Cl WD7 156 E7
Raphael Dr WD2 167 D7
Rapper Ct LU3 63 D8
Rasehill Cl WD3 165 C4
Rathlin HP3 139 B8
Ratty's La EN11 135 D6
Raven Cl WD3 165 D2
Raven Ct AL10 130 A4
Ravenbank Rd LU2 46 C5
Ravenfield Rd AL7 110 F6
Ravenhill Way LU4 44 B4
Ravens La HP4 122 D4
Ravens Wharf HP4 122 D4
Ravenscroft
Harpenden AL5 107 D6
Hoddesdon EN10 134 F3
Watford WD2 154 E4
Ravenscroft Pk EN5 171 D5
Ravenscroft Sch N20 171 F2
Ravensdell HP1 123 F4
Ravensthorpe LU2 46 B4
Ravenswood Pk HA6 175 A4
Rawdon Dr EN11 135 A5
Ray's Hill HP5 120 C2
Rayburn Rd HP1 124 A5
Raydon Rd EN8 162 D7
Rayfield AL8 89 D1
Rayleigh Ho WD5 153 F7
Raymer Cl AL1 127 E4
Raymond Cl WD5 153 D7
Raymond Cotts SG5 21 E4
Raymond Ct EN6 159 C5
Raymonds Cl AL7 110 E4
Raymonds Plain AL7 110 E4
Raynham Rd CM23 77 B8
Raynham St SG13
Raynham Way LU2
Raynsford Rd SG12
Raynton Rd EN3
Readings The WD3
Recreation Ground CM24
Rectory Cl
Bishop's Stortford CM23
Essendon AL9
Hunsdon SG12
Rectory Gdns AL10
Rectory La
Berkhamsted HP4
Farnham CM23
Kings Langley WD4
Lilley LU2
Rickmansworth WD3
Shenley WD7,AL2
Stevenage SG1
Watton at Stone SG14
Welwyn SG3
Rectory Rd
Rickmansworth WD3
Welwyn Garden City AL8
Rectory Wood CM20
Red House Cl SG12
Red Lion Cl WD2
Red Lion Cotts SG5
Red Lion Ct 5 CM23
Red Lion La
Hemel Hempstead HP3
Sarratt WD3
Red Lodge WD6
Red Lodge Gdns HP4
Red Rails LU1
Red Rails Ct LU1
Red Rd WD6
Redan Rd SG12
Redbourn Ind Est AL3
Redbourn Inf Sch AL3
Redbourn Jun Sch AL3
Redbourn La AL3,AL5
Redbourn Rd
Hemel Hempstead HP2
St Albans AL3
Redbourn Recn Ctr AL3
Redbournbury La AL3
Redbournbury Water Mill
AL3
Redbrick Row CM22
Redcar Dr SG1
Redding Ho WD1
Redding La AL3
Reddings
Hemel Hempstead HP3
Welwyn Garden City AL8
Reddings Ave WD2
Reddings Cty Prim Sch
The HP3
Reddings The WD6
Redferns Cl LU1
Redferns Ct LU1
Redgrave Gdns LU3
Redhall Cl AL10
Redhall Dr AL10
Redhall La
Colney Heath AL4
Sarratt WD3
Redheath Cl WD2
Redhill Rd SG5
Redhoods Way E SG6
Redhoods Way W SG6
Redhouse The EN10
Redlands Rd EN3
Redmire Cl LU4
Redoubt Cl SG4
Redricks La CM21
Redvers Cl CM23
Redwell Ct EN8
Redwing Cl SG2
Redwing Gr WD5
Redwood Cl WD1
Redwood Dr
Hemel Hempstead HP3
Luton LU3
Redwood Rise WD6
Redwood Way EN5
Redwoods Hertford AL8
Welwyn Garden City AL8
Reed Cl AL2
Reed Fst Sch SG8
Reed Pl AL5
Reedham Cl AL2
Reedings Jun Sch CM21
Reedings Way CM21
Reeds Cres WD1
Reeds The AL7
Reedsdale LU2
Reeves Ave LU3
Reeves Pightle SG8
Regal Cl SG11
Regal Ct 4 SG5
Regal Way WD2
Regency Cl CM23
Regency Ct
Hemel Hempstead HP2
Hoddesdon EN10
Regent Cl
Kings Langley WD4
St Albans AL4
Welwyn Garden City AL7
Regent Ct SG5
Regent Gate EN8
Regent St Luton LU1
Stotfold SG5
Watford WD2
Regents Cl WD7
Regina Cl EN5

eginald Rd HA6 . . . . 174 F3
eginald St LU2 . . . . 45 E1
endlesham Ave WD7 . . . . . 155 F2
endlesham Sq LU3 . . . . 93 B2
endlesham Rd EN2 . . . . . . 161 B1
endlesham Way WD3 . . . . 164 C3
ennie Ct EN3 . . . . 163 A1
ennison Ct EN7 . . . . 147 F4
enshaw Cl LU2 . . . . 46 E2
epton Cl LU3 . . . . 44 F6
epton Gn AL3 . . . . 127 D6
epton Way WD5 . . . . 166 A4
eson Way HP1 . . . . 123 E4
eston Cl WD6 . . . . 157 B1
eston Path LU2 . . . . 46 C2
etford Cl WD6 . . . . 157 A1
etreat The WD5 . . . . 153 C8
evels Cl SG14 . . . . 113 D8
evels Rd SG14 . . . . 113 D8
eynard Copse CM23 . . . . . 58 F1
eynard Way SG13 . . . . . . 114 B6
eynard's Way AL2 . . . . . . 140 F2
eynards Rd AL6 . . . . 89 C7
eynolds Cl 11 F1
eynolds Cl HP1 . . . . 124 A4
eynolds Cres AL4 . . . . 128 B8
hee Spring SG7 . . . . 13 B1
hodes Ave CM23 . . . . 76 F1
hodes Memorial Mus &
Commonwealth Ctr
CM23 . . . . 77 A6
hodes Way WD2 . . . . 167 D8
hymes HP1 . . . . 124 B5
ib Cl SG11 . . . . 55 E2
rib Vale SG14 . . . . 92 D1
ibbledale Al2 . . . . 142 F4
ibbledale HP4 . . . . 124 E6
ibocon Way LU4 . . . . 44 B7
ibston Cl WD7 . . . . 156 D6
Rice Cl HP2 . . . . 124 F4
Richard Ct EN5 . . . . 171 E6
Richard Hale Sch SG13 . . 113 D5
Richard Stagg Cl AL1 . . . . 128 C1
Richard Wittington
Jun Mix Inf Sch CM23 . . . 76 E1
Richards Cl Bushey WD2 . 168 D2
Luton LU1 . . . . 63 B6
Richards Ct LU1 . . . . 63 B5
Richardson Cl AL2 . . . . . . 142 E4
Richardson Cres EN7 . . . . 147 B6
Richardson Pl AL4 . . . . 129 B1
Richfield Rd WD2 . . . . 168 C2
Richmond Cl
Bishop's Stortford CM23 . . . 76 C7
Cheshunt EN8 . . . . 148 C2
Ware SG12 . . . . 93 B3
Richmond Ct
4 Hatfield AL10 . . . . 130 B3
Hoddesdon EN10 . . . . . . 134 F3
Luton LU2 . . . . 45 F1
Potters Bar EN6 . . . . 159 C8
Richmond Dr WD1 . . . . . . 166 E7
Richmond Gdns HA3 . . . . 176 F3
Richmond Hill LU2 . . . . 45 F2
Richmond Hill Sch LU2 . . . 45 E2
Richmond Rd EN6 . . . . 159 C8
Richmond Way WD3 . . . . 166 C5
Richmond Wlk AL4 . . . . . . 128 D7
Rickfield Cl AL10 . . . . 130 A3
Rickmansworth La SL9 . . . 172 A5
Rickmansworth Park
Jun Mix Inf Sch WD3 . . . . 165 C2
Rickmansworth Rd
Chorleywood WD3 . . . . 164 F6
Harefield UB9 . . . . 173 D3
Northwood HA6 . . . . 174 D3
Pinner HA5 . . . . 175 C1
Watford WD1 . . . . 166 E5
Rickmansworth Sch
WD3 . . . . 165 F3
Rickmansworth Sta
WD3 . . . . 165 D2
Rickyard Cl LU2 . . . . 46 B3
Rickyard Mdw Al3 . . . . . . 106 A5
Rickyard The Ashwell SG7 . . 4 D3
Letchworth SG6 . . . . 22 C1
Riddel Gdns SG7 . . . . 23 F8
Riddy Hill Cl SG4 . . . . 35 A6
Riddy La Hitchin SG4 . . . . . 35 A6
Luton LU3 . . . . 45 C5
Riddy The SG4 . . . . 35 A6
Ridge Ave Harpenden AL5 . 85 E4
Letchworth SG6 . . . . 23 A6
Ridge Ct LU2 . . . . 46 A1
Ridge La WD1 . . . . 153 F2
Ridge Lea HP1 . . . . 123 F2
Ridge Rd SG6 . . . . 23 A6
Ridge St WD2 . . . . 154 B1
Ridge The Barnet EN5 . . . 171 F4
Letchworth SG6 . . . . 23 A6
Northwood HA6 . . . . 174 F4
Ridge View HP23 . . . . 100 C5
Ridgedown AL3 . . . . 106 A5
Ridgefield WD1 . . . . 153 E2
Ridgehurst Ave WD2 . . . . 153 F5
Ridgeview Cl EN5 . . . . 171 D3
Ridgeway
Berkhamsted HP4 . . . . . . 121 F4
Harpenden AL5 . . . . 85 E4
Kensworth Common LU6 . . 82 E8
Little Hadham SG11 . . . . . . 57 E4
Stevenage SG1 . . . . 50 F5
Welwyn Garden City AL7 . 111 B6
Ridgeway Cl HP3 . . . . 138 F5
Ridgeway Ct HA5 . . . . 176 A3
Ridgeway The
Codicote SG4 . . . . 67 F1

Ridgeway The, continued
Cuffley EN6 . . . . 146 A4
Hadley Wood EN2,EN4 . . 160 D3
Hertford SG14 . . . . 112 F7
Hitchin SG5 . . . . 34 D6
Radlett WD7 . . . . 155 F2
St Albans AL4 . . . . 93 C3
Ware SG12 . . . . 93 C3
Watford WD1 . . . . 153 E2
Ridgewood Dr AL5 . . . . . . 85 E4
Ridgewood Gdns AL5 . . . . 85 E4
Ridgmont Rd AL1 . . . . 127 E2
Ridgway Rd LU2 . . . . 45 F1
Ridings The
Bishop's Stortford CM23 . 76 D4
Hertford SG14 . . . . 113 A5
Latimer HP5 . . . . 150 D3
Luton LU3 . . . . 45 C1
Markyate AL3 . . . . 83 E6
Stevenage SG2 . . . . 51 B3
Ridler Rd EN1 . . . . 161 E1
Ridlins End SG2 . . . . 51 C2
Rigby Pl LU3 . . . . 163 A2
Rigery La SG11 . . . . 72 F6
Riley Rd EN3 . . . . 162 C1
Ringmer Ct LU2 . . . . 46 C3
Ringshall Dr HP4 . . . . 102 C8
Ringshall Rd HP4 . . . . 81 B3
Ringtale Pl SG7 . . . . 13 B1
Ringway Rd AL2 . . . . 141 C4
Ringwood Rd LU2 . . . . 45 D7
Ripley Rd Enfield EN2 . . . 161 A1
Luton LU4 . . . . 44 C1
Ripley Way Cheshunt EN7 . 148 B1
Hemel Hempstead HP1 . . 123 E4
Ripon Rd SG1 . . . . 37 A2
Ripon Way
Borehamwood WD6 . . . . 170 D4
Luton LU2 . . . . 128 D7
Rise The Borehamwood WD6 . 170 C3
Park Street AL2 . . . . 141 D6
Risedale Cl WD3 . . . . 138 E8
Risedale Hill HP3 . . . . 138 E8
Risedale Rd HP3 . . . . 138 E8
Rising Hill Cl HA6 . . . . . . 174 C4
Risingholme Cl
Bushey WD2 . . . . 168 B2
Harrow HA3 . . . . 176 E2
Risingholme Rd HA3 . . . . 176 E1
Ritcroft Cl HP3 . . . . 125 B2
Ritcroft Dr HP3 . . . . 125 B2
Ritcroft St HP3 . . . . 125 B2
Ritz Ct EN6 . . . . 159 A8
Rivenhall End AL11 . . . . . 111 C6
River Ave EN11 . . . . 135 B7
River Cl EN8 . . . . 163 A5
River Ct Ickleford SG5 . . . . 21 F4
Sacombe SG14 . . . . 92 E4
Sawbridgeworth CM21 . . . . 97 F3
River Gn SG9 . . . . 40 E8
River Hill AL3 . . . . 84 B2
River Lee Ctry Pk EN9 . . . 149 B1
River Mead SG5 . . . . 21 C2
River Meads SG12 . . . . . . 115 C4
River Park Ind Est HP4 . . . 122 A5
River Pk HP1 . . . . 124 A1
River View AL7 . . . . 89 F2
River Way Harlow CM20 . 118 B5
Luton LU3 . . . . 44 E5
Riverbanks Cl EN8 . . . . 86 C4
Riverfield La CM21 . . . . . . 97 E3
Riverford Cl AL5 . . . . 86 B4
Riverhill CM20 . . . . 117 C2
Rivermill Ct SG8 . . . . 7 C7
Rivers Hospl The CM21 . . . 97 C1
Riversend Rd HP3 . . . . . . 138 C8
Rivershill SG14 . . . . 70 E3
Riverside
Bishop's Stortford CM23 . . . 76 F7
Buntingford SG9 . . . . 40 E7
London Colney AL2 . . . . . 142 E4
Welwyn AL6 . . . . 89 B5
Riverside Ave LU6 . . . . . . 135 A1
Riverside Cl
Kings Langley WD4 . . . . . 139 B2
St Albans AL1 . . . . 127 E1
Riverside Cotts SG12 . . . . 115 C6
Riverside Ct Harlow CM20 . 118 C6
St Albans AL1 . . . . 127 E1
Riverside Dr WD3 . . . . . . 165 D1
Riverside Est AL5 . . . . 86 C4
Riverside Gdns HP4 . . . . . 122 A5
Riverside Mews
Hoddesdon EN10 . . . . . . 148 E8
10 Ware SG12 . . . . 93 D1
Riverside Path EN8 . . . . . 148 C2
Riverside Rd Luton LU3 . . . 45 A5
St Albans AL1 . . . . 127 E1
Watford WD1 . . . . 167 B3
Riverside Wlk 10 CM23 . . . 76 F7
Riversmead EN11 . . . . 135 A5
Riversmeet SG14 . . . . 113 B5
Rivett Cl SG7 . . . . 23 A5
Roan Wlk SG8 . . . . 7 E6
Roaring Meg Ret & L Pk
SG1 . . . . 50 E3
Robbery Bottom La AL6 . . 90 A8
Robbs Cl HP1 . . . . 124 A6
Robe End HP1 . . . . 123 F5
Robert Allen Ct 3 LU1 . . . 63 E6
Robert Ave AL1 . . . . 141 C7
Robert Cl EN6 . . . . 158 E6
Robert Humbert Ho SG6 . . 23 A5
Robert Saunders Ct SG6 . . 22 E4
Robert Tebbutt Ct SG5 . . . 34 E6

Robert Wallace Cl CM23 . . 58 F1
Robert Cl EN8 . . . . 148 E1
Roberts La SL9 . . . . 172 B5
Roberts Rd WD1 . . . . 167 C4
Roberts Way AL10 . . . . . . 129 F3
Roberts Wood Dr SL9 . . . 172 A5
Robertson Cl EN10 . . . . . . 148 A5
Robeson Way WD6 . . . . . 170 C8
Robin Cl SG12 . . . . 115 C3
Robin Ct AL5 . . . . 86 B4
Robin Hill HP4 . . . . 122 C3
Robin Hood Dr
Bushey WD2 . . . . 167 F8
Harrow HA3 . . . . 176 F3
Robin Hood La AL10 . . . . 130 A6
Robin Hood Mdw HP2 . . . 124 F8
Robin Mead AL7 . . . . 90 A1
Robin Way AL7 . . . . 146 E3
Robina Cl HA6 . . . . 174 F2
Robins Cl AL2 . . . . 142 E4
Robins Nest Hill SG13 . . . 132 C6
Robins Rd HP3 . . . . 125 A1
Robins Way AL10 . . . . 129 F2
Robinsfield HP1 . . . . 124 A3
Robinson Ave EN7 . . . . . . 147 B3
Robinson Cl CM23 . . . . 76 F5
Robinson Cres WD2 . . . . . 168 C1
Robinsway EN9 . . . . 163 E5
Robinswood LU2 . . . . 45 E5
Robsons Cl EN8 . . . . 148 D3
Rochdale Ct 6 LU1 . . . . . . 63 E6
Rochester Ave LU2 . . . . . . 46 C4
Rochester Dr WD2 . . . . . . 154 C4
Rochester Way
Croxley Green WD3 . . . . . 166 B5
Royston SG8 . . . . 7 D8
Rochford Ave EN9 . . . . . . 163 D5
Rochford Cl
Cheshunt EN10 . . . . 148 E5
Stansted Mountfitchet CM24 . 59 E5
Rochford Rd CM23 . . . . 59 C1
Rock Rd SG8 . . . . 7 C8
Rockfield Ave SG12 . . . . . 115 C4
Rockingham Gate WD2 . . 168 C3
Rockingham Way SG1 . . . . 50 E4
Rockleigh SG14 . . . . 113 C6
Rockley Rd LU3 . . . . 63 A7
Rockliffe Ave WD4 . . . . . . 139 A1
Rockways HP5 . . . . 170 F3
Rodgers Cl WD6 . . . . 169 D3
Rodings The EN5 . . . . 171 E5
Rodney Ave AL1 . . . . 128 A1
Rodney Cres EN11 . . . . . . 135 A8
Roe Cl SG5 . . . . 34 A1
Roe End La AL3 . . . . 83 B4
Roe Green Cl AL10 . . . . . . 129 F4
Roe Green Ctr AL10 . . . . . 129 F4
Roe Green La AL10 . . . . . 129 F5
Roe Hill Cl AL10 . . . . 129 F5
Roebuck Cl Hertford SG13 . 114 A6
Luton LU1 . . . . 63 B6
Roebuck Ct 1 SG2 . . . . 50 F1
Roebuck Gate SG2 . . . . . . 50 F1
Roebuck Jun & Inf
Sch SG2 . . . . 50 F2
Roebuck Ret Pk SG2 . . . . . 50 E2
Roecroft Lower Sch SG5 . . 11 F6
Roedean Ave EN3 . . . . . . 162 C1
Roedean Cl LU2 . . . . 46 D3
Roedean Ho 8 WD1 . . . . . 167 C7
Roefields Cl HP3 . . . . 138 A7
Roehyde Way AL10 . . . . . 129 E2
Roestock Gdns AL4 . . . . . 129 E1
Roestock La AL4 . . . . 129 E1
Rofant Rd HA6 . . . . 174 E4
Rogate Rd LU2 . . . . 46 C5
Roge de Clare CE Fst Sch
SG13 . . . . 114 C2
Rogers Ruff HA6 . . . . 174 C2
Rokewood Mews 3 SG12 . 93 D2
Roland St AL1 . . . . 128 B2
Rolleston Cl SG12 . . . . 93 C3
Rollswood Rd AL7 . . . . . . 110 E3
Rollswood Rd AL6 . . . . 89 B8
Rollys La SG7 . . . . 4 D4
Roman Gdns
Kings Langley WD4 . . . . . 139 B1
Lechworth SG6 . . . . 22 C6
Roman La SG7 . . . . 24 A8
Roman Mews 7 EN11 . . . 135 A7
Roman Rd AL5 . . . . 85 F4
Roman Rise CM21 . . . . 97 D2
Roman St 8 EN11 . . . . . . 135 A7
Roman Vale CM17 . . . . . . 118 C5
Romany Cl LU3 . . . . 45 B3
Romany Ct HP2 . . . . 124 E5
Romeland Elstree WD6 . . 169 D3
St Albans AL3 . . . . 127 C3
Waltham Abbey EN9 . . . . 163 C6
Romeland Hill AL3 . . . . . . 127 C3
Romilly Dr WD1 . . . . 175 F6
Rondini Ave LU3 . . . . 45 B3
Rook Tree Cl SG6 . . . . 12 A6
Rook Tree La SG6 . . . . 12 A6
Rookery Dr LU2 . . . . 45 E6
Rookery The Hatfield AL3 . 144 D8
Stansted Mountfitchet CM24 . 59 E8
Westmill SG9 . . . . 40 E3
Rookery Yd SG1 . . . . 50 C7

Rookes Cl SG6 . . . . 23 B3
Rooks Cl AL8 . . . . 110 D5
Rooks Hill
Rickmansworth WD3 . . . . 165 D5
Welwyn Garden City AL8 . 110 C5
Rooks Nest La SG8 . . . . . . 16 A5
Rookwood Dr SG2 . . . . 51 B1
Rosary Ct EN6 . . . . 145 B1
Rosary Gdns WD2 . . . . . . 168 E2
Rose Acre AL3 . . . . 105 F6
Rose Cl AL10 . . . . 130 A8
Rose Cotts Arlesey SG15 . . 11 A6
Meesden SG9 . . . . 30 A5
Wyddial SG9 . . . . 28 A3
Rose Ct
Hammond Street EN7 . . . 148 A4
St Albans AL3 . . . . 128 C5
Rose Gdns WD1 . . . . 167 A4
Rose La Essendon AL9 . . . 131 C5
Wheathampstead AL4 . . . . 87 C2
Rose Lawn WD2 . . . . 168 B1
Rose Mdw SG11 . . . . 41 E4
Rose Mead EN6 . . . . 145 C1
Rose Vale EN11 . . . . 135 A6
Rose Wlk Royston SG8 . . . . . 7 C7
St Albans AL4 . . . . 128 C5
Rose Wlk The WD2 . . . . . 154 C1
Rosebank LU2 . . . . 45 F3
Roseacre Gdns AL7 . . . . . 111 D6
Roseacres SG11 . . . . 97 D3
Rosebank EN9 . . . . 163 E6
Roseberry Ct WD1 . . . . . . 167 A8
Rosebery Ave AL5 . . . . 85 F1
Roseberry Mews LU7 . . . . . 45 D4
Rosebery Rd WD2 . . . . . . 168 B2
Rosebery Way HP23 . . . . 100 B5
Rosebriar Wlk WD2 . . . . . 153 F3
Rosecroft Ct HA6 . . . . 174 C4
Rosecroft Dr WD1 . . . . . . 153 E3
Rosecroft La AL6 . . . . 90 A8
Rosedale AL7 . . . . 89 F2
Rosedale Ave EN7 . . . . . . 147 F2
Rosedale Cl
Bricket Wood AL2 . . . . . . 140 C5
Luton LU3 . . . . 44 C7
Rosedale Way EN7 . . . . . . 148 A3
Rosehill HP1 . . . . 123 E4
Rosehill Cl EN11 . . . . 134 F6
Rosehill Ct HP1 . . . . 124 A1
Rosehill Gdns WD5 . . . . . 153 C7
Rosehill Hospl SG6 . . . . . . 22 D2
Roselands Ave EN11 . . . . 114 F1
Roselands Prim Sch
EN11 . . . . 114 F1
Roseley Cotts CM20 . . . . 117 F2
Rosemary Cl CM17 . . . . . 118 C4
Rosemont Cl SG6 . . . . 22 C6
Rosewood Ct HP1 . . . . . . 123 E4
Rosewood Dr EN2 . . . . . . 161 A4
Roslyn Cl EN10 . . . . 134 E2
Roslyn Rd WD1 . . . . 167 B6
Ross Cl HA3 . . . . 63 B6
Ross Cres WD3 . . . . 154 A4
Ross Ct SG2 . . . . 51 B7
Ross Haven Pl HA6 . . . . . 174 F2
Ross Way HA6 . . . . 174 F6
Rossfold Rd LU3 . . . . 44 D8
Rossgate HP1 . . . . 124 A5
Rossgate Prim Sch HP1 . . 124 A5
Rossington Ave WD6 . . . . 156 E1
Rossington Cl EN1 . . . . . . 162 B3
Rossiter Fields EN5 . . . . . 171 F3
Rosslyn Cres LU3 . . . . 45 C5
Rosslyn Rd WD1 . . . . 167 B6
Rossway Dr WD2 . . . . 168 D4
Rossway La HP4 . . . . 121 A7
Roswell Cl EN8 . . . . 148 E1
Rothamsted Ave AL5 . . . . . 86 A1
Rothamsted Ct AL5 . . . . . . 86 A1
Rothamsted
Experimental Sta AL5 . . 107 A8
Rother Cl WD2 . . . . 154 C5
Rother Field LU2 . . . . 46 D3
Rotheram Ave LU1 . . . . 63 B5
Rotherfield Rd EN3 . . . . . 162 D2
Rothesay Ct HP4 . . . . 122 A4
Rothesay Rd LU1 . . . . 63 D7
Roughdown Ave HP3 . . . . 138 A8
Roughdown Rd HP3 . . . . . 138 B8
Roughdown Villas Rd
HP3 . . . . 138 A8
Roughs The HA6 . . . . 174 E7
Roughwood Cl WD1 . . . . 153 E1
Round Diamond Prim Sch
SG1 . . . . 51 B8
Roundabout Ho HA6 . . . . 175 A2
Roundabout La AL6 . . . . . . 89 F8
Roundcroft EN7 . . . . 147 F5
Roundfield Ave AL5 . . . . . . 86 D3
Roundhaye AL5 . . . . 55 D3
Roundhedge Way EN2 . . . 160 F2
Roundhills EN9 . . . . 163 E4
Roundings The SG13 . . . . 114 C2
Roundmoor Dr EN8 . . . . . 148 E2
Roundway The HP1 . . . . . 166 F2
Roundwood HP3 . . . . 138 E4
Roundwood Cl
Hitchin SG4 . . . . 22 C2
Oaklands AL5 . . . . 89 D8
Roundwood Dr AL8 . . . . . 110 C7
Roundwood Gdns AL5 . . . . 85 E2
Roundwood La AL5 . . . . . . 85 E3
Roundwood Park Sch
AL5 . . . . 85 E2
Roundwood Pk AL5 . . . . . . 85 E3

Roundwood Prim Sch
AL5 . . . . 85 E2
Rounton Rd EN9 . . . . 163 E6
Rousebarn La WD3 . . . . . 166 C7
Rowan Cl
Bricket Wood AL2 . . . . . . 155 A8
Harrow HA7 . . . . 176 F4
Luton LU1 . . . . 63 B7
Shenley WD7 . . . . 156 E6
St Albans AL4 . . . . 128 C3
Weston SG4 . . . . 37 B8
Rowan Cres
Letchworth SG6 . . . . 23 E7
Stevenage SG1 . . . . 50 E7
Rowan Dr EN10 . . . . 148 F6
Rowan Gr SG4 . . . . 35 A4
Rowan Way AL5 . . . . 107 C8
Rowan Wlk 6 AL10 . . . . . 130 A2
Rowans AL7 . . . . 90 A1
Rowans Prim Sch The
AL7 . . . . 90 A1
Rowans The Baldock SG7 . . 23 E7
Hemel Hempstead HP1 . . 123 A4
Hoddesdon EN10 . . . . . . 134 F4
Rowcroft HP1 . . . . 123 E2
Rowelfield LU2 . . . . 46 C1
Rowington Cl LU2 . . . . 46 C2
Rowland Pl HA6 . . . . 174 E3
Rowland Rd SG1 . . . . 50 F4
Rowland Way SG6 . . . . 22 F6
Rowlands Ave HA5 . . . . . 176 B4
Rowlands Cl EN8 . . . . 148 D1
Rowlands Ct 3 EN8 . . . . . 148 D1
Rowlatt Ct AL1 . . . . 127 E4
Rowlatt Dr AL3 . . . . 127 A1
Rowley Cl WD1 . . . . 167 E3
Rowley Gdns EN8 . . . . . . 148 D3
Rowley Green Rd EN5 . . . 171 A4
Rowley La Barnet EN5 . . . 170 F5
Borehamwood WD6 . . . . 170 D7
Rowley Wlk HP2 . . . . 125 C8
Rowley's Rd SG13 . . . . . . 113 F7
Rowney Gdns CM21 . . . . 118 C8
Rowney Rd AL1 . . . . 72 B5
Rowney Wood CM21 . . . . . 97 E1
Rows The CM20 . . . . 117 D1
Roxley Cotts SG6 . . . . 23 B2
Roy Rd HA6 . . . . 174 F3
Royal Ave EN8 . . . . 162 E6
Royal Ct HP3 . . . . 138 E8
Royal Masonic Sch WD3 . 165 De
Royal National
Orthopaedic Hospl
HA7 . . . . 169 B1
Royal Oak La SG5 . . . . 27 D5
Royal Oak Gdns 6 CM23 . 76 F6
Royal Oak La SG5 . . . . 20 D4
Royal Rd AL1 . . . . 128 B3
Royal Veterinary Coll
AL9 . . . . 144 D3
Royce Cl EN10 . . . . 134 F2
Roydon Cl LU4 . . . . 44 A4
Roydon Ct HP2 . . . . 105 A3
Roydon Lodge Chalet Est
CM19 . . . . 116 C1
Roydon Rd Harlow CM19 . 116 E1
Stanstead Abbotts SG12 . 115 E4
Roydon Sta CM19 . . . . . . 116 B2
Royse Gr SG8 . . . . 7 D4
Roysia Mid Sch SG8 . . . . . . 7 D8
Royston Cl SG14 . . . . 113 B6
Royston & District Mus
SG8 . . . . 7 C6
Royston Gr HA5 . . . . 176 A4
Royston Hospl SG8 . . . . 7 D4
Royston Park Rd HA5 . . . 176 A5
Royston Rd Baldock SG7 . . 13 D2
Barkway SG8 . . . . 17 C5
Barley SG8 . . . . 8 B1
St Albans AL1 . . . . 128 B2
Royston Sta SG8 . . . . 7 C7
Rucklers La WD4 . . . . 138 C4
Ruckles Cl SG1 . . . . 50 E5
Rudd Cl SG2 . . . . 51 B3
Rudham Gr SG6 . . . . 23 C3
Rudolf Steiner Sch WD4 . 138 E2
Rudolph Rd WD2 . . . . 168 A3
Rudyard Cl LU4 . . . . 44 D3
Rue de St Lawrence EN9 . 163 C5
Rueley Dell Rd LU2 . . . . . . 32 D2
Rufford Cl WD1 . . . . 153 F2
Rugby Way WD3 . . . . 166 B4
Ruins The AL3 . . . . 106 B5
Rumballs Cl HP3 . . . . 139 A8
Rumballs Rd HP3 . . . . 139 A8
Rumbold Rd EN11 . . . . . . 135 C8
Rumsley EN7 . . . . 148 A4
Runcie Cl AL4 . . . . 128 A7
Runcorn Cres HP2 . . . . . . 124 F7
Rundells LU3 . . . . 44 C8
Runfold Ave LU3 . . . . 45 A5
Runham Cl LU4 . . . . 44 A4
Runham Rd HP3 . . . . 124 E1
Runley Rd LU1 . . . . 62 F7
Runnalow SG6 . . . . 22 E7
Runsley AL7 . . . . 90 A1
Rural Bygones Mus LU7 . . 80 D4
Rusham Ct AL2 . . . . 141 C5
Rush Cl SG12 . . . . 115 C4
Rushall Gn LU2 . . . . 46 C2
Rushby Mead SG6 . . . . 23 A5
Rushby Pl SG6 . . . . 23 A5
Rushby Wlk SG6 . . . . 23 A6
Rushden Rd SG8 . . . . 26 A8

Rushen Dr SG13 . . . . .114 C3
Rushendon Furlong LU7 . . .80 E5
Rushes Ct CM23 . . . . .77 A5
Rushfield
 Potters Bar EN6 . . . . .158 E6
 Sawbridgeworth CM21 . . . . . .97 E2
Rushfield Rd SG12 . . . . .93 F3
Rushleigh Ave EN8 . . . . .148 D1
Rushleigh Gn CM23 . . . . .76 D4
Rushmere La HP5 . . . . .136 B3
Rushmoor Cl WD3 . . . . .173 D8
Rushmore Cl LU1 . . . . .62 E4
Rushton Ave WD2 . . . . .154 A8
Rushton Ct EN8 . . . . .148 D2
Ruskin Ave EN9 . . . . .163 E5
Ruskin Cl EN7 . . . . .147 E5
Ruskin La SG4 . . . . .35 C7
Rusper Gn LU2 . . . . .46 D3
Russell Ave AL3 . . . . .127 D3
Russell Cl
 Kensworth Common LU6 . . . .82 E8
 Moor Park HA6 . . . . .174 C5
Russell Ct SG1 . . . . .51 B2
Russell Cres WD2 . . . . .153 F4
Russell Ct AL2 . . . . .141 A1
Russell La WD1 . . . . .153 D3
Russell Pl HP3 . . . . .138 B8
Russell Rd Enfield EN1 . . . . .161 F1
 Moor Park HA6 . . . . .174 C6
Russell Rise LU1 . . . . .63 D6
Russell Sch The WD3 . . . . . .164 B5
Russell St Hertford SG14 . . . .113 C6
 Luton LU1 . . . . .63 D6
Russett Way WD1 . . . . .167 B2
Russell's Ride EN8 . . . . .162 E8
Russellcroft Rd AL8 . . . . .110 C7
Russet Ct EN7 . . . . .147 E5
Russet Dr Shenley WD7 . . . . .156 E7
 St Albans AL4 . . . . .128 C8
Russett Ho AL7 . . . . .111 D6
Russett Wood AL7 . . . . .111 D5
Rutherford Cl
 Borehamwood WD6 . . . . . . .170 C7
 Stevenage SG1 . . . . .50 D6
Rutherford Way WD2 . . . . . . .168 E1
Ruthin Cl LU1 . . . . .63 D5
Ruthven Ave EN8 . . . . .162 D6
Rutland Cres LU2 . . . . .64 A7
Rutland Ct LU2 . . . . .64 A7
Rutland Hall LU2 . . . . .64 A7
Rutland Pl WD2 . . . . .168 D1
Rutts The WD2 . . . . .168 D1
Ryall Cl AL2 . . . . .140 E2
Ryan Way WD2 . . . . .167 C8
Ryans Ct LU2 . . . . .45 F1
Rydal Ct WD2 . . . . .154 B7
Rydal Mount EN6 . . . . .158 E6
Rydal Way LU3 . . . . .44 F5
Ryde Sch The AL9 . . . . .130 C8
Ryde The AL9 . . . . .130 C8
Ryder Ave SG5 . . . . .21 D3
Ryder Cl Bovingdon HP3 . . . .137 A4
 Bushey WD2 . . . . .168 B3
 Hertford SG13 . . . . .114 B7
Ryder Seed Mews AL1 . . . . .127 D2
Ryder Way SG5 . . . . .21 D3
Ryders Ave AL4 . . . . .129 E3
Rye Cl AL5 . . . . .86 B4
Rye Gdns SG2 . . . . .13 B1
Rye Hill Harpenden AL5 . . . . .86 B4
 ■ Luton LU2 . . . . .45 D1
Rye House Gatehouse
 EN11 . . . . .135 D8
Rye House Sta EN11 . . . . . . .135 C8
Rye Mead Cotts EN11 . . . . . .135 C8
Rye Rd EN11 . . . . .135 C8
Rye St CM23 . . . . .58 F1
Ryecroft Hatfield AL10 . . . . . .129 F3
 Stevenage SG1 . . . . .50 E7
Ryecroft Cl HP2 . . . . .125 C2
Ryecroft Cres EN5 . . . . .171 B4
Ryecroft Ct AL4 . . . . .128 F3
Ryecroft Way LU2 . . . . .46 A4
Ryefield Cl EN11 . . . . .115 B2
Ryefield LU3 . . . . .31 A1
Ryefield Cres HA6 . . . . .175 A1
Ryelands AL7 . . . . .110 F3
Ryelands Prim Sch EN11 . . .135 B7
Rylands Heath LU2 . . . . .46 F2
Ryley Cl SG16 . . . . .10 B5
Ryman Ct WD3 . . . . .164 C3
Rymill Cl HP3 . . . . .137 A3
Ryton Cl LU1 . . . . .63 B6

S

Saberton Cl AL3 . . . . .105 F4
Sabine Ho WD5 . . . . .153 F7
Sacombe Gn LU3 . . . . .31 B1
Sacombe Green Rd SG12 . . .71 E4
Sacombe Pound SG12 . . . . . .71 E3
Sacombe Rd
 Hemel Hempstead HP1 . . . . .123 F5
 Hertford SG14 . . . . .92 F4
 Stapleford SG14 . . . . .92 B4
Sacombs Ash La SG10 . . . . . .96 E7
Sacred Heart High Sch
 HA3 . . . . .176 E1
Sacred Heart Inf Sch LU2 . . .46 A3
Sacred Heart Jun Sch
 Luton LU2 . . . . .46 A3
 St Albans AL3 . . . . .127 B1
Sacred Heart
 RC Prim Sch SG12 . . . . .93 D1

Sacred Heart RC Prim Sch
 The WD7 . . . . .167 F3
Saddlers Cl
 Baldock SG7 . . . . .23 E8
 Barnet EN5 . . . . .171 B4
 Bishop's Stortford CM23 . . . .76 C4
 Borehamwood WD6 . . . . . . .170 D3
 Pinner HA5 . . . . .176 A4
Saddlers Path WD6 . . . . .170 D4
Saddlers Pl SG8 . . . . .7 C7
Saddlers Wlk WD4 . . . . .139 A2
Sadleir Rd AL1 . . . . .127 E1
Sadler Cl EN7 . . . . .147 C6
Sadlers Way SG14 . . . . .113 A6
Sadlier Rd SG11 . . . . .55 E2
Saffron Cl Arlesey SG15 . . . .11 A7
 Hoddesdon EN11 . . . . .134 F7
 Luton LU2 . . . . .45 D7
Saffron Green Fst Sch
 WD6 . . . . .170 E5
Saffron Hill SG6 . . . . .22 E6
Saffron La HP1 . . . . .124 B4
Saffron Mdw SG11 . . . . .55 E2
Saffron St SG8 . . . . .7 F5
Sainfoin End HP2 . . . . .125 A5
St Adrian's RC Prim Sch
 AL1 . . . . .141 C8
St Agnell's Farm Mews
 HP2 . . . . .105 A1
St Agnells Ct HP2 . . . . .125 A7
St Agnells La HP2 . . . . .125 A8
St Alban & St Stephen
 RC Inf Sch AL1 . . . . .127 F2
St Alban & St Stephen
 RC Jun Sch AL1 . . . . .128 A3
St Alban's Cath AL3 . . . . . . .127 D3
St Albans City Hospl
 AL3 . . . . .127 C5
St Albans City Sta AL1 . . . . .127 F3
St Albans Dr SG1 . . . . .36 E1
St Albans Girls' Sch AL3 . . .127 E7
St Albans High Sch
 for Girls AL1 . . . . .127 E4
St Albans Hill HP3 . . . . .124 F1
St Albans La WD5 . . . . .140 A5
St Albans Link SG11 . . . . .36 E1
St Albans Music
 Sch AL3 . . . . .127 D6
St Albans RC Prim Sch
 CM20 . . . . .117 F2
St Albans Rd Barnet EN5 . . .171 C7
 Codicote SG4 . . . . .88 F7
 Harpenden AL5 . . . . .107 B6
 Hemel
 Hempstead HP2,HP3 . . . . . .124 E2
 Potters Bar EN5 . . . . .158 C3
 Redbourn AL3 . . . . .106 D3
 Ridge EN6 . . . . .157 F8
 Sandridge AL4 . . . . .108 B1
 St Albans AL4 . . . . .128 A8
 Watford WD1,WD2 . . . . .154 B2
St Albans Rd E AL10 . . . . . . .130 B6
St Albans Rd W AL4 . . . . . . .129 D5
St Albans Sch AL3 . . . . .127 C3
St Albert the Great
 RC Prim Sch HP3 . . . . .125 A2
St Aldates Ct LU3 . . . . .45 B3
St Andrew St SG14 . . . . .113 C6
St Andrew's Ave AL5 . . . . . . .85 F1
St Andrew's CE Prim Sch
 Hertford SG14 . . . . .112 F7
 Hitchin SG4 . . . . .35 A7
St Andrew's Cl LU1 . . . . .63 B1
St Andrew's Ho CM20 . . . . . .117 F2
St Andrew's Pl ❷ SG4 . . . . . .34 F6
St Andrew's Rd HP3 . . . . . . .138 D7
St Andrews CE Prim Sch
 Much Hadham SG10 . . . . . . .74 F2
 Stanstead Abbotts SG12 . . . .115 D4
St Andrews Dr SG1 . . . . .36 F2
St Andrews Mews
 ■ Hertford SG14 . . . . .113 C6
 Luton LU3 . . . . .45 A8
St Andrews Rd WD1 . . . . . . .175 D7
St Andrews Terr WD1 . . . . . .175 C5
St Andrews Wlk LU1 . . . . .63 C1
St Ann's Rd LU1 . . . . .63 F7
St Anna Rd EN5 . . . . .171 D4
St Anne's Cl EN7 . . . . .148 A3
St Anne's Ct ❷ SG5 . . . . .34 F8
St Anne's Pk SG10 . . . . .115 A4
St Anne's Rd Hitchin SG5 . . .34 F8
 London Colney AL2 . . . . .142 D4
St Annes Cl WD1 . . . . .175 C6
St Anthonys Ave HP3 . . . . . .125 B1
St Anthonys RC Prim Sch
 WD1 . . . . .166 E4
St Audrys Cl AL10 . . . . .130 B2
St Audreys Gn AL7 . . . . .110 F5
St Augusta Ct AL3 . . . . .127 D5
St Augustine Ave LU3 . . . . . .45 C3
St Augustine Cl ■ SG5 . . . . .34 F8
St Augustine's
 RC Prim Sch EN11 . . . . . . .135 B6
St Augustines Cl EN10 . . . . .134 F3
St Augustines Dr EN10 . . . . .134 F3
St Barnabas Ct
 Harrow HA3 . . . . .176 C2
 Hemel Hempstead HP2 . . . .125 A3
St Bartholomew's
 CE Prim Sch HP23 . . . . . . .100 D1
St Barts Cl AL4 . . . . .128 D2
St Bernadette's
 RC Prim Sch AL2 . . . . .142 D4
St Bernard's Cl LU3 . . . . .45 C3
St Bernard's Rd AL3 . . . . . . .127 E4
St Brelades Pl AL4 . . . . .128 D7
St Catharine's Rd EN10 . . . .135 A4

St Catherine of Siena
 RC Jun Mix Inf
 Sch WD2 . . . . .154 D6
St Catherine's
 CE Prim Sch SG12 . . . . .93 B2
St Catherines Ave LU3 . . . . . .45 B3
St Catherines Ct CM23 . . . . . .76 E7
St Christopher Sch SG6 . . . . .22 F3
St Clement Danes Sch
 WD3 . . . . .164 D7
St Clement's CE Jun Sch
 EN8 . . . . .148 E4
St Clements Ct EN9 . . . . .163 C6
St Columba's Coll AL3 . . . . . .127 C1
St Cross Ct EN11 . . . . .135 A4
St Cross RC Prim Sch
 EN11 . . . . .135 A4
St Cuthbert Mayne
 RC Jun Sch HP1 . . . . .124 B4
St Cuthberts Gdns ■
 HA5 . . . . .175 F3
St Cuthberts Rd EN11 . . . . . .115 C1
St David's Cl HP2 . . . . .125 D2
St David's Dr EN10 . . . . .134 F4
St Davids Cl SG4 . . . . .36 F2
St Dominic RC Prim Sch
 AL5 . . . . .107 B8
St Dunstan's Rd SG12 . . . . . .116 D8
St Edmund's Coll SG11 . . . . .73 A8
St Edmund's Way CM17 . . . .118 C4
St Edmunds HP4 . . . . .122 C3
St Edmunds Wlk AL4 . . . . . . .128 D2
St Edward's Coll N20 . . . . . . .171 B1
St Elizabeth's Sch & Home
 SG10 . . . . .96 C6
St Elmo Ct SG4 . . . . .34 F5
St Ethelbert Ave LU3 . . . . .45 C4
St Etheldreda's Dr AL10 . . . .130 C5
St Evroul Ct ❺ SG12 . . . . .93 D2
St Faiths Cl SG4 . . . . .22 B1
St Francis Cl
 Buntingford SG9 . . . . .40 F6
 Potters Bar EN6 . . . . .159 C5
 Watford WD1 . . . . .167 B1
St Francis' Coll SG6 . . . . .22 E4
St Francis de Sales
 Ind Prim Sch HP23 . . . . .99 F3
St George's CE Inf Sch
 EN3 . . . . .162 D3
St George's Dr WD1 . . . . .175 E6
St George's Rd
 Enfield EN1 . . . . .161 F1
 Hemel Hempstead HP3 . . . .138 C7
 Watford WD2 . . . . .154 B1
St George's Sch AL5 . . . . .86 B2
St George's Way SG1 . . . . . . .50 D5
St Giles' Ave EN6 . . . . .158 B7
St Giles' CE Prim Sch
 EN6 . . . . .158 A7
St Giles Rd SG4 . . . . .67 F2
St Helen's CE Prim Sch
 AL4 . . . . .108 D8
St Helen's Cl AL4 . . . . .108 D8
St Helen's Sch HA6 . . . . .174 E4
St Heliers Rd AL4 . . . . .128 B8
St Hilda's Sch
 Bushey WD2 . . . . .168 B2
 Harpenden AL5 . . . . .85 F2
St Ignatius Coll EN1 . . . . . . .162 B2
St Ippolyts CE Prim Sch
 SG4 .35 B3
St Ives Cl Luton LU3 . . . . .45 B3
 Welwyn AL6 . . . . .89 F3
St James Ctr CM20 . . . . .118 A4
St James Rd AL5 . . . . .86 B4
St James Way CM23 . . . . .76 C3
St James's Ct AL5 . . . . .86 B3
St James's Rd EN7 . . . . .147 D3
St Joan of Arc RC Sch
 WD3 . . . . .165 C2
St John Cl LU1 . . . . .63 B5
St John Fisher RC Jun
 Mix Inf Sch AL4 . . . . .128 C6
St John The Baptist
 CE Prim Sch SG12 . . . . . . .115 A5
St John's Ave LU2 . . . . .46 A1
St John's CE Prim Sch
 Hatfield AL8 . . . . .109 F5
 Welwyn Garden City AL6 . . . .89 F2
St John's Cl EN6 . . . . .159 C6
St John's Cres CM24 . . . . .59 E7
St John's Ct
 Harpenden AL5 . . . . .107 C7
 ■ Hertford SG13 . . . . .113 D6
St John's La CM24 . . . . .59 E7
St John's Prim Sch EN2 . . . .161 B2
St John's RC Jun Mix Inf
 Sch SG7 . . . . .23 B7
St John's Rd Arlesey SG15 . .11 A4
 Harpenden AL5 . . . . .107 C7
 Hemel Hempstead HP1 . . . .124 B1
 Hitchin SG4 . . . . .34 F6
 Stansted Mountfitchet CM24 . .59 E7
 Watford WD1 . . . . .167 B7
St John's St SG13 . . . . .113 D6
St John's Terr EN2 . . . . .161 D2
St John's Well La HP4 . . . . . .122 B5
St John's Well La HP4 . . . . . .122 B5
St Johns SG11 . . . . .55 E3
St Johns CE Inf Sch
 WD7 . . . . .155 F4
St Johns Cl AL6 . . . . .89 C6
St Johns Ct Luton LU1 . . . . . .63 B5
 St Albans AL1 . . . . .128 B5

St Johns La SG12 . . . . .115 A6
St Johns Wlk CM17 . . . . .118 C4
St Joseph's Cl LU3 . . . . .45 A4
St Joseph's Inf Sch LU3 . . . .45 A4
St Joseph's Jun Sch LU3 . . .45 A4
St Joseph's
 RC Jun Mix Inf Sch CM23 .76 E6
St Joseph's RC Prim Sch
 Hertford SG14 . . . . .113 A7
 South Oxhey WD1 . . . . .175 C6
St Joseph's RC Sch EN8 . . .162 E7
St Joseph's Rd EN8 . . . . . . .162 E6
St Joseph's Sch SG14 . . . . . .113 A4
St Joseph's Wlk AL5 . . . . . . .107 A8
St Julian's Rd AL1 . . . . .127 D1
St Katharines Cl SG5 . . . . . . .21 D3
St Katherine's Way HP4 . . . .121 F7
St Laurence Dr EN10 . . . . . . .148 F8
St Lawrence CE Jun Sch
 EN9 . . . . .163 F6
St Lawrence Cl
 Abbots Langley HP3 . . . . . . .139 E1
 Bovingdon HP3 . . . . .137 A4
St Lawrence Way AL2 . . . . . .140 F1
St Lawrences Ave LU3 . . . . . .45 C3
St Leonard's Ct AL4 . . . . .108 C1
St Leonard's Rd LU4 . . . . . . .113 D8
St Leonards Cl
 Hertford SG13 . . . . .113 E8
 Watford WD2 . . . . .167 E5
St Leonards Cres AL4 . . . . . .108 C1
St Leonards Rd EN9 . . . . . . .149 D6
St Luke's Ave EN2 . . . . .161 D1
St Luke's Cl LU4 . . . . .44 E2
St Luke's Sch AL3 . . . . .106 A6
St Magnus Ct HP3 . . . . .125 C1
St Margaret Clitherow
 RC Prim Sch SG2 . . . . .50 F2
St Margaret of Scotland
 Inf Sch LU1 . . . . .63 B5
St Margaret of Scotland
 Jun Sch LU1 . . . . .63 B5
St Margaret's Cl HP4 . . . . . . .122 D3
St Margaret's Rd SG12 . . . . .115 B2
St Margaret's Sch WD2 . . . . .168 A2
St Margarets SG2 . . . . .50 F2
St Margarets Cl AL3 . . . . .45 B3
St Margarets Ct LU3 . . . . .31 A6
St Margarets Sta SG12 . . . . .115 C4
St Margarets Way HP2 . . . . .125 D3
St Mark's Cl SG5 . . . . .21 D1
St Marks Cl AL4 . . . . .129 B1
St Martha's Jun Sch
 EN5 . . . . .171 E5
St Martin de Porres
 RC Inf Sch LU4 . . . . .44 A4
St Martin de Porres
 RC Jun Sch LU4 . . . . .44 A4
St Martin's Ave LU2 . . . . .45 F2
St Martin's Rd SG3 . . . . .69 A5
St Martin's Sch HA6 . . . . . . .174 D5
St Martins Cl
 Harpenden AL5 . . . . .86 C4
 South Oxhey WD1 . . . . .175 C6
St Mary's Ave
 Berkhamsted UB2 . . . . .121 D6
 Moor Park HA6 . . . . .174 E5
 Stotfold SG5 . . . . .11 F6
St Mary's CE Fst Sch
 HP4 . . . . .121 E6
St Mary's CE High Sch
 EN7 . . . . .148 B1
St Mary's
 CE Jun Mix Inf Sch AL9 . .144 B8
St Mary's CE Jun Sch
 SG12 . . . . .93 D3
St Mary's CE Prim Sch
 CM24 . . . . .59 E7
St Mary's Cl
 Letchworth SG6 . . . . .22 F2
 Pirton SG5 . . . . .20 D4
 Redbourn AL3 . . . . .106 A4
St Mary's Ct
 ■ Hemel Hempstead HP2 . .124 D4
 Potters Bar EN6 . . . . .159 B7
 Welwyn AL6 . . . . .89 F2
St Mary's Ctyd ❺ SG12 . . . . .93 D1
St Mary's Dr CM24 . . . . .59 F5
St Mary's Inf Sch SG7 . . . . . .23 E6
St Mary's Jun Mix Sch
 SG7 .23 E6
St Mary's La SG14 . . . . .112 F3
St Mary's Prim Sch AL6 . . . . .89 A4
St Matthew's Inf Sch LU2 . . .45 E1
St Matthews Cl Luton LU2 . . .63 B8
 Watford WD1 . . . . .167 D3
St Meryl Jun Mix Inf Sch
 WD1 . . . . .175 E7

St Michael's Ct AL3 127
St Michael's Mount SG4 35
St Michael's RC Sch
 WD2 154
St Michael's Rd EN10 135
St Michael's St AL3 127
St Michaels Ave HP3 125
St Michaels Cl
 Harlow CM20 117
 Harpenden AL5 107
St Michaels Ct SG1 51
St Michaels Dr WD2 154
St Michaels Rd SG4 35
St Michaels View AL10 130
St Michaels Way HA6 149
St Mildreds Ave LU3 45
St Monicas Ave LU3 45
St Neots Cl WD6 157
St Nicholas Ave AL5 86
St Nicholas CE Jun Mix Inf
 Sch Harpenden AL5 86
 Letchworth SG6 12
St Nicholas CE Prim Sch
 SG2 .50
St Nicholas Cl WD6 169
St Nicholas Ct AL5 85
St Nicholas Elstree
 CE Prim Sch WD6 169
St Nicholas House Sch
 HP3 139
St Nicholas Mount HP1 123
St Nicholas Sch CM17 118
St Ninian's Ct ❼ LU2 63
St Olam's Cl LU3 45
St Olives SG5 11
St Pancras Ho SG8 2
St Panct's CE Inf Sch
 EN11 135
St Paul's CE Prim Sch
 WD4 152
St Paul's Gdns LU1 63
St Paul's Rd
 Hemel Hempstead HP2 124
 Luton LU1 63
St Paul's Walden Sch SG4 . .49
St Paul's Walden Prim Sch
 SG4 .66
St Pauls CE Prim Sch
 WD3 153
St Pauls Ct ❸ SG2 50
St Pauls Pl AL1 128
St Pauls RC Prim Sch
 EN7 148
St Pauls Way
 Waltham Abbey EN9 163
 Watford WD2 167
St Peter's New SG12 11
St Peter's CE Prim Sch
 WD3 165
St Peter's Cl Barnet EN5 . . .171
 Bushey WD2 168
 Rickmansworth WD3 165
 St Albans AL1 127
St Peter's Rd AL1 127
St Peter's Sch AL1 127
St Peter's St AL1 127
St Peters Cl Hatfield AL10 . .130
 London Colney AL2 142
St Peters Hill HP23 100
St Peters Rd LU1 63
St Peters Way WD3 164
St Philip Howard
 RC Prim Sch AL10 130
St Raphaels Ct AL1 128
St Ronans Ct AL4 155
St Rose's Inf Sch HP1 124
St Saviours View AL1 127
St Saviours's Cres LU1 63
St Stephan's Ave AL3 141
St Stephen's Cl AL3 141
St Stephen's Hill AL1 127
St Stephen's Rd EN3 162
St Stephens CE Prim Sch
 AL3 141
St Teresa's Fst & Mid
 RC Sch HA3 176
St Teresa's RC Prim Sch
 WD7 167
St Thomas' Dr HA5 175
St Thomas More RC
 Jun Mix Inf Sch SG6 22
St Thomas More RC
 Prim Sch HP4 122
St Thomas of Canterbury
 RC Prim Sch SG11 55
St Thomas Pl AL4 108
St Thomas's Rd AL1 127
St Vincent de Paul
 RC Prim Sch SG1 51
St Vincent Dr AL1 128
St Vincent Gdns LU4 44
St Vincent's Way EN6 159
St Winifreds Ave LU3 45
St Yon Ct AL4 128
Sale Dr SG7 13
Salisbury Ave
 Harpenden AL5 86
 St Albans AL1 128
Salisbury Cl
 Bishop's Stortford CM23 76
 Potters Bar EN6 159
Salisbury Cres EN8 162
Salisbury Gdns AL7 111
Salisbury Ho AL3 127
Salisbury Jun Sch LU3 45
Salisbury Rd Baldock SG7 . . .13
 Barnet EN5 171
 Enfield EN3 162
 Harpenden AL5 86

Salisbury Rd continued
Hoddesdon EN11 . . . . **135** C8
Luton LU1 . . . .**63** D6
Stevenage SG1 . . . .**37** A2
Watford WD2 . . . .**154** C1
Welwyn Garden City AL7 . . . .**111** A5
Salisbury Sq Hatfield AL9 . . . . .**130** C6
ly Hertford SG14 . . . .**113** D6
ally Deards La AL6 . . . .**68** B3
Salmon Cl AL7 . . . .**90** A1
Salmons Cl SG12 . . . .**93** D4
Saltdean Cl LU2 . . . .**46** B3
Salter's Cl HP4 . . . .**121** F6
Salters CM23 . . . .**76** C4
Salters Cl WD3 . . . .**165** E1
Salters Gdns WD1 . . . .**167** A8
Saltfield Cres LU4 . . . .**44** C4
Salusbury La SG5 . . . .**33** C2
Salvatorian Coll HA3 . . . .**176** E1
Salwey Cres EN10 . . . .**134** F3
Samian Gate AL3 . . . .**126** F1
Sampson Ave EN5 . . . .**171** D4
Samuel Lucas
Jun Mix Inf Sch SG5 . . . .**34** D7
Sancroft Rd HA3 . . . .**176** F6
Sanctuary Cl UB9 . . . .**173** C3
Sandalls Spring HP1 . . . .**123** F5
Sandalwood Cl LU3 . . . .**45** B7
Sanday Cl HP3 . . . .**125** B1
Sandbrook La HP23 . . . .**79** C1
Sandell Cl LU2 . . . .**45** E8
Sanderling Cl SG6 . . . .**22** E8
Sanders Cl
Hemel Hempstead HP3 . . . .**138** F7
London Colney AL2 . . . .**142** D4
Sanders Rd HP3 . . . .**139** A7
Sandfield Rd AL1 . . . .**128** A3
Sandgate Rd LU4 . . . .**44** D2
Sandhurst Ct AL5 . . . .**107** D6
Sandifield AL10 . . . .**130** B2
Sandle Rd CM23 . . . .**77** A7
Sandmere Cl HP2 . . . .**125** A2
Sandon Jun Mix Inf Sch
SG9 . . . .**15** C1
Sandon Rd EN8 . . . .**148** C1
Sandover Cl SG4 . . . .**35** B6
Sandown Rd
Stevenage SG1 . . . .**37** C1
Watford WD2 . . . .**154** C1
Sandown Road Ind Est
WD2 . . . .**154** C2
Sandpit Hill Cotts HP23 . . . . . .**120** B3
Sandpit La AL1,AL4 . . . .**128** C5
Sandpit Rd AL7 . . . .**110** E4
Sandridge Cl HP2 . . . .**105** A1
Sandridge Ct AL4 . . . .**128** D7
Sandridge Rd AL1 . . . .**127** F5
Sandridge Sch AL4 . . . .**108** D1
Sandridgebury La
Sandridge AL3,AL4 . . . .**108** A2
St Albans AL3 . . . .**127** E8
Sandringham Cres AL4 . . . .**128** C8
Sandringham Gdns 6
CM23 . . . .**76** E5
Sandringham Rd
Potters Bar EN6 . . . .**145** B1
Watford WD2 . . . .**154** C2
Sandringham Sch AL4 . . . .**128** B7
Sandringham Way EN8 . . . .**162** D5
Sandy Cl SG14 . . . .**113** B6
Sandy Gr SG2 . . . .**51** C5
Sandy La Bushey WD2 . . . .**168** C6
Moor Park HA6 . . . .**175** A5
Sandy Lodge HA6 . . . .**174** E8
Sandy Lodge Ct HA6 . . . .**174** E5
Sandy Lodge La HA6 . . . .**174** E8
Sandy Lodge Rd HA6 . . . .**174** C8
Sandy Lodge Way HA6 . . . .**174** E4
Sandycroft Rd HP6 . . . .**150** C1
Sanfoin Rd LU4 . . . .**44** A4
Sanfoine Cl SG4 . . . .**35** C1
Santers La EN6 . . . .**158** E6
Santingfield N LU1 . . . .**63** B6
Santingfield S LU1 . . . .**63** B6
Sappers Cl CM21 . . . .**97** F2
Saracen Est HP27 . . . .**125** B5
Saracens Head HP22 . . . .**129** E3
Sark Ho Enfield EN3 . . . .**162** D1
10 Watford WD1 . . . .**166** F3
Sarratt Ave HP2 . . . .**125** A8
Sarratt Jun Inf Sch
WD3 . . . .**152** A3
Sarratt La
Rickmansworth WD3 . . . .**165** C6
Sarratt WD3 . . . .**165** D8
Sarratt Rd WD3 . . . .**165** C8
Sarum Pl HP2 . . . .**124** E7
Sarum Rd LU3 . . . .**44** F4
Satinwood Cl 1 HP4 . . . .**124** E1
Saturn Way HP2 . . . .**124** F6
Sauncey Ave AL5 . . . .**86** B3
Sauncey Wood AL5 . . . .**86** E4
Sauncey Wood La AL5 . . . .**86** E6
Saunders Cl
Cheshunt EN8 . . . .**148** D4
Letchworth SG6 . . . .**23** C7
Savanna Ct WD1 . . . .**166** F5
Savill Cl EN7 . . . .**147** C6
Savoy Cl UB9 . . . .**173** D1
Sawbridgeworth Rd
Hatfield Heath CM22 . . . .**98** E3
Little Hallingbury CM22 . . . .**98** B6
Sawbridgeworth Sta
CM21 . . . .**98** A3
Sawells EN10 . . . .**134** F2
Sawtry Cl LU3 . . . .**45** A6
Sawtry Way WD6 . . . .**157** A1

Sawyers La EN6 . . . .**158** D5
Sawyers Way HP2 . . . .**124** F3
Sax Ho SG6 . . . .**11** E1
Saxon Ave SG6 . . . .**11** F1
Saxon Cl Harpenden AL5 . . . .**86** C4
Letchworth SG6 . . . .**11** F1
Saxon Ct WD6 . . . .**169** E8
Saxon La SG12 . . . .**45** C2
Saxon Rd Luton LU3 . . . .**45** C2
Welwyn AL6 . . . .**89** B3
Wheathampstead AL4 . . . .**108** D7
Saxon Way Baldock SG7 . . . .**13** B1
Waltham Abbey EN9 . . . .**163** C6
Saxtead Cl LU2 . . . .**46** D1
Sayer Way SG3 . . . .**68** F4
Sayers Gdns HP4 . . . .**122** A6
Sayes Gdns CM21 . . . .**97** F2
Sayesbury Ave CM21 . . . .**97** E3
Sayesbury Rd CM21 . . . .**97** E2
Saywell Rd LU2 . . . .**46** B1
Scammell Way WD1 . . . .**166** F3
Scarborough Ave SG1 . . . .**50** B7
Scatterdells La WD4 . . . .**138** A2
Scholar's Hill SG12 . . . .**95** A4
Scholars Ct AL4 . . . .**143** C8
Scholars Mews AL8 . . . .**110** D8
Scholars The WD1 . . . .**167** C4
Scholars Wlk 4 AL10 . . . .**130** A2
School Cl Essendon AL9 . . . .**131** F6
Stevenage SG2 . . . .**51** B3
School Gdns HP4 . . . .**123** B6
School La Ardeley SG2 . . . .**38** F3
Aston SG2 . . . .**51** E2
Barley SG8 . . . .**9** A1
Bricket Wood AL2 . . . .**155** A7
Bushey WD2 . . . .**168** A2
Essendon AL9 . . . .**131** F6
Great Offley SG5 . . . .**33** C3
Harlow CM20 . . . .**117** E2
Hatfield AL10 . . . .**130** C6
Luton LU4 . . . .**44** E3
Preston SG4 . . . .**48** E5
Tewin AL6 . . . .**90** E2
Watton at Stone SG14 . . . .**70** E3
Welwyn AL6 . . . .**89** B4
Weston SG4 . . . .**24** C1
School Mead WD5 . . . .**153** D7
School Rd EN6 . . . .**145** C1
School Row HP1 . . . .**123** F2
School Wlk SG6 . . . .**23** B6
Schoolfields SG6 . . . .**23** C5
Schubert Rd WD6 . . . .**169** F7
Scot Gr HA5 . . . .**175** D3
Scotfield Ct LU2 . . . .**46** D3
Scots Hill WD3 . . . .**165** F3
Scots Hill Cl WD3 . . . .**165** F3
Scotscraig WD7 . . . .**157** C4
Scott Ave SG12 . . . .**115** B4
Scott Cl SG8 . . . .**2** D1
Scott Rd
Bishop's Stortford CM23 . . . .**76** E6
Luton LU3 . . . .**44** F2
Stevenage SG2 . . . .**51** B6
Scott's Grotto SG12 . . . .**114** D8
Scott's Rd SG12 . . . .**114** D8
Scotts Cl SG12 . . . .**114** D8
Scotts Hill La WD3 . . . .**165** F3
Scotts View AL8 . . . .**110** C5
Scottswood Cl WD2 . . . .**167** E7
Scottswood Rd WD2 . . . .**167** E7
Scratchwood Nature Trail
NW7 . . . .**170** D2
Scriveners Cl HP2 . . . .**124** E3
Scrubbits Sq WD7 . . . .**156** A4
Scrubbits Park Rd WD7 . . . . . .**156** A4
Seabrook LU4 . . . .**44** B3
Seabrook Rd WD5 . . . .**139** D4
Seacroft Gdns WD1 . . . .**175** D7
Seaford Cl LU2 . . . .**46** C3
Seaforth Dr EN8 . . . .**162** D5
Seal Cl LU4 . . . .**44** D3
Seaman Cl AL2 . . . .**141** D6
Searches La WD4 . . . .**140** C4
Seaton Rd
Hemel Hempstead HP2 . . . .**124** E1
London Colney AL2 . . . .**142** D5
Luton LU4 . . . .**44** F3
Sebright Rd Barnet EN5 . . . . . .**171** E6
Hemel Hempstead HP1 . . . .**124** A1
Markyate AL3 . . . .**83** E5
Sebright Sch AL3 . . . .**83** C4
Secker Cres HA3 . . . .**176** C2
Second Ave
Letchworth SG6 . . . .**23** C6
Watford WD2 . . . .**154** D4
Sedbury Cl LU3 . . . .**45** A6
Sedge Gn EN9 . . . .**135** E3
Sedgwick Cl HP2 . . . .**105** B1
Sedgwick Rd LU4 . . . .**44** B7
Sedley Cl EN1 . . . .**162** B1
Seebohm Cl SG5 . . . .**21** C1
Seeleys CM17 . . . .**118** C4
Sefton Ave HA3 . . . .**176** D2
Sefton Cl AL1 . . . .**142** C4
Sefton Rd SG1 . . . .**37** B1
Selbourne Rd LU4 . . . .**45** A2
Selby Ave AL3 . . . .**127** D3
Selden Hill HP2 . . . .**124** D2
Sele Mill SG14 . . . .**113** B6
Sele Rd SG14 . . . .**113** B6
Sele Sch The SG14 . . . .**112** F6
Selina Cl LU3 . . . .**44** C7
Sell Cl EN7 . . . .**147** B5
Sellers Cl WD6 . . . .**170** C8
Sells Rd SG12 . . . .**93** C3
Sellwood Dr EN5 . . . .**171** D4
Selsey Dr LU2 . . . .**46** D4
Selwyn Ave AL10 . . . .**129** E4
Selwyn Cres AL10 . . . .**129** E5

Selwyn Dr AL10 . . . .**129** E5
Sempill Rd HP3 . . . .**124** E1
Senate Pl SG1 . . . .**37** B3
Sentis Ct HA6 . . . .**174** F4
Sequin Cl CM22 . . . .**168** D1
Sequoia Pk HA5 . . . .**176** B4
Serby Ave SG8 . . . .**7** C8
Sergehill La WD5 . . . .**140** A5
Serpentine Cl SG7 . . . .**37** C2
Service Industry Bays
CM20 . . . .**117** F2
Service Rd The EN6 . . . .**159** A7
Seven Acres HA6 . . . .**175** A4
Sevenoaks Cl HA6 . . . .**174** C2
Severalls The LU2 . . . .**46** B3
Severn Dr EN1 . . . .**162** A1
Severn Way SG1 . . . .**50** C5
Severnmead HP2 . . . .**124** E6
Severnvale AL2 . . . .**142** F4
Sewardstone Rd EN9 . . . .**163** D3
Sewardstone St EN9 . . . .**163** C5
Sewell Cl AL4 . . . .**128** E3
Sewell Harris Cl CM20 . . . .**117** F1
Sewells AL8 . . . .**89** D2
Sexton Cl EN7 . . . .**147** B6
Seymour Cl LU1 . . . .**63** F5
Seymour Cres HP2 . . . .**124** E3
Seymour Ct HP4 . . . .**121** E6
Seymour Mews CM21 . . . .**118** E7
Seymour Rd
Berkhamsted HP4 . . . .**121** E6
Luton LU1 . . . .**63** F5
St Albans AL3 . . . .**127** D5
Shackledell SG2 . . . .**50** F2
Shacklegate La SG4 . . . .**66** E5
Shackleton Spring SG2 . . . .**51** A3
Shackleton Way
Abbots Langley WD5 . . . .**154** A7
Welwyn Garden City AL7 . . . . . .**111** D6
Shady Bush Cl WD2 . . . .**168** C2
Shady La WD1 . . . .**167** B7
Shaftenhoe End Rd
Barley SG8 . . . .**9** A1
Nuthampstead SG8 . . . .**8** B8
Shaftesbury Cl
Croxley Green WD3 . . . .**166** C4
Stevenage SG1 . . . .**50** E4
Shaftesbury Ind Ctr SG6 . . . . . .**23** B7
Shaftesbury Quay 9
SG14 . . . .**113** D6
Shaftesbury Rd Luton LU4 . . . . .**45** B1
Watford WD1 . . . .**167** C4
Shaftesbury Sch HA3 . . . .**176** B2
Shaftesbury Way
Kings Langley WD4 . . . .**139** C3
Royston SG8 . . . .**7** E5
Shakespeare Cl SG8 . . . .**7** D8
Shakespeare Ct EN11 . . . .**115** A2
Shakespeare Ind Est
WD24 . . . .**154** A1
Shakespeare Rd
Harpenden AL5 . . . .**86** C1
Luton LU4 . . . .**44** B2
Shakespeare St WD24 . . . .**154** A1
Shalcross Dr EN8 . . . .**148** F1
Shalcross Cres 6 AL10 . . . .**130** A2
Shambrook Rd EN7 . . . .**147** B6
Shangani Rd CM23 . . . .**76** F5
Shanklin Cl
Goff's Oak EN7 . . . .**147** F2
Luton LU3 . . . .**45** A7
Shanklin Gdns WD1 . . . .**175** C6
Shantock Hall La HP3 . . . .**136** E1
Shantock La HP3 . . . .**136** A6
Sharmans Cl AL6 . . . .**89** F4
Sharose Cl AL3 . . . .**83** E5
Sharpcroft 1 HP2 . . . .**124** D5
Sharpenhoe Rd LU3 . . . .**31** A5
Sharpes La HP1 . . . .**123** B1
Sharples Gn LU3 . . . .**45** A8
Sharps Way Hitchin SG4 . . . .**22** A1
Hitchin SG4 . . . .**35** A8
Shaw Cl Bushey WD2 . . . .**176** E8
Cheshunt EN8 . . . .**148** C3
Shaw's Corner AL6 . . . .**88** A4
Shaws The AL7 . . . .**111** C5
Shearers The CM23 . . . .**76** C4
Shearing Lower Rd CM21 . . . . . .**98** A2
Shearing Mill La CM21 . . . .**97** F2
Shearing Rd CM17 . . . .**118** F4
Sheerhanger La HP23 . . . .**138** A7
Shefton Rise HA6 . . . .**175** A3
Sheldon Cl EN7 . . . .**147** E5
Shelford Rd EN5 . . . .**171** E3
Shelley Cl Hitchin SG4 . . . .**35** C7
Moor Park HA6 . . . .**174** F5
Royston SG8 . . . .**2** D1
Shelley Ct Cheshunt EN7 . . . . . .**148** A3
10 Harpenden AL5 . . . .**86** A1
Waltham Abbey EN9 . . . .**163** F6
Shelley La UB9 . . . .**173** A3
Shelley Rd LU4 . . . .**44** B2
Shelton Way LU2 . . . .**46** A3
Shendish Edge HP3 . . . .**138** F6
Shenley Ct HP2 . . . .**125** B8

Shenley Hill WD7 . . . .**156** B4
Shenley La AL2 . . . .**142** C4
Shenley Prim Sch WD7 . . . .**156** F5
Shenley Rd
Borehamwood WD6 . . . .**170** B6
Hemel Hempstead HP2 . . . .**105** B1
Radlett WD7 . . . .**156** C4
Shenley WD7,AL2 . . . .**156** E8
Shenleybury Cotts WD7 . . . . . .**156** E8
Shenleybury Villas WD7 . . . . . .**156** E8
Shenstone Hill HP4 . . . .**122** E5
Shenval Ho CM20 . . . .**118** A4
Shephall Gn SG2 . . . .**51** B2
Shephall Green Inf Sch
SG2 . . . .**51** B2
Shephall View SG1 . . . .**51** A3
Shephall Way SG2 . . . .**51** C3
Shepherd Cl SG8 . . . .**7** D5
Shepherd Inf Sch WD3 . . . .**165** A1
Shepherd Jun Mix Inf Sch
WD3 . . . .**165** A1
Shepherd's La WD3 . . . .**164** E2
Shepherd's Row AL3 . . . .**106** B5
Shepherds Cl CM23 . . . .**76** E4
Shepherds Cl SG14 . . . .**92** C1
Shepherds Gn HP1 . . . .**123** E2
Shepherds La SG1 . . . .**50** A6
Shepherds La HP1 . . . .**123** E2
Shepherds Mead SG5 . . . .**21** F2
Shepherds Row SG2 . . . .**51** A7
Shepherds Way
Brookmans Park AL9 . . . .**145** C3
Harpenden AL5 . . . .**85** D4
Rickmansworth WD3 . . . .**165** B2
Shepherds Wlk WD2 . . . .**176** D8
Shepley Mews EN3 . . . .**163** A2
Sheppard Cl EN1 . . . .**162** B1
Sheppards Cl AL3 . . . .**127** E6
Shepperton Cl WD6 . . . .**170** D8
Sheppey's La WD5 . . . .**139** E3
Sheraton Cl EN5 . . . .**171** E4
Sheraton Ho WD3 . . . .**164** C5
Sheraton Mews WD1 . . . .**166** E5
Sherborne Ave LU2 . . . .**45** D6
Sherborne Cotts WD1 . . . .**167** C4
Sherborne Pl HA6 . . . .**174** D4
Sherborne Way WD3 . . . .**166** B5
Sherbourne Cl HP2 . . . .**124** E2
Sherd Cl LU3 . . . .**44** F7
Sheredes Cty Prim Sch
EN11 . . . .**134** F4
Sheredes Dr EN11 . . . .**134** F4
Sheredes Sch EN11 . . . .**134** F5
Sherfield Ave WD3 . . . .**173** E8
Sheridan Cl HP1 . . . .**124** B2
Sheridan Rd Luton LU2 . . . .**45** C2
Watford WD1 . . . .**167** D2
Sheriden Wlk EN10 . . . .**134** E3
Sheriff Way WD2 . . . .**154** A5
Sheringham Ave SG1 . . . .**36** A6
Sheringham Cl LU2 . . . .**45** C7
Sherington Ave HA5 . . . .**176** A3
Sherland Ct WD7 . . . .**156** A4
Shernbroke Rd EN9 . . . .**163** F5
Sherrards Mews AL8 . . . .**89** B1
Sherrardspark Rd AL8 . . . .**110** D8
Sherrardswood Sch AL6 . . . .**89** D4
Sherwood Ave
Potters Bar EN6 . . . .**158** E7
St Albans AL4 . . . .**128** B6
Sherwood Cl 2 CM23 . . . .**76** F7
Sherwood Ho HA2 . . . .**153** F8
Sherwood Pl 1 HP2 . . . .**124** F7
Sherwood Rd LU4 . . . .**45** A2
Sherwoods Rd WD1 . . . .**167** D8
Sherwoods Rise AL5 . . . .**107** D8
Shetland Cl WD6 . . . .**170** D3
Shetland Ho 10 WD1 . . . .**166** F3
Shillington Rd SG5 . . . .**20** B5
Shillitoe Ave SG6 . . . .**45** A8
Shingle Cl LU3 . . . .**44** C8
Shinc Cl EN10 . . . .**148** E5
Shire La
Chalfont St Peter WD3 . . . .**172** C4
Chorleywood WD3 . . . .**164** D3
Maple Cross WD3 . . . .**172** B5
Tring HP23 . . . .**120** B4
Shiremeade WD6 . . . .**169** F4
Shires The Luton LU2 . . . .**45** D1
Royston SG8 . . . .**7** C8
Shirley Cl Cheshunt EN8 . . . .**148** C2
Hoddesdon EN11 . . . .**148** F7
Stevenage SG1 . . . .**51** C8
Shirley Rd
Abbots Langley WD5 . . . .**153** F7
Luton LU1 . . . .**63** C8
St Albans AL1 . . . .**127** F2
Shootersway HP4 . . . .**121** E4
Shootersway La HP4 . . . .**121** F4
Shootersway Pk HP4 . . . .**121** F3
Shoplands AL8 . . . .**89** D2
Shoreham Cl SG1 . . . .**50** A8
Short Hale LU7 . . . .**80** C3
Short La Aston SG2 . . . .**51** E4
Bricket Wood AL2 . . . .**140** E2
Shortcroft CM23 . . . .**77** D7
Shortlands Gn AL7 . . . .**110** F5
Shortlands Pl CM23 . . . .**76** F8
Shortmead Dr EN8 . . . .**162** F6
Shothanger Way HP3 . . . .**137** D6
Shott La SG6 . . . .**23** A5
Shottfield Cl AL4 . . . .**108** D2
Shrub Hill Rd HP1 . . . .**123** F2
Shrubbery Gr SG8 . . . .**7** C6
Shrubbery The HP1 . . . .**123** E4
Shrublands AL3 . . . .**145** A5
Shrublands Ave HP4 . . . .**122** A4
Shrublands Rd HP4 . . . .**122** A5

Shrublands The EN6 . . . .**158** E6
Shugars Gn HP23 . . . .**100** B5
Sibley Ave AL5 . . . .**107** E7
Sibley Cl LU2 . . . .**46** B3
Sibthorpe Rd AL9 . . . .**144** D7
Siccut Rd SG4 . . . .**35** E4
Sicklefield Cl EN7 . . . .**147** E6
Siddons Rd SG2 . . . .**51** C6
Sidford Cl HP1 . . . .**123** F3
Sidings The Hatfield AL10 . . . . .**129** E4
Hemel Hempstead HP2 . . . .**124** D3
Hoddesdon EN11 . . . .**135** A1
Sidmouth Cl WD1 . . . .**175** B8
Sidney Terr CM23 . . . .**76** F6
Silam Rd SG1 . . . .**50** E5
Silecroft Rd LU2 . . . .**64** B8
Silk Mill Ct WD1 . . . .**167** B2
Silk Mill Rd Redbourn AL3 . . . .**106** B4
Watford WD1 . . . .**167** B2
Silk Mill Way HP23 . . . .**100** A5
Silkin Ct SG2 . . . .**51** D3
Silver La AL3 . . . .**176** D3
Silver Ct SG5 . . . .**34** F8
Silver Dell WD2 . . . .**153** F4
Silver Hill WD6 . . . .**157** B3
Silver St Anstey SG9 . . . .**29** A5
Ashwell SG7 . . . .**4** H7
Goff's Oak EN7 . . . .**147** D1
Guilden Morden SG8 . . . .**14** C2
Luton LU1 . . . .**63** E7
Stansted Mountfitchet CM24 . . . .**59** D6
Waltham Abbey EN9 . . . .**163** C6
Silver Trees AL2 . . . .**140** F1
Silverbirch Ave SG5 . . . .**11** F8
Silverdale Rd WD2 . . . .**167** E4
Silverfield EN10 . . . .**134** F1
Silverthorn Dr HP3 . . . .**139** B7
Silverwood Cl HA6 . . . .**174** C2
Simmonds Rise HP3 . . . .**124** D1
Simon Balle Sch SG13 . . . .**113** E5
Simon Dean HP3 . . . .**137** A4
Simpson Cl LU4 . . . .**44** D2
Simpson Dr SG7 . . . .**23** F8
Simpsons Cl SG2 . . . .**23** F8
Sinderby Cl WD6 . . . .**169** E8
Sinfield Cl SG1 . . . .**51** A5
Singlets La AL3 . . . .**84** C2
Sir Frederic Osborn Sch
AL7 . . . .**111** B7
Sir Herbert Janes Village
The LU4 . . . .**44** D4
Sir James Altham Pool
WD1 . . . .**175** E5
Sir John Lawes Sch AL5 . . . .**86** C3
Sir John Newsom Sch
AL7 . . . .**110** E3
Sir Peter's Way HP4 . . . .**81** E6
Sirita Cl HA3 . . . .**176** D1
Sirus Rd HA6 . . . .**175** A5
Sish Cl SG1 . . . .**50** D6
Sish La SG1 . . . .**50** D6
Siskin Cl
Borehamwood WD6 . . . .**170** A5
Watford WD2 . . . .**167** E5
Sisson Cl SG2 . . . .**51** C2
Sitwell Gr HA7 . . . .**176** F5
Six Acres HP3 . . . .**139** A8
Six Hills Way SG1,SG2 . . . .**50** C4
Sixth Ave Letchworth SG6 . . . . .**23** C6
Watford WD24 . . . .**154** D4
Skegness Rd SG1 . . . .**50** B8
Skegsbury La SG4 . . . .**65** F1
Skelton Cl LU3 . . . .**31** B1
Skidmore Way WD3 . . . .**165** E1
Skimpans Cl AL9 . . . .**144** D7
Skimpot Rd LU4 . . . .**44** A5
Skinners St CM23 . . . .**76** C4
Skipton Cl SG2 . . . .**68** F8
Skua Cl LU4 . . . .**44** A5
Skye Ho 11 WD1 . . . .**166** F3
Skylark Cnr SG2 . . . .**51** D3
Skys Wood Rd AL4 . . . .**128** B7
Skyswood Prim Sch AL4 . . . . .**128** C6
Slade Cl WD7 . . . .**156** A4
Sleaford Gn WD1 . . . .**175** D7
Sleapcross Gdns AL4 . . . .**129** C2
Sleaps Hyde SG2 . . . .**51** C1
Sleapshyde La AL4 . . . .**129** C2
Sledale HP2 . . . .**124** E6
Sleets End HP1 . . . .**124** B5
Slimmons Dr AL4 . . . .**128** A7
Slip End Lower Sch LU1 . . . .**63** B1
Slip La SG3,AL6 . . . .**68** C4
Slipe La EN10 . . . .**148** F7
Slipe The LU7 . . . .**80** A7
Slippers Hill HP2 . . . .**124** D4
Sloan Ct SG1 . . . .**50** F6
Sloansway AL7 . . . .**90** A1
Slowmans AL2 . . . .**141** C3
Slype The AL5,AL4 . . . .**87** B5
Small Acre HP1 . . . .**123** F3
Smallcroft AL7 . . . .**111** B7
Smallford La AL4 . . . .**129** B2
Smallwood Cl AL4 . . . .**108** E7
Smarts Gn EN7 . . . .**147** F5
Smeaton Cl EN9 . . . .**163** E7
Smeaton Rd EN3 . . . .**162** D1
Smith St WD1 . . . .**167** C5
Smith's End La Barley SG8 . . . . .**17** F8
Nuthampstead SG8 . . . .**18** A8
Smithfield HP2 . . . .**124** D5
Smiths La EN7 . . . .**147** B6
Smiths Lane Mall 5 LU1 . . . .**63** E7
Smiths Sq SG13 . . . .**63** E7
Smithy The SG11 . . . .**57** B2

Smug Oak Bsns Ctr AL2 ....141 B3
Smug Oak La AL2 ....141 D1
Snailswell La SG5 ....21 E5
Snatchup AL3 ....106 A5
Snells Mead SG9 ....40 F7
Snipe The SG4 ....24 B1
Snowdrop Cl CM23 ....76 C6
Snowford Cl 1 LU3 ....45 A7
Snowley Par CM23 ....59 B1
Soham Rd EN3 ....162 F2
Solar Cl WD1 ....166 F4
Solar Way EN3 ....162 F3
Solesbridge Cl WD3 ....164 F6
Solesbridge La WD3 ....165 B7
Sollershott E SG6 ....22 F4
Sollershott Hall SG6 ....22 F4
Sollershott W SG6 ....22 E4
Solomon's Hill WD3 ....165 D2
Solway HP2 ....124 F5
Solway Rd N LU3 ....45 A4
Solway Rd S LU3 ....45 A3
Somerby Cl EN10 ....135 B2
Someries Inf Sch LU2 ....46 C3
Someries Jun Sch LU2 ....46 C3
Someries Rd
Harpenden AL5 ....86 C4
Hemel Hempstead HP1 ....123 F5
Somers Rd AL9 ....144 C7
Somers Sq AL9 ....144 C8
Somers Way WD2 ....168 C2
Somerset Cl LU1 ....63 E5
Somerset Ave LU2 ....46 A1
Somerset Rd EN3 ....163 A1
Somersham AL7 ....111 D6
Sonia Cl WD1 ....167 C2
Southouse Spring AL3 ....127 F7
Soper Mews EN3 ....163 A1
Sopers Rd EN6 ....146 F2
Sopwell La AL1 ....127 D2
Sorrel Cl Luton LU3 ....45 B8
Royston SG8 ....7 F5
Sorrel Garth SG4 ....35 A6
Sotheron Rd WD1 ....167 C6
Souberie Ave SG6 ....22 F5
Souldern St WD1 ....167 B4
South App HA6 ....174 D7
South Bank Rd HP4 ....121 F6
South Block CM21 ....97 F7
South Charlton Mead La
EN11 ....135 D5
South Cl Baldock SG7 ....23 F7
Barnet EN5 ....171 E6
Chiswellgreen AL2 ....141 A6
Pinner HA5 ....175 D2
Royston SG8 ....7 B7
South Cottage Dr WD3 ....164 F4
South Cottage Gdns
WD3 ....164 F4
South Dr Cuffley EN6 ....146 E1
St Albans AL1 ....128 E4
South Drift Way LU1 ....63 B5
South Hill Cl SG4 ....35 A6
South Hill Prim Sch HP1 ....124 C2
South Hill Rd HP1 ....124 C3
South Ley AL7 ....110 E3
South Ley Ct AL7 ....110 E3
South Luton High Sch
LU1 ....63 F5
South Ordnance Rd EN3 ....163 A2
South Par EN9 ....163 C6
South Park Ave WD3 ....164 F4
South Park Gdns HP4 ....122 B5
South Pl Harlow CM20 ....118 A4
Hitchin SG5 ....34 D8
South Rd Baldock SG7 ....24 A7
Bishop's Stortford CM23 ....77 A5
Chorleywood WD3 ....164 C4
Harlow CM20 ....118 A4
Luton LU1 ....63 D6
Standon SG11 ....56 F2
South Riding AL2 ....141 A1
South St
Bishop's Stortford CM23 ....76 F6
Hertford SG14 ....114 D6
Stansted Abbotts SG12 ....115 C4
South Street
Commercial Ctr 1 CM23 ....76 F6
Southview SG6 ....22 E7
South View Rd HA5 ....175 B4
South Way
Abbots Langley WD5 ....153 E6
Hatfield AL10 ....130 B2
Waltham Abbey EN9 ....163 C3
South Weald Dr EN9 ....163 D6
Southacre Way HA5 ....175 C2
Southall Cl SG12 ....93 D2
Southbrook CM21 ....97 E1
Southdown Cl 2 EN8 ....148 D3
Southdown Ct AL10 ....130 A2
Southdown Ho AL5 ....107 C8
Southdown Ind Est AL5 ....107 C7
Southdown Rd
Harpenden AL5 ....107 B8
Hatfield AL10 ....130 A2
Southend Cl SG1 ....50 D7
Southern Ave SG16 ....10 C3
Southern Rise LU2 ....85 F7
Southern Terr EN11 ....115 B1
Southern Way
Letchworth SG6 ....22 E8
Studham LU6 ....142 C8
Southernwood Cl HP2 ....125 A4
Southerton Way WD7 ....156 E6
Southfield Barnet EN5 ....171 D3
Braughing SG11 ....55 F7

Southfield continued
Welwyn Garden City AL7 ....110 D4
Southfield Ave WD2 ....154 C1
Southfield Rd
Cheshunt EN8 ....162 E7
Hoddesdon EN11 ....135 A7
Southfield Sch AL10 ....130 B1
Southfield Way AL4 ....128 D6
Southfields Letchworth SG6 ....11 F1
Standon SG11 ....55 E2
Southgate SG1 ....50 D4
Southgate Cotts WD3 ....165 E2
Southgate E 5 AL5 ....86 A2
Southgate Ho 1 EN8 ....148 D1
Southgate Rd EN6 ....159 C6
Southlynn Ho 2 LU2 ....63 F8
Southmead Cres EN8 ....148 F1
Southmill Rd CM23 ....77 A5
Southmill Trad Ctr CM23 ....77 A6
Southsea Ave WD1 ....167 A5
Southsea Rd SG1 ....50 B8
Southside 28 A3
Southview Cl EN7 ....147 E5
Southview Rd AL5 ....86 D3
Southwark Cl SG1 ....37 B2
Southwold Cl SG2 ....50 A6
Southwold Rd WD1 ....154 C2
Sovereign Cl WD1 ....167 A5
Sovereign Pk HP2 ....125 B5
Sowerby Ave LU2 ....46 C2
Sparhawke SG6 ....12 A1
Sparrow Cl LU4 ....44 A4
Sparrow Dr SG2 ....51 D4
Sparrows Herne WD2 ....168 C2
Sparrows Way WD2 ....168 C1
Sparrowswick Ride AL3 ....127 C8
Spayne Cl LU3 ....45 B8
Spear Cl LU3 ....44 E6
Speedwell Cl LU3 ....45 A8
Speke Cl SG2 ....51 D5
Spellbrook La E CM22 ....97 F8
Spellbrook La W CM23 ....97 E7
Spellbrook Prim Sch
CM23 ....97 F7
Spencer Ave 5 SG5 ....34 D8
Spencer Ave EN7 ....147 E5
Spencer Cl CM24 ....59 E6
Spencer Gate AL1 ....127 E5
Spencer Ho SG5 ....11 F6
Spencer Jun Sch AL3 ....127 E6
Spencer Mews AL1 ....127 E7
Spencer Pl AL4 ....108 C2
Spencer Rd Harrow HA3 ....176 E1
Luton LU3 ....45 C2
Spencer St Hertford SG13 ....113 E7
St Albans AL3 ....127 D3
Spencer Wlk WD3 ....165 C4
Spenser Cl SG8 ....2 D1
Spenser Rd AL5 ....86 C1
Sphere Ind Est The AL1 ....128 A2
Spicer St AL3 ....127 C3
Spicersfield EN7 ....148 A4
Spindle Berry Cl AL6 ....90 A7
Spinney Cl EN7 ....147 C1
Spinney La CM20 ....118 A1
Spinney Rd AL4 ....128 D5
Spinney St SG13 ....113 E4
Spinney The Baldock SG7 ....23 E7
Berkhamsted HP4 ....121 F3
Edmonton N18 ....148 B1
Harpenden AL5 ....86 B3
Hertford SG13 ....113 F6
Hoddesdon EN10 ....134 F4
Potters Bar EN6 ....159 D8
Stansted Mountfitchet CM24 ....59 D7
Watford WD1 ....167 A8
Welwyn Garden City AL7 ....110 E5
Spinneys Dr AL3 ....127 B1
Spires The EN5 ....171 E6
Spittlesea Rd LU2 ....64 C7
Spooners Dr AL2 ....141 C4
Spratts La LU6 ....82 F8
Spreckley Cl SG16 ....10 B5
Spring Cl Barnet EN5 ....171 D4
Borehamwood WD6 ....170 A8
Harefield UB9 ....173 D2
Latimer HP5 ....150 D3
Spring Court Rd EN2 ....161 A1
Spring Crofts WD2 ....168 A4
Spring Dr SG2 ....69 B8
Spring Field Rd HP4 ....122 A6
Spring Glen AL10 ....129 C3
Spring Hills CM20 ....117 B1
Spring La Cottered SG9 ....39 C5
Hemel Hempstead HP1 ....124 A4
Spring Mews CM21 ....97 E2
Spring Pl 1 LU1 ....63 D6
Spring Rd
Harpenden AL5 ....85 A4
Letchworth SG6 ....22 E4
Letchworth SG6 ....22 E6
Spring View Rd SG12 ....114 F8
Spring Way HP2 ....124 F5
Spring Wlk WD3 ....134 C2
Springall Rd WD3 ....168 D1
Springfield
Borehamwood WD6 ....170 A8
Northaw EN6 ....159 E8
Springfield Cres AL5 ....86 B5
Springfield Cl
Bishop's Stortford CM23 ....76 E8
Rickmansworth WD3 ....165 B1

Springfield Rd
Cheshunt EN8 ....162 E7
Hemel Hempstead HP2 ....124 F4
Luton LU3 ....45 C6
St Albans, Smallford AL4 ....129 B3
St Albans, The Camp AL1 ....128 A2
Watford WD2 ....154 B6
Springfields
Hoddesdon EN10 ....134 F4
Waltham Abbey EN9 ....163 E5
Welwyn Garden City AL7 ....110 D4
Springfields Ho AL8 ....110 C4
Springhall Ct CM21 ....97 E2
Springhall La CM21 ....97 E1
Springhall Rd CM21 ....97 E2
Springhead SG7 ....24 B1
Springle La SG13 ....114 F2
Springmead Jun Mix Inf
Sch AL7 ....111 C7
Springs Cotts EN10 ....148 E7
Springs The
Cheshunt EN10 ....148 E6
Hertford SG13 ....113 F7
Springshott SG6 ....22 E5
Springwell Ave LU3 ....173 A8
Springwell Cl LU3 ....173 A8
Springwood EN7 ....148 A5
Springwood Cl UB9 ....173 D2
Springwood Wlk AL4 ....128 D6
Spruce Way AL4 ....141 B4
Spur Cl WD5 ....153 D6
Spur The Cheshunt EN8 ....148 D3
Stevenage SG1 ....50 E4
Spurcroft LU3 ....31 C1
Spurs Cl SG4 ....35 B7
Square The Braughing SG11 ....55 F7
Buckland SG9 ....27 D5
Hemel Hempstead HP1 ....124 C3
Hoddesdon EN10 ....148 E8
Much Hadham SG10 ....74 F3
Redbourn AL3 ....105 F6
Sawbridgeworth CM21 ....97 E2
Watford WD1 ....154 B2
Squires Ct CM23 ....76 C8
Squires Ct EN11 ....135 A5
Squires Ride HP2 ....104 F1
Squirrel Chase HP1 ....123 E4
Squirrels Cl 1 CM23 ....76 F8
Squirrels The
Bushey WD2 ....168 D3
Hertford SG13 ....114 B6
Welwyn Garden City AL7 ....111 C5
Stable Ct AL1 ....127 E5
Stable Mews AL1 ....127 E4
Stacey Cl 9 CM23 ....76 F6
Stacklands AL8 ....110 B4
Stacklands AL10 ....110 B4
Staddles CM22 ....98 B8
Stadium Est The LU4 ....44 B1
Stadium Way CM19 ....116 F1
Stafford Cl EN8 ....148 B2
Stafford Ct EN10 ....135 A3
Stafford Dr EN10 ....135 A3
Stafford Ho
Bishop's Stortford CM23 ....77 A6
Hoddesdon EN10 ....135 A3
Stafford Rd HA3 ....176 C3
Staffords CM17 ....118 E4
Stag Ct WD1 ....154 C5
Stag Green Ave AL9 ....130 C2
Stag La Berkhamsted HP4 ....122 B5
Chorleywood WD3 ....164 C3
Stag Hill HP4 ....159 E3
Stainer Rd
Borehamwood WD6 ....156 D1
Radlett WD6 ....169 D8
Stains Cl EN8 ....148 F3
Stake Piece Rd SG8 ....7 C5
Stakers Ct AL5 ....86 B1
Stamford Ave SG8 ....7 D7
Stamford Ct 5 Harrow HA3 ....176 F1
Potters Bar EN6 ....159 D7
Stamford Ct SG8 ....7 D7
Stamford Rd WD1 ....167 B7
Stamford Yd SG8 ....7 C6
Stanborough Ave WD6 ....157 B1
Stanborough Cl AL8 ....110 C5
Stanborough La AL8 ....110 C4
Stanborough Prim Sch
WD2 ....154 A4
Stanborough Rd AL8 ....110 C4
Stanborough Sch
Watford WD2 ....154 A4
Welwyn Garden City AL8 ....110 B4
Stanbury Ave WD1 ....153 E2
Standalone Farm SG6 ....22 D7
Standard Rd EN3 ....162 E2
Standfield WD5 ....139 E1
Standhill Cl SG4 ....34 F6
Standhill Rd SG4 ....34 F6
Standon Bsns Pk SG11 ....56 A5
Standon Ct SG11 ....55 F1
Standon Hill SG11 ....55 D2
Standon Rd SG1 ....56 E3
Standring Rise HP3 ....138 B8
Stane Cl CM23 ....58 F1
Stane Fields SG6 ....23 B3
Stane St SG7 ....13 A1
Stanelow Cres SG1 ....55 D2
Stanfields Ct CM20 ....117 E1
Stanford Rd LU2 ....46 A1
Stangate Cres WD6 ....170 C4
Stanhope Ave HA3 ....176 C2
Stanhope Rd Barnet EN5 ....171 D3
Cheshunt EN8 ....148 A1
St Albans AL1 ....128 A4
Stanier Rise HP4 ....121 F7

Stanley Ave AL2 ....141 A6
Stanley Dr AL10 ....130 B3
Stanley Gdns
Borehamwood WD6 ....169 E8
Tring HP23 ....99 F3
Stanley Livingstone Ct
LU1 ....63 D6
Stanley Rd Baldock SG13 ....113 E5
Northwood HA6 ....175 A2
Stevenage SG2 ....51 B7
Streatley LU3 ....31 A5
Watford WD1 ....167 C5
Stanley St LU1 ....63 D6
Stanmore Chase AL4 ....128 D2
Stanmore Cres AL4 ....44 F4
Stanmore Rd
Stevenage SG1 ....50 D7
Watford WD1 ....167 B8
Stanmount Rd AL2 ....141 A6
Stannington Path WD6 ....170 A8
Stanstead Dr EN11 ....135 B8
Stansted Dr EN11 ....135 B8
Stansted Rd
Hertford SG13 ....114 A6
Hertford Heath SG13 ....114 D5
Hoddesdon EN11 ....115 B1
Stansted Hill SG10 ....75 A1
Stapleford
Jun Mix Inf Sch SG14 ....92 A6
Stapleford Cl LU2 ....46 A4
Stapleford Rd LU2 ....46 C4
Stapleton Cl EN6 ....159 D8
Stapleton Rd WD6 ....157 B1
Stapley Rd AL1 ....127 D4
Stapylton Rd EN5 ....171 C6
Star Holme Ct SG12 ....93 E1
Star St SG12 ....93 E1
Starkey Cl EN7 ....147 C6
Starlight Way AL4 ....128 C1
Starling La EN6 ....146 F3
Startpoint LU1 ....63 C7
Station App Cheshunt EN8 ....162 E5
Chorleywood WD3 ....164 D5
Harlow CM20 ....118 C5
Harpenden AL5 ....86 B1
Kings Langley WD4 ....139 B1
Northwood HA6 ....174 E3
Radlett WD7 ....156 A4
South Oxhey WD1 ....175 D7
Station Cl
Brookmans Park AL9 ....144 E5
Potters Bar EN6 ....158 F8
Station Rd 18 SG13 ....93 D1
Station Footpath WD4 ....139 B1
Station Mews SG6 ....159 A8
Station Par SG6 ....22 D6
Station Rd Aldbury HP23 ....101 B5
Arlesey SG15 ....11 A4
Ashwell SG7 ....12 F1
Baldock SG7 ....23 F7
Berkhamsted HP4 ....122 D4
Bishop's Stortford CM23 ....77 A7
Braughing SG11 ....55 E5
Bricket Wood AL2 ....155 A8
Brookmans Park AL9 ....144 D6
Buntingford SG9 ....40 F7
Cheddington LU7 ....79 F8
Cuffley EN6 ....146 F2
Harlow CM17 ....118 C4
Harpenden AL5 ....86 C2
Hemel Hempstead HP1 ....124 C1
Hertingfordbury SG14 ....112 B3
Hoddesdon EN10 ....135 A3
Holdbrook EN9 ....163 A5
Kings Langley WD4 ....139 B1
Knebworth SG3 ....69 A5
Letchworth SG6 ....22 F6
Long Marston HP23 ....79 B4
Lower Stondon SG16 ....10 A4
Luton, High Town LU1 ....63 E7
Luton, Leagrave LU4 ....44 E5
Much Hadham SG10 ....74 E1
Pitstone LU7 ....80 E5
Radlett WD7 ....156 A4
Rickmansworth WD3 ....165 D2
Sawbridgeworth CM21 ....97 E3
St Albans AL1 ....128 A3
Standon SG11 ....55 E2
Stapleford SG14 ....92 A6
Stansted Mountfitchet CM24 ....59 E6
Steeple Morden SG7,SG8 ....5 C5
Tring HP23 ....100 D4
Ware SG12 ....93 E1
Watford WD1 ....167 B5
Watton at Stone SG14 ....70 D3
Welwyn AL6 ....89 F3
Wheathampstead AL4 ....87 D1
Station Terr Hitchin SG4 ....35 A8
Park Street AL2 ....141 D5
Station Way SG6 ....22 E6
Staveley Rd LU4 ....44 D5
Steeplands WD2 ....168 B2
Steeple View CM23 ....76 F8
Sten Cl EN3 ....163 A2

Stephens Cl LU2 ....46 A4
Stephens Gdns LU2 ....46 A4
Stephens Way AL3 ....105 F7
Stephenson Cl SG8 ....7 B8
Stephenson Way WD2 ....167 D7
Stepnells HP23 ....80 A6
Stepping Stones The LU3 ....44 E8
Sterling Ave EN8 ....162 D9
Sterling Rd EN2 ....161 D7
Stevenage Cres WD6 ....169 E7
Stevenage Mus SG1 ....50 E6
Stevenage Rd Hitchin SG4 ....34 F7
Knebworth SG2,SG3 ....68 F7
Little Wymondley SG4 ....68 F7
Little Wymondley, Titmore
Green SG4 ....35 E6
Stevenage St SG1 ....35 C7
Stevenage Rise HP2 ....124 F7
Stevenage Sta SG1 ....50 C5
Stevens Gn WD2 ....168 C3
Steward Cl EN4 ....148 E1
Steward Cl WD5 ....154 A2
Steward Rd AL5 ....86 B2
Stewarts The CM23 ....76 E6
Stirling Bsns Pk EN8 ....162 F5
Stirling Cl Hitchin SG4 ....35 C2
Stevenage SG2 ....69 C2
Stirling Cnr EN5 ....170 D2
Stirling Ho WD6 ....170 C5
Stirling Way
Borehamwood WD6 ....170 D4
Watford WD5 ....154 A2
Welwyn Garden City AL7 ....111 E6
Stoat Cl SG13 ....114 A6
Stobarts Cl SG12 ....68 F6
Stock Bank SG8 ....8 D1
Stockbreach Cl AL10 ....130 A6
Stockbreach Rd AL10 ....130 A6
Stockens Dell SG3 ....68 E8
Stockens Gn SG3 ....68 E8
Stockers Farm Rd WD3 ....173 D8
Stockfield Ave EN11 ....135 B8
Stockholm Way LU3 ....44 E8
Stocking Hill SG9 ....39 B8
Stocking La SG9 ....18 C1
Stockings La SG13 ....132 C6
Stockingstone Rd LU2 ....45 E3
Stockmen Field CM23 ....76 C6
Stockport Rd WD3 ....164 C2
Stocks Mdw HP2 ....125 A4
Stocks Rd HP23 ....101 D7
Stockwell Ct EN7 ....148 A3
Stockwell La EN7 ....148 B3
Stockwood Craft Mus
& Gdns LU1 ....63 D4
Stockwood Cres LU1 ....63 D6
Stockwood Ct 18 LU1 ....63 D6
Stone Cross CM20 ....117 D1
Stonecroft SG8 ....68 F5
Stonecross Rd AL10 ....130 B7
Stonehill
Jun Mix Inf Sch SG4 ....35 A5
Stonehills AL8 ....110 D7
Stonelea Rd HP3 ....138 F8
Stoneleigh Cl EN8 ....148 E1
Stoneleigh Ave SG1 ....162 B1
Stoneleigh Ct
Cheshunt EN8 ....162 D6
Luton LU3 ....45 B7
Stoneley Rd EN11 ....115 B1
Stoneley SG6 ....12 C3
Stonemason Cl AL3 ....86 A3
Stonemead AL8 ....89 D3
Stonesdale LU4 ....44 C4
Stoneways Cl LU4 ....44 C6
Stoney Cl HP4 ....122 C5
Stoney Comm CM24 ....59 C5
Stoney Common Rd CM24 ....59 D5
Stoney Croft HP23 ....101 C5
Stoney La
Bovingdon HP3 ....137 C5
Chipperfield HP3 ....137 A3
Hemel Hempstead HP1 ....137 A8
Stoney Pl CM24 ....59 E5
Stoneycroft
Hemel Hempstead HP1 ....124 A3
Welwyn Garden City AL7 ....111 A7
Stoneyfield Dr CM24 ....59 E6
Stoneygate Rd LU4 ....44 D3
Stonnells Cl SG6 ....22 F8
Stony Croft SG1 ....50 E6
Stony Hills SG4 ....92 C7
Stony La
Chenies HP5,HP6 ....150 L1
Great Offley LU2,SG4 ....47 C4
Stonyshotts EN9 ....163 E6
Stooksdale HP22 ....60 A3
Stopsley High Sch LU2 ....46 A4
Stopsley Inf Sch LU2 ....46 A4
Stopsley Jun Sch LU2 ....46 A4
Stopsley Way LU2 ....46 A3
Storehouse La SG4 ....34 F6
Storey St EN3 ....163 B2
Storey St HP3 ....138 D7
Stormont Rd SG5 ....21 F1
Stormont Sch EN6 ....159 D8
Stornoway HP3 ....125 B1
Stort Lodge CM23 ....76 F8
Stort Mill CM20 ....118 B6
Stort Rd CM23 ....76 F8
Stort Valley Ind Pk CM23 ....59 B2
Stortford Hall Ind Pk
CM23 ....77 B8
Stortford Hall Pk CM23 ....77 B8
Stortford Hall Rd 3 CM23 ....77 B8

fford Rd
field Heath CM22 ....98 E4
ddesdon EN11 ....135 C7
le Hadham SG11 ....57 C2
ndon SG15 ....55 F2
fold Rd SG5 ....11 F6
fold Rd Arlesey SG15 ....11 C7
xworth SG7 ....3 C1
chin SG6 ....22 C4
chworth SG6 ....11 D3
w The A10 ....117 F2
w Mead HA3 ....176 D2
fford Cl EN16 ....159 A7
fford Rd SG3 ....69 A5
fford Gate EN6 ....159 A7
fford Rd EN5 ....163 B7
fts The EN9 ....163 B7
andburgh Pl HP3 ....125 B1
angers Way LU4 ....44 C4
angeways WD1 ....134 E4
atfield Dr EN10 ....134 E4
atfield Rd WD6 ....170 A7
atford Lodge WD1 ....167 B8
w Mead Rd Luton LU4 ....45 B1
atford WD1 ....167 A7
atford Way
  icket Wood AL2 ....140 F2
  emel Hempstead HP3 ....138 B8
atford WD1 ....167 A7
athmore Ave
  tchin SG5 ....21 F1
  ton LU1 ....63 F5
athmore Ct SG5 ....21 F1
athmore Inf Sch SG5 ....21 C2
athmore Rd SG4 ....46 C6
athmore Wlk LU1 ....63 F6
atton Ave LU2 ....161 D2
atton Gdns LU2 ....45 D4
raw Plait SG15 ....110 F4
awberry Field
  Hatfield AL10 ....130 A2
awberry Fields SG12 ....93 B2
awfields AL7 ....111 B7
awmead AL10 ....130 B7
awplaiters Cl SG3 ....69 A2
aws Hadley Ct HP22 ....160 B2
ayfield Rd EN2 ....161 B2
ream Woods
  un Mix Inf Sch AL10 ....130 B4
reet The Braughing SG11 ....55 F7
  hipperfield WD4 ....138 A1
  readley SG11 ....53 F3
  urneux Pelham SG9 ....43 A4
  sheering CM22 ....98 E1
  Wallington SG7 ....25 C8
retton Way WD6 ....169 F7
ringers La SG2 ....51 E2
ripling Way WD1 ....167 A3
roma Cl HP3 ....125 C1
ronnell Cl LU2 ....45 A3
ronsay HP3 ....125 C1
roud Wood Bsns Ctr
  AL2 ....141 E4
uart Cl WD6 ....169 D3
uart Dr Hitchin SG4 ....35 B7
  Royston SG8 ....7 D8
uart Ho EN9 ....89 B3
uart St LU1 ....63 D7
uart Way EN7 ....162 B8
uarts Cl EN3 HP3 ....122 E4
uart Gl WD2 ....154 B7
tudham La Dagnall HP4 ....81 F1
  Whipsnade LU6 ....82 A7
tudham Lower Sch LU6 ....82 B4
tudio Way WD6 ....170 C8
tudios The WD2 ....168 A3
tudlands Rise SG8 ....7 E6
tudlands Rise Fst Sch
  SG8 ....7 E6
tudley Rd LU3 ....45 D1
turgeon's Rd SG4 ....22 B2
turia Cl SG14 ....113 D3
turlas Way EN8 ....162 D6
turmer Cl AL4 ....128 C3
turrock Way SG6 ....35 C6
tylemans La CM22 ....77 B5
tyles Cl LU2 ....46 C2
uch Cl SG6 ....23 B7
udbury Ct AL1 ....127 E2
udbury Rd LU4 ....44 B6
  Borehamwood WD6 ....170 D4
  London Colney AL2 ....142 C6
uffolk Cl AL4 ....144 A3
uffolk Rd
  Potters Bar EN6 ....158 C7
  Royston SG8 ....7 E6
ugar La HP1 ....123 B1
ulgrave Cres HP23 ....100 C5
ullivan Cres WD1 ....173 D1
ullivan Way WD6 ....169 C3
ummer Ct HP22 ....124 D5
ummer Dale AL4 ....89 C1
ummer Gr WD6 ....169 D3
ummer Hill WD6 ....170 A4
ummer St LU1 ....63 C1
ummer Wlk AL3 ....83 E5
ummercroft
  Jun & Inf Schs CM23 ....77 C8
ummerfield AL10 ....130 A2
ummerfield Cl AL2 ....142 C5
ummerfield Rd Luton LU1 ....62 F8
  Watford WD1 ....154 A4
ummerhill Ct LU1 ....127 F4
ummerhouse La
  Harefield UB9 ....173 A3

Summerhouse La continued
  Radlett WD2 ....168 C8
Summerhouse Way WD5 ....139 F1
Summers Rd AL2 ....142 C7
Summers Way AL2 ....142 E4
Summersend Rd AL1 ....128 C7
Summerswood Fst Sch
  WD6 ....170 B5
Summerswood La WD6 ....157 E4
Summit Rd EN6 ....144 E1
Sumpter Yd AL1 ....127 D3
Sun Hill SG8 ....7 C5
Sun La AL5 ....86 A2
Sun Sq ⊡ HP1 ....124 D4
Sun St Baldock SG7 ....23 E8
  Hitchin SG5 ....34 E6
  Sawbridgeworth CM21 ....97 F1
  Waltham Abbey EN9 ....163 C6
Sunbury Ct ⊡ EN5 ....171 E5
Sunderland Ave AL1 ....128 A4
Sundew Rd HP1 ....123 F2
Sundon Park Jun Sch
  LU3 ....44 C8
Sundon Park Rd LU3 ....44 C7
Sunmead Rd HP2 ....124 D5
Sunningdale
  Bishop's Stortford CM23 ....76 E6
  Luton LU2 ....45 F3
Sunningdale Mews AL7 ....89 F2
Sunny Bank LU7 ....79 F7
Sunny Bank Prim Sch
  EN6 ....159 A5
Sunny Hill SG9 ....40 F7
Sunnybank Rd EN6 ....159 A6
Sunnydell AL2 ....141 B5
Sunnyhill AL9 ....130 D8
Sunnyhill Rd
  Hemel Hempstead HP1 ....124 B3
  Maple Cross WD3 ....172 D4
Sunnyside
  Lower Nazeing EN9 ....135 F1
  Stansted Mountfitchet CM24 ....59 E6
Sunnyside Rd SG4 ....35 A5
Sunridge Ave LU2 ....45 E2
Sunrise Cres HP3 ....138 E8
Sunset Dr LU2 ....45 F3
Sunset View EN5 ....171 E7
Surrey Pl HP23 ....100 A3
Surrey St LU1 ....63 F6
Surrey Street Prim Sch
  LU1 ....63 F6
Sursham Ct AL3 ....83 E5
Sussex Cl EN11 ....135 A7
Sussex Pl LU2 ....46 D2
Sussex Rd WD2 ....168 C5
Sutcliffe Cl Bushey WD2 ....168 F5
  Stevenage SG1 ....51 A8
Sutherland Ave EN6 ....146 D3
Sutherland Ct EN5 ....171 E5
Sutherland Ct
  Moor Park WD1 ....166 C2
  Welwyn Garden City AL7 ....110 F7
Sutherland Pl LU1 ....63 D5
Sutherland Way EN6 ....146 E3
Sutton Acres CM22 ....98 D7
Sutton Cl Hoddesdon EN10 ....134 E4
  Tring HP23 ....100 A5
Sutton Cres EN5 ....171 D4
Sutton Gdns LU3 ....44 D6
Sutton Path HA6 ....170 A6
Sutton Rd St Albans AL1 ....128 B3
  Watford WD1 ....167 C6
Swallow Cl Bushey WD2 ....168 C1
  Luton LU4 ....44 A4
  Rickmansworth WD3 ....165 C2
Swallow Ct Hertford SG14 ....110 F6
  Welwyn Garden City AL7 ....110 F6
Swallow End AL7 ....110 F6
Swallow Gdns AL10 ....130 A8
Swallow Oaks WD5 ....153 F7
Swallowdale La HP2 ....125 B6
Swallowfields AL7 ....110 E6
Swallows CM7 ....118 C4
Swallows The AL3 ....89 F2
Swan Cl WD3 ....165 D2
Swan ⊡
  Bishop's Stortford CM23 ....76 F6
  Welwyn Garden City AL7 ....110 E6
Swan Ct AL5 ....86 C2
Charley Sq SG8 ....1 F4
Swan Mead
  Hemel Hempstead HP3 ....138 F6
  Luton LU4 ....44 B4
Swan & Pike Rd EN3 ....163 A1
Swan St SG7 ....4 D4
Swanfield Rd EN8 ....162 E6
Swanglands La SG3 ....69 B4
Swanhill AL7 ....111 A7
Swanland Rd EN6 ....144 B3
Swanley Bar La EN6 ....145 B3
Swanley Cres EN6 ....145 B2
Swanley Ct WD2 ....154 C2
Swanstand SG3 ....23 D4
Swanston Grange LU4 ....44 B2
Swanston Path WD1 ....175 C2
Swansedale Rd LU3 ....45 A6
Sweet Briar
  Bishop's Stortford CM23 ....76 B6
  Welwyn Garden City AL7 ....111 A4
Sweetbriar Cl HP1 ....124 A6
Swepstens Mead SG2 ....51 C7
Swift Cl Letchworth SG6 ....22 E8
  Royston SG8 ....2 D1
  Stanstead Abbotts SG12 ....115 C3
Swiftfields AL7 ....111 A7
Swifts Green Cl LU2 ....46 B5

Swifts Green Rd LU2 ....46 B5
Swinburne Ave SG5 ....21 C1
Swinburne Cl SG8 ....2 D1
Swing Gate Fst Sch HP4 ....122 D3
Swing Gate La HP4 ....122 D2
Swingate SG1 ....50 D5
Swinnell Cl SG8 ....2 B5
Swiss Ave WD1 ....166 E6
Swiss Cl WD1 ....166 E6
Sword Cl LU10 ....134 D3
Sworders Yd ⊡ CM23 ....76 F7
Sycamore Ave AL10 ....130 A4
Sycamore Cl Bushey WD2 ....167 C7
  Hammond Street EN7 ....147 F4
  Hitchin SG4 ....35 A4
  Watford WD2 ....154 B4
Sycamore Dr
  Park Street AL2 ....141 D4
  Tring HP23 ....100 B4
Sycamore Rd WD3 ....166 D4
Sycamore Rise HP4 ....122 D3
Sycamores The
  Baldock SG7 ....23 E8
  Bishop's Stortford CM23 ....77 B6
  Hemel Hempstead HP3 ....137 F8
  Radlett WD7 ....156 B5
  St Albans AL1 ....127 D2
Sydney Rd WD1 ....154 D1
Sylam Cl LU3 ....44 E7
Sylvan Cl HP3 ....125 A2
Sylvan Way AL7 ....111 C5
Sylvandale AL7 ....111 C5
Sylvia Ave HA5 ....175 F4
Symonds Green La SG1 ....50 A6
Symonds Green Rd SG1 ....50 A7
Symonds Rd SG5 ....34 D8

T

Tabbs Cl SG6 ....23 B7
Tacitus Ct ⊡ SG1 ....51 C8
Tailors CM23 ....76 B5
Takeley Cl EN4 ....163 D6
Talbot Ave WD1 ....167 E2
Talbot Cl HP3 ....124 D1
Talbot Rd Harrow HA3 ....176 F1
  Hatfield AL10 ....130 A8
  Luton LU2 ....45 E4
  Rickmansworth WD3 ....165 E1
Talbot St Hertford SG13 ....113 E6
  Hitchin SG5 ....34 C8
Talbot Way SG1 ....12 B1
Talisman St SG4 ....35 C6
Tall Trees Hitchin SG4 ....46 A1
  Royston SG8 ....7 E6
Tallack Cl HA3 ....176 E3
Tallents Cres AL5 ....86 D3
Tallis Way WD6 ....169 E8
Tamar Cl HP2 ....124 F8
Tamar Gn HP2 ....124 F8
Tamarisk Cl AL3 ....127 D7
Tameton Cl LU2 ....46 F2
Tamworth Rd SG13 ....113 F7
Tancred Rd LU2 ....148 A4
Tanfield Cl EN7 ....148 A4
Tanfield Ct LU2 ....46 E1
Tanglewood
  Harpenden AL5 ....85 F2
  Welwyn AL6 ....90 A7
Tanglewood Cl HA7 ....176 E8
Tanner Ho WD1 ....167 B2
Tanners Cl AL1 ....127 C4
Tanners Cres SG13 ....113 C4
Tanners Hill WD5 ....154 A8
Tanners Wood Cl WD5 ....153 F7
Tanners Wood Ct WD5 ....153 E7
Tanners Wood
  Jun Mix Inf Sch WD5 ....153 E7
Tanners Wood La WD5 ....153 F7
Tannery Cl SG8 ....7 C6
Tannery Drift SG8 ....7 C6
Tannery Drift Sch SG8 ....7 C6
Tannery The SG9 ....40 E7
Tannery Yd SG4 ....34 C6
Tansfield Dr EN1 HP4 ....124 F5
Tansmore Cl ⊡ HP2 ....124 F5
Tansycroft AL7 ....111 D7
Tansycroft Cl HA6 ....174 C4
Tanworth Gdns HA5 ....175 C1
Tany's Dell CM20 ....118 A3
Tany's Dell Cty Prim Sch
  CM20 ....118 A3
Tanyard La AL6,SG4 ....69 B6
Tapster St EN5 ....171 F6
Taransay HP3 ....125 B1
Tarlings CM20 ....117 F3
Tarpan Way EN10 ....148 F8
Tarrant SG1 ....36 B1
Tarrant Dr AL5 ....107 D7
Tassell Hall AL1 ....105 E6
Tate Gdns WD2 ....168 E2
Tatlers La SG2 ....51 E4
Tatsfield Ave LU3 ....149 D8
Tattershall Dr HP2 ....105 B1
Tattle Hill SG14 ....91 E2
Tatton Way HP22 ....60 B3
Tauber Cl WD6 ....169 F5
Taunton Rd LU2 ....46 B1
Taverners HP2 ....124 B1
Taverners Way HP1 ....135 A6
Taverners Way SG6 ....22 D3
Tavistock Ct
  Potters Bar EN6 ....159 D8
  St Albans AL1 ....141 D8
Tavistock Cres LU2 ....46 E5
Tavistock Rd WD2 ....167 D8

Tavistock St LU1 ....63 E6
Taylor Cl Harefield UB9 ....173 C1
  St Albans AL4 ....128 A8
Taylor St LU2 ....63 F8
Taylor Trad Est SG13 ....114 B7
Taylor's La EN5 ....34 F6
Taylor's La EN5 ....171 F8
Taylor's Rd SG5 ....11 F8
Taylors Ave EN11 ....135 A5
Taywood Cl SG2 ....51 B2
Teal Dr HA6 ....174 C3
Teal Ho WD1 ....154 E3
Teasdale Cl SG8 ....2 D1
Teasel Cl SG8 ....7 E5
Tedder Ave SG16 ....10 B5
Tedder Rd HP2 ....125 A4
Tees Side SG13 ....114 B7
Teesdale
  Hemel Hempstead HP2 ....124 E6
  Luton LU4 ....44 C5
Telford Ave SG2 ....51 B6
Telford Cl WD2 ....154 D4
Telford Ct ⊡ Hatfield AL10 ....129 F1
  St Albans AL1 ....127 E2
Telford Rd AL2 ....142 C4
Telford Way LU1 ....63 D8
Telmere Ind Est ⊡ LU1 ....63 E6
Telscombe Way LU2 ....46 C3
Temperance St AL3 ....127 C3
Tempest Ave EN6 ....159 D7
Templar Ave SG7 ....23 F6
Templars Dr HA3 ....176 D4
Templars La SG4 ....48 D8
Temple Bank CM20 ....118 B5
Temple Cl Cheshunt EN7 ....162 A8
  Luton LU2 ....45 C5
  Preston SG5 ....34 B4
  Watford WD1 ....166 F7
Temple Ct Baldock SG7 ....92 D1
  Potters Bar EN6 ....158 D8
Temple Fields SG14 ....92 D1
Temple Gdns
  Letchworth SG6 ....23 C8
  Moor Park WD3 ....174 B6
Temple La SG12 ....92 F8
Temple Mead
  Hemel Hempstead HP2 ....124 D5
  Roydon CM19 ....116 B1
Temple View AL3 ....127 C5
Templefields Ent Ctr
  CM20 ....118 A3
Templepan La WD3 ....152 E2
Templewood AL8 ....89 D1
Templewood
  Jun Mix Inf Sch AL8 ....110 D8
Tempsford AL7 ....111 D6
Tempsford Ave WD6 ....170 D5
Tensford Ct HA2 ....176 C1
Tenby Gdns LU3 ....44 E3
Tenby Mews LU1 ....44 E3
Tene The SG7 ....23 F8
Tennand Ct EN7 ....147 F5
Tennison Ave WD6 ....170 B4
Tennyson Ave
  Hitchin SG4 ....35 C7
  Waltham Abbey EN9 ....163 E5
Tennyson Cl SG8 ....2 B1
Tennyson Ho LU1 ....63 E5
Tennyson Road Prim Sch
  LU1 ....63 E5
Tenterfield Ho AL6 ....89 C4
Tenth Ave LU3 ....44 C2
Tenzing Gr LU1 ....63 C6
Tenzing Rd HP2 ....125 A3
Teresa Gdns EN8 ....162 D2
Terminus St CM20 ....117 D1
Terrace Gdns WD1 ....167 B7
Terrace The
  Essendon AL9 ....131 E6
  Redbourn AL3 ....106 A5
  Tring HP23 ....100 A3
Tewin Cl AL4 ....128 C7
Tewin Ct AL7 ....110 F7
Tewin Rd Welwyn AL6 ....90 C5
Tewin Rd AL7 ....111 A8
Tewin Water
  Hemel Hempstead HP2 ....125 C3
  Welwyn Garden City AL7 ....110 F7
Thackeray Cl SG2 ....2 D1
Thames Ave HP2 ....124 F8
Thames Ct SG8 ....45 B3
Thames Tallis
  Cty Inf Sch The EN9 ....163 F6
Thamesdale AL7 ....111 D6
Thanet Ho ⊡ WD1 ....166 F3
Thatchers Croft HP2 ....124 E7
Thatchers End HA4 ....35 D8
Thatchers The CM23 ....76 C5
Thaxted Cl LU2 ....46 F2
Thaxted Way WD1 ....163 D6
Thaynesfield EN6 ....159 D8
The Riverside Club
  (Tennis Ctr) HA4 ....174 B3
Theabald's Grove Sta
  EN8 ....162 D7
The Dby Cl LU3 ....44 F6
Thele Ave SG12 ....115 D4
Thele Est SG12 ....115 E4
Thelway Cl EN11 ....115 B1
Thellusson Way WD3 ....164 C1
Thelusson Ct WD7 ....156 A3
Theobald Bsns Ctr SG4 ....22 A3

Theobald Cres HA3 ....176 D3
Theobald St
  Borehamwood WD6 ....169 F7
  Radlett WD7 ....156 D2
Theobald's La
  Cheshunt EN8 ....162 B7
  Cheshunt EN8 ....162 D7
Theobald's Rd EN6 ....146 F1
Theobalds Park
  Coll EN7 ....162 A6
Theobalds Park Rd EN2 ....161 B3
Therfield Fst Sch SG8 ....15 F7
Therfield Heath
  Nature Reserve SG8 ....7 B5
Therfield Rd AL3 ....127 D6
Thetford Gdns LU2 ....45 E6
Thieves' La SG14 ....112 F7
Third Ave Letchworth SG6 ....23 C7
  Luton LU3 ....44 D7
  Watford WD2 ....154 D4
Thirlestane AL1 ....127 F4
Thirlestone Rd LU4 ....44 D1
Thirlmere SG1 ....37 C2
Thirlmere Dr AL1 ....128 B1
Thirlmere Gdns HA6 ....174 C4
Thirsk Rd WD6 ....157 A1
Thirston Path WD6 ....170 A7
Thistle Cl HP1 ....123 E2
Thistle Gr AL7 ....111 C7
Thistle Rd LU1 ....63 F7
Thistlecroft HP1 ....124 B2
Thistles The HP1 ....124 B4
Thistley La SG4 ....34 B4
Thomas Alleyne Sch The
  SG1 ....50 C8
Thomas Coram
  CE Mid Sch The HP4 ....122 D2
Thomas Ct HP4 ....121 F5
Thomas Heskin Ct ⊡
  CM23 ....77 F7
Thomas Rochford Way
  EN8 ....148 F4
Thomas Watson
  Cottage Homes The
  EN5 ....171 E5
Thomas Way SG8 ....2 D1
Thompson Way WD3 ....165 A1
Thompsons Cl
  Goff's Oak EN7 ....147 F2
  Harpenden AL5 ....86 A1
Thompsons Mdw SG8 ....1 F4
Thorley Ctr CM23 ....76 D4
Thorley High CM23 ....76 F2
Thorley Hill CM23 ....76 F5
Thorley Hill Jun Mix Inf Sch
  CM23 ....76 F4
Thorley La Bishop's
  Stortford, Thorley CM23 ....76 B4
  Bishop's Stortford, Thorley
  Houses CM23 ....76 B4
  Bishop's Stortford, Thorley
  Street CM23 ....76 B4
Thorley Park Rd CM23 ....76 D4
Thorn Ave WD2 ....168 C1
Thorn Gr CM23 ....77 B6
Thorn Grove
  Jun Mix Inf Sch CM23 ....77 B6
Thorn Tree Dr HP23 ....99 F4
Thornage Cl LU2 ....45 D7
Thornbera Cl CM23 ....76 F4
Thornbera Gdns CM23 ....76 F4
Thornbera Rd CM23 ....76 F4
Thornbury Cl
  Hoddesdon EN11 ....115 B2
  Stevenage SG2 ....69 A8
Thornbury Gdns WD6 ....170 C5
Thorncroft HP3 ....125 B1
Thorndyke Ct HA5 ....175 F3
Thorne Cl HP1 ....124 B1
Thorne Ho AL1 ....127 E4
Thorne Way HP22 ....99 B4
Thorneycroft Dr EN3 ....163 A2
Thornfield Rd WD6 ....176 E8
Thornhill Rd Luton LU4 ....44 F2
  Moor Park HA6 ....174 A4
Thornquay Gr HA5 ....176 A4
Thornton Rd Barnet EN5 ....171 F6
  Potters Bar EN6 ....145 C1
Thornton St
  Hertford SG14 ....113 D6
  St Albans AL3 ....127 C4
Thorntondale ⊡ LU4 ....44 C5
Thorpe Cres WD1 ....167 C2
Thorpe Rd AL1 ....128 D2
Thorpefield Cl AL4 ....128 D6
Thrales Cl LU3 ....44 E7
Three Cherrytrees La
  HP2 ....125 B7
Three Close La HP4 ....122 C4
Three Closes SG5 ....20 C4
Three Corners HP3 ....125 A1
Three Horse Shoes La SG4 ....67 D5
Three Rivers Mus
  of Local History WD3 ....165 C2
Three Stiles SG2 ....52 E4
Three Valleys Way WD2 ....167 E4
Thremhall Ave CM23 ....77 F8
Thresher Cl CM23 ....76 F4
Thricknells Cl LU3 ....44 C7
Thrift Farm La WD6 ....170 C7
Thristers Cl SG6 ....23 B3
Throcking La SG9 ....27 C1
Thrums WD2 ....154 B2

Thrush Ave AL10 ...130 A3
Thrush Gn WD3 ...165 C2
Thrush La E6 ...146 F3
Thumbswood AL7
Thumbswood Inf Sch
AL7 ...111 A5
Thumpers HP2 ...124 E5
Thunder Hall 1 SG12 ...93 D2
Thundercourt SG12 ...93 D2
Thundridge CI AL7 ...111 B5
Thurgood Rd EN11 ...135 A8
Thurlow CI SG1 ...36 D2
Thurnall Ave SG8 ...7 D5
Thurston CI SG7 ...23 F8
Tibbles CI WD2 ...154 E4
Tibbs Hill Rd WD5 ...139 F1
Tiberius Rd LU3 ...44 F6
Tichborne WD3 ...172 D5
Tile Kiln CI HP3 ...125 B2
Tile Kiln Cres HP3 ...125 B2
Tile Kiln La HP3 ...125 B2
Tilecroft AL8 ...89 D1
Tilehouse CI WD6 ...169 F6
Tilehouse La UB9 ...172 C2
Tilehouse St SG5 ...34 E6
Tilekiln EN2 ...147 F2
Tilgate LU2 ...46 D3
Tillers Link SG2 ...51 A2
Tilloton Rd HA3 ...176 B3
Tilsworth Wlk AL4 ...128 C8
Timber Dch SG14 ...92 A2
Timber Ridge WD3 ...165 D5
Timbercroft AL7 ...89 F1
Timbers Ct AL5 ...85 F2
Times CI SG5 ...21 D2
Timplings Row HP1 ...124 B5
Timworth CI LU2 ...46 D1
Tingeys CI AL3 ...106 A5
Tinkers La HP23 ...121 A6
Tinsley CI LU1 ...63 B5
Tintagel CI
Hemel Hempstead HP2 ...124 D8
Luton LU3 ...45 A4
Tintern CI Harpenden AL5 ...85 C4
Stevenage SG2 ...69 A7
Tinwell Mews WD18 ...170 D4
Tippendell La AL2 ...141 C5
Tippet CI SG1 ...50 D3
Titan Ct LU4 ...44 F1
Titan Rd HP2 ...124 F6
Titchfield Rd EN3 ...162 E2
Tithe Barn CI AL1 ...141 C8
Tithe CI WD2 ...67 F1
Titian Ave WD2 ...168 E2
Titmore Ct SG4 ...35 E2
Titmus CI SG1 ...50 E6
Tiverton Ct AL5 ...107 E6
Tiverton Rd EN6 ...159 E8
Toddington Rd LU4 ...44 C6
Toland CI LU4 ...44 C1
Tolcarne Dr HA5 ...175 A1
Tollgate CI WD3 ...164 F5
Tollgate Rd
Colney Heath AL4,AL9 ...143 E7
Enfield EN3 ...162 D4
Welham Green AL4 ...144 A4
Tollpit End HP1 ...124 A6
Tollsworth Way SG11 ...55 D3
Tolmers Ave EN6 ...146 E3
Tolmers Gdns EN6 ...146 F2
Tolmers Mews SG13 ...146 E6
Tolmers Rd EN6 ...146 E3
Tolpits CI WD1 ...166 F4
Tolpits La WD1 ...166 E2
Tom's Hill WD3 ...152 E3
Tomkins CI WD6 ...169 E8
Toms Croft HP2 ...124 E2
Toms Field AL6 ...129 E4
Toms Hill Rd HP23 ...101 D5
Toms La WD4,WD5 ...139 D3
Tomshill CI HP23 ...101 D5
Tonwell St Mary's
CE Prim Sch SG12 ...92 E7
Tooke CI HA5 ...175 E2
Toorack Rd HA3 ...176 D1
Tooveys Mill CI WD4 ...139 A2
Topstreet Way AL5 ...107 C8
Torquay Cres SG1 ...50 B7
Torquay Dr LU4 ...44 D4
Torridge Wlk 2 HP2 ...124 F8
Torrington CI EN6 ...159 D7
Torrington Rd HP4 ...122 A4
Tortoiseshell Way HP4 ...121 F6
Torwood CI HP4 ...121 F4
Torworth Rd WD6 ...157 A1
Tot La CM23 ...59 D4
Totteridge Comm N20 ...171 C1
Totteridge Pk N20 ...171 C1
Totteridge Rd EN3 ...162 D2
Totteridge Village N20 ...171 F1
Totton Mews AL3 ...106 B5
Totts La SG2 ...38 C1
Toulmin Dr AL3 ...142 D5
Tovey CI AL2 ...142 D5
Tower CI
Berkhamsted HP4 ...122 A3
Kneesworth SG8 ...2 A5
Little Wymondley SG4 ...35 B3
Tower Ct LU2 ...46 A1
Tower Ctr 10 EN11 ...135 A7
Tower Hill
Chipperfield HP3,WD4 ...137 F1
Much Hadham SG10 ...74 F2
Tower Hill La AL4 ...108 A4
Tower Hts EN11 ...135 A6

Tower Prim Sch SG12 ...93 E3
Tower Rd Codicote SG4 ...67 F2
Luton LU2 ...63 F2
Ware SG12 ...93 F2
Tower St SG14 ...113 C8
Tower View SG4 ...66 D6
Tower Way LU2 ...63 F2
Towers Rd
Hemel Hempstead HP2 ...124 E4
Pinner HA5 ...175 E2
Stevenage SG1 ...50 D4
Towers The SG1 ...50 D4
Town Ctr AL10 ...130 A6
Town Farm
Cheddington LU7 ...80 A7
Wheathampstead AL4 ...108 D8
Town Farm CI SG4 ...1 F4
Town Farm Cres SG1 ...51 C7
Town Fields AL10 ...130 A6
Town La LU7 ...80 A8
Town La SG2 ...52 E4
Town Mead Rd EN9 ...163 C5
Town Sq SG1 ...50 D5
Towne Rd SG8 ...7 D5
Townfield WD3 ...165 C2
Townley SG6 ...23 D4
Townsend HP2 ...124 D5
Townsend Ave AL1 ...127 E4
Townsend CE Sch AL3 ...127 C8
Townsend CI Barkway SG8 ...17 C3
Harpenden AL5 ...85 F1
Townsend Dr AL3 ...127 D5
Townsend La AL5 ...85 F1
Townsend Rd AL5 ...86 A2
Townsend Way HA6 ...175 A3
Townshend St SG13 ...113 E6
Townsley CI LU1 ...63 C6
Tracey CI 12 LU1 ...63 E6
Trafalgar Ave EN10 ...134 F2
Trafford CI Stanley Ind SG7 ...156 E7
Stevenage SG1 ...36 E2
Traherne CI 2 SG4 ...34 F5
Trajan Gate SG2 ...37 D1
Trapstyle Rd SG12 ...93 A2
Travellers CI AL4 ...144 C8
Travellers La
Hatfield AL9,AL10 ...130 B2
Welham Green AL9 ...130 C1
Treacle La SG9 ...25 F3
Treacy CI WD2 ...176 C8
Trebellan Dr HP2 ...124 E2
Tree CI HP3 ...125 B1
Tree Ct WD6 ...169 D3
Treehanger CI HP23 ...100 B4
Treetops AL6 ...89 E7
Treetops CI HA6 ...174 B1
Trefoil CI LU4 ...44 A4
Trefusis Wlk WD1 ...166 E8
Tremaine Gr HP2 ...124 E7
Trent CI Stanley WD7 ...156 E7
Stevenage SG1 ...50 E8
Trent Rd LU3 ...45 B4
Tresco Rd HP4 ...121 F5
Trescott CI LU2 ...46 E2
Tresilian Sq HP1 ...123 E2
Treslian Sq 1 HP1 ...123 E2
Trevalga Way HP2 ...124 E7
Trevellance Way SG4 ...154 D6
Trevelyan Way HP4 ...122 B6
Trevera Ct EN11 ...135 A7
Trevera Ct EN11 ...135 A7
Trevor CI HA3 ...176 F3
Trevor Rd SG4 ...35 A8
Trevose Way WD1 ...175 C2
Trewenna Dr EN6 ...159 D7
Triangle The SG4 ...34 F6
Trident Ave AL10 ...129 E6
Trident Ind Est EN11 ...135 C2
Trident Rd WD2 ...153 F5
Triggs Way LU2 ...46 E3
Trimley CI LU4 ...44 B5
Trinder Rd EN5 ...171 B5
Tring Bsns Ctr HP23 ...99 E4
Tring Ford Rd HP23 ...100 A7
Tring Rd HP23 ...99 C3
Tring Wharf HP23 ...166 E2
Trinity CI
Bishop's Stortford CM23 ...76 F4
Northwood HA6 ...174 E4
Trinity Ct SG12 ...113 C8
Trinity Gr SG14 ...113 C8
Trinity Hall CI WD2 ...167 C6
Trinity La EN8 ...162 E7
Trinity Mews HP2 ...125 D2
Trinity PI SG1 ...50 D6
Trinity Rd
Hertford Heath SG13 ...114 C3
Luton LU2 ...45 A4
Stevenage SG1 ...50 C6
Stotfold SG5 ...11 F7
Ware SG12 ...93 E2
Trinity Sch CM23 ...76 F6
Trinity Wlk SG13 ...114 C3
Tristram Rd SG4 ...22 B2
Tring Hyde HP2 ...124 F8
Trojan Terr CM21 ...97 E3
Troon Gdns LU2 ...45 E7
Trooper Rd HP23 ...101 C5
Trotter's Gap SG12 ...115 E4
Trotters Bottom EN5 ...158 B2
Trotts Hill Prim Sch SG1 ...36 F1
Trout Rise WD3 ...165 B6

Troutstream Way WD3 ...165 B5
Trouvere Pk HP1 ...124 C5
Trowbridge Gdns LU2 ...45 E3
Trowley Bottom AL3 ...105 B8
Trowley Hill Rd AL3 ...84 B1
Trowley Hts AL3 ...84 B2
Trowley Rise WD5 ...153 F8
Truemans Rd SG12 ...21 D2
Trumper Rd SG1 ...36 A1
Trumpington Dr AL1 ...141 D8
Truncals LU1 ...63 D5
Trundlers Way HP2 ...168 E1
Truro Gdns LU3 ...45 C5
Trust Cotts HP4 ...81 A1
Trust Rd EN8 ...162 E5
Tucker St WD1 ...167 C4
Tucker's Row 4 CM23 ...76 F6
Tudor Ave Cheshunt EN7 ...162 B8
Watford WD2 ...154 D2
Tudor CI Cheshunt EN7 ...162 B8
Hatfield AL10 ...129 F2
Hunsdon SG12 ...116 D8
Stevenage SG1 ...36 C1
Tudor Cres EN2 ...161 C1
Tudor Ct
Borehamwood WD6 ...169 E7
Hitchin SG5 ...34 D6
Kneesworth SG8 ...2 B4
Stevenage SG1 ...36 C1
Wadesmill AL3 ...165 A1
Sawbridgeworth CM21 ...97 E3
Tudor Dr WD2 ...154 D2
Tudor Jun Mix Inf Sch
HP3 ...124 E1
Tudor Manor Gdns WD2 ...154 D7
Tudor Par WD3 ...165 A2
Tudor Rd Harrow HA3 ...176 D1
Luton LU3 ...45 B2
Pinner HA5 ...175 C1
St Albans AL3 ...127 E7
Welwyn AL6 ...89 E3
Wheathampstead AL4 ...108 E8
Tudor Rise EN10 ...134 E2
Tudor Way Hertford SG14 ...113 A7
Rickmansworth WD3 ...165 A2
Waltham Abbey EN9 ...163 D6
Tudor Wlk WD2 ...154 D7
Tuffnells Way AL5 ...85 D4
Tunfield Rd EN11 ...115 B1
Tunnel Wood CI WD1 ...153 F2
Tunnel Wood Rd WD1 ...153 F2
Tunnmeade CM20 ...117 A1
Turf La SG4 ...36 B4
Turkey St EN1,EN3 ...162 C2
Turkey Street Sta EN1 ...162 C2
Turmore Dale AL8 ...110 C5
Turn Braemar WD7 ...156 C8
Turnberry CI WD1 ...175 C7
Turnberry Dr AL2 ...140 E1
Turner CI SG1 ...36 C2
Turner Rd WD2 ...168 C5
Turners CI Bramfield SG14 ...91 C4
Harpenden AL5 ...86 C4
Turners Cres CM23 ...76 C4
Turners Ct EN8 ...162 D8
Turners Hill
Cheshunt EN8 ...148 D1
Hemel Hempstead HP2 ...124 E2
Turners Orch WD3 ...164 D4
Turners Rd N LU2 ...46 A2
Turners Rd S LU2 ...46 A2
Turnford CI EN8 ...148 E3
Turnford Villas EN8 ...148 F5
Turnpike Dr LU3 ...31 C1
Turnpike Gn HP2 ...124 F7
Turnpike La SG5 ...21 E3
Turnstones The WD2 ...154 C3
Turpin CI EN3 ...162 F1
Turpin's Ride SG8 ...7 D5
Turpin's Rise SG2 ...50 F1
Turpin's Way SG7 ...23 F7
Turpins Chase AL6 ...89 F7
Turpins CI SG14 ...112 F6
Turpins Ride AL6 ...89 F7
Tuthill Ct SG8 ...15 E7
Tuxford CI WD6 ...156 E1
Tweed CI HP4 ...122 B5
Twelve Acres AL7 ...110 E4
Twelve Leys HP22 ...60 B3
Twickenham Gdns HA3 ...176 E3
Twigden CI LU3 ...44 E5
Twin Foxes SG3 ...69 A1
Twinwoods SG1 ...50 F4
Twist The HP23 ...100 D2
Twitchell The SG7 ...23 F8
Two Acres AL7 ...110 F3
Two Beeches HP2 ...124 F8
Two Dells La HP5 ...136 A4
Two Oaks Dr AL6 ...90 C6
Two Waters Prim Sch
HP3 ...138 D6
Two Waters Rd
Hemel Hempstead HP3 ...124 C1
Hemel Hempstead HP3 ...138 D8
Twyford Bsns Ctr The
CM23 ...77 A4
Twyford Bury La CM22 ...77 A4
Twyford Dr LU2 ...45 E5
Twyford Gdns CM23 ...76 F4
Twyford Mill CM23 ...77 A3
Twyford Rd
Bishop's Stortford CM23 ...77 A4
St Albans AL4 ...128 D7
Tye Green SG9 ...49 B8
Tye End SG2 ...69 B8
Tyfield CI EN8 ...148 B3
Tylers AL5 ...86 D1
Tylers CI Buntingford SG9 ...40 D7
Kings Langley WD4 ...138 F3

Tylers Cswy SG13 ...132 C1
Tylers Hill Rd HP5 ...150 A8
Tylers Mead LU2 ...45 E5
Tylers Way WD2 ...168 E4
Tylers Wood AL6 ...90 C6
Tylersfield WD5 ...154 A8
Tynedale AL2 ...142 F4
Tynemouth Dr EN1 ...162 A1
Tyne CI HP2 ...124 D5
Tysoe Ave EN3 ...162 F4
Tythe Rd LU4 ...44 C6
Tyttenhanger Gn AL1 ...142 E8

U

Uckfield Rd EN3 ...162 D2
Ufford CI HA3 ...176 B3
Ufford Rd HA3 ...176 B3
Ullswater CI SG1 ...37 C2
Ullswater Rd HP3 ...125 C1
Underacres CI HP2 ...124 A4
Underhill Jun & Inf Schs
EN5 ...171 E4
Underwood Rd SG1 ...36 C2
Union Chapel Ho 1 AL1 ...63 E6
Union Gn HP2 ...124 D4
Union St Barnet EN5 ...171 E6
Luton LU1 ...63 E6
Union Terr SG9 ...40 E7
Unity Rd EN3 ...162 C1
University CI WD2 ...168 A5
University of Hertfordshire
AL10 ...129 F3
University
of Hertfordshire
(Hertford Campus)
SG13 ...113 A5
Unwin CI SG6 ...22 E4
Unwin PI SG2 ...51 C3
Unwin Rd SG2 ...51 C3
Updale CI EN6 ...158 E6
Upland Dr AL7 ...145 B6
Uplands Braughing SG11 ...55 F6
Croxley Green WD3 ...165 F3
Stevenage SG2 ...44 D8
Ware SG12 ...93 F2
Uplands Ave SG4 ...35 B6
Uplands CI LU1 ...63 E4
Uplands The
Bricket Wood AL2 ...140 E1
Harpenden AL5 ...107 A4
Upper Ashlyns Rd HP4 ...122 B3
Upper Barn HP3 ...138 F8
Upper Bourne End La
HP1 ...137 B8
Upper Clabdens SG12 ...93 F2
Upper Culver Rd AL1 ...127 F5
Upper Dagnall St AL3 ...127 D3
Upper George St LU1 ...63 E6
Upper Gn AL6 ...90 D3
Upper Green Rd AL6 ...90 E3
Upper Hall Pk HP4 ...122 E2
Upper Heath Rd AL1 ...127 F5
Upper Highway WD5 ...153 D6
Upper Hill Rise WD3 ...165 B3
Upper Hitch WD1 ...167 E1
Upper Icknield Way
Aldbury LU7 ...80 E1
Aston Clinton HP22 ...99 A3
Tring HP23 ...100 D8
Upper King St SG8 ...7 D6
Upper Lattimore Rd AL1 ...127 E3
Upper Marlborough Rd
AL1 ...127 E3
Upper Marsh La EN11 ...135 A5
Upper Maylins SG6 ...23 C3
Upper Paddock Rd WD1 ...167 E3
Upper Pk CM20 ...117 B1
Upper Sales HP1 ...123 F2
Upper Sean SG2 ...51 A3
Upper Shot AL7 ...111 A7
Upper Shott EN7 ...147 F5
Upper Station Rd WD7 ...156 A4
Upper Tail AL7 ...175 E7
Upper Tilehouse St SG5 ...34 E7
Upperfield Rd AL7 ...110 F5
Upperstone CI SG5 ...11 F6
Upshire Rd EN9 ...163 F7
Upton Ave AL3 ...127 D4
Upton CI Luton LU2 ...45 D6
Luton LU2 ...45 D6
Upton Lodge CI WD2 ...168 C2
Upton Rd WD2 ...167 B6
Upwell Rd LU2 ...46 B2
Urban Rd CM23 ...77 B7
Uxbridge Rd AL3 ...173 A8
Uxbridge Rd
(Harrow Weald) HA3 ...176 D3
Uxbridge Rd
(Hatch End) HA5 ...175 F3
Uxbridge Rd (Pinner)
HA5 ...175 D2
Uxbridge Rd (Stanmore)
HA7 ...176 F4

Valence Dr EN7 ...14...
Valency CI HA6 ...17...
Valerian Way SG2 ...5...
Valerie CI AL4 ...12...
Valerie Ct WD2 ...16...
Valeside SG14 ...11...
Vallance PI AL5 ...10...
Vallans CI SG12 ...9...
Vallansgate SG2 ...5...
Valley CI Hertford SG13 ...11...
Pinner HA5 ...17...
Studham LU6 ...8...
Waltham Abbey EN9 ...16...
Whipsnade HP4 ...9...
Valley Gn HP2 ...10...
Valley Gn The AL8 ...11...
Valley La AL3 ...
Valley Rd
Berkhamsted HP4 ...12...
Letchworth SG6 ...2...
Rickmansworth WD3 ...165...
St Albans AL3 ...127...
Studham LU6 ...82...
Welwyn Garden City AL8 ...110...
Valley Rise Lea Valley AL4 ...8...
Royston SG8 ...7...
Watford WD2 ...154...
Valley Sch The SG2 ...5(...
Valley The SG4 ...66...
Valley View Barnet EN5 ...171...
Goff's Oak EN7 ...147...
Valley Way SG2 ...51...
Valley Wlk WD3 ...166...
Valleyside HP1 ...123...
Valpy CI HP23 ...100...
Vanda Cres AL1 ...127...
Vantorts CI CM21 ...97...
Vantorts Rd CM21 ...97...
Vardon Rd SG2 ...50...
Varna CI LU3 ...4...
Varney CI
Hammond Street EN7 ...148...
Hemel Hempstead HP1 ...123...
Varney Rd HP1 ...123...
Vaughan Read AL3 ...106...
Vaughan Rd
Harpenden AL5 ...86...
Stotfold SG5 ...
Vauxhall Rd
Hemel Hempstead HP2 ...125...
Luton LU1,LU2 ...46...
Vauxhall Way LU2 ...46...
Vega Cres HA6 ...
Vega Rd WD2 ...168...
Velizy Ave CM20 ...117...
Venetia Rd LU2 ...
Ventnor Gdns LU3 ...45...
Ventura Pk AL2 ...141...
Venus Hill HP3 ...151...
Ver Rd Redbourn AL3 ...106...
St Albans AL3 ...127...
Vera Ct WD1 ...167...
Vera La AL6 ...90...
Verdure CI WD2 ...154...
Verity Way SG1 ...51...
Verlys AL10 ...130...
Verney CI
Berkhamsted HP4 ...121...
Tring HP23 ...100...
Vernon Ave EN3 ...162...
Vernon CI CM23 ...76...
Vernon Dr LU9 ...173...
Vernon Rd Luton LU1 ...63...
Watford WD2 ...167...
Vernon's CI AL1 ...127...
Veronica Ho AL7 ...111...
Verulam CI AL7 ...110...
Verulam Gdns LU3 ...44...
Verulam Rd Hitchin SG5 ...34...
St Albans AL3 ...127...
Verulam Sch AL1 ...128...
Verulamium Mus AL3 ...127...
Verulamium Roman Town
AL3 ...127...
Verwood Rd AL5 ...176...
Vespers CI LU4 ...44...
Vesta Ave AL1 ...141...
Vestry CI LU1 ...63...
Veysey CI HP1 ...124...
Viaduct Cotts LU1 ...85...
Viaduct Rd SG12 ...114...
Viaduct Way AL7 ...89...
Vian Ave EN3 ...162...
Vicarage CI Arlesey SG15 ...11...
Bishop's Stortford CM23 ...76...
Hemel Hempstead HP1 ...124...
Northaw EN6 ...145...
Shillington SG5 ...19...
St Albans AL1 ...141...
Standon AL3 ...141...
Vicarage Cswy SG13 ...114...
Vicarage Gdns
Flamstead AL3 ...84...
Marsworth HP23 ...84...
Potten End HP4 ...123...
Vicarage La
Bishop's Stortford CM23 ...137...
Kings Langley WD4 ...138...
Pitstone LU7 ...80...
Stapleford SG14 ...92...
Vicarage Rd
Buntingford SG9 ...40...
Berkhamsted HP4 ...122...
Marsworth HP23 ...84...
Pitstone LU7 ...80...
Potten End HP4 ...123...
Ware SG12 ...93...

carage Rd continued
Watford WD1 ....167 A4
Wigginton HP23 ....100 D1
carage Road Prec WD1 ....167 B5
carage St LU1 ....63 F7
carage Wood CM20 ....118 A1
cerons Pl CM23 ....76 D4
ctoria C Fst Sch HP4 ....122 C4
ctoria Cl
 Rickmansworth WD3 ....165 D2
 Stevenage SG1 ....50 D7
ctoria Cres SG8 ....7 D7
ctoria Ct WD1 ....167 C6
ctoria Dr SG5 ....12 A5
ctoria La EN5 ....171 C5
ctoria Pl HP4 ....124 D3
ctoria Rd
 Bushey WD2 ....168 B3
 7 Harpenden AL5 ....86 B1
 Waltham Abbey EN9 ....133 A1
 Watford WD2 ....154 A1
ctoria St Luton LU1 ....63 E6
 St Albans AL1 ....127 E3
ctoria Way SG5 ....34 D8
ctory Cres SG8 ....7 E5
ctory Rd HP4 ....122 A5
ctory Way SG5 ....171 F6
view Point SG1 ....50 A5
view Rd EN6 ....159 C7
cigors Croft ■ LU3 ....129 F4
cilla C E SG12 ....63 D8
cilla Rd LU2 ....63 D8
cillage Ct AL4 ....128 D7
cillage Sq SG4 ....49 F1
cilliers Cl LU4 ....44 D3
cilliers Cres AL4 ....128 D3
cilliers Rd WD1 ....167 E3
cilliers St SG13 ....113 E6
cilliers-Sur-Marne Ave CM23 ....76 D4
cincent Cl
 Vincent Cl EN5 ....148 E3
cincent Ct HA6 ....174 F2
cincent Rd LU4 ....44 D5
cincenzo Cl AL9 ....144 C8
cine Cl AL8 ....110 E8
cine Gr CM20 ....117 E5
cines The SG5 ....11 E6
cineyards Rd EN5 ....94 A2
cinters Ave SG1 ....50 F5
ciolet Ave EN2 ....161 D1
ciolet Way WD3 ....165 C5
ciolets La SG9 ....43 B5
cirgil Dr EN8 ....148 F8
cirginia Cl LU2 ....45 F3
ciscount Cl LU3 ....45 A5
ciscount Ct ■ LU2 ....45 D1
civian Cl WD1 ....167 A1
civian Gdns WD1 ....167 A1
cixen Dr SG13 ....114 A6
cyse Cl EN5 ....171 C5

W

Wacketts EN7 ....148 A4
Waddesdon Cl LU2 ....46 D2
Waddeston Ct EN2 ....161 E1
Waddington Rd ■ AL3 ....127 D3
Wade The AL7 ....111 A3
Wades The AL10 ....130 A2
Wadesmill Rd
 Tonwell SG14 ....92 D3
 Ware SG12 ....93 D2
Wadham Rd WD5 ....153 F8
Wadhurst Ave LU3 ....45 C4
Wadley Cl ■ HP2 ....124 F2
Wadnall Way SG3 ....68 F3
Waggon Rd EN4 ....159 E2
Waggoners Yd ■ SG12 ....93 D2
Wagon Rd EN4 ....159 E2
Wagon Way WD3 ....165 C6
Wain Cl EN6 ....159 B5
Wakefield Wlk EN8 ....162 E8
Walcot Ave LU2 ....46 B1
Waldeck Rd LU3 ....63 C8
Waldegrave Pk AL5 ....86 D1
Walden End SG1 ....50 E4
Walden Rd LU3 ....44 B8
Walden Rd AL8 ....110 D8
Waleran Cl HA7 ....176 F4
Waleys Cl LU3 ....44 E8
Walfords Cl CM17 ....118 C4
Walk The EN6 ....159 B7
Walkern Prim Sch SG2 ....52 D5
Walkern Rd Benington SG2 ....52 D5
 Stevenage SG1 ....50 D8
 Watton at Stone SG14 ....107 C7
Walkers Cl AL5 ....85 F1
Walker's Cl SG7 ....23 F8
Walkers Ct SG7 ....23 F8
Walkers Rd AL5 ....107 B7
Wall Hall (Univ Campus) WD2 ....155 B3
Wallace Way SG4 ....22 A2
Waller Ave LU4 ....44 F3
Waller Dr HA6 ....175 A2
Waller Street Mall ■ LU1 ....63 F7
Waller's Cl
 Chiswellgreen AL2 ....141 B4
Walkers Way EN11 ....115 B1
Wallingford Wlk AL1 ....141 D8
Wallington Rd SG7 ....13 D1
Walnut Ave SG7 ....24 A7
Walnut Cl
 Chiswellgreen AL2 ....141 B4

Walnut Cl continued
 Hitchin SG4 ....35 A6
 Luton LU2 ....46 B4
 Much Hadham SG10 ....74 F2
 Royston SG8 ....11 F6
 Stotfold SG5 ....11 F6
Walnut Cotts CM21 ....97 E3
Walnut Ct
 Welwyn Garden City AL7 ....110 E3
 Wheathampstead AL4 ....108 D8
Walnut Dr CM23 ....76 D3
Walnut Gn
 Hemel Hempstead HP2 ....124 D3
 Welwyn Garden City AL7 ....110 E3
Walnut Ho AL7 ....110 F3
Walnut Tree Ave CM23 ....77 B6
Walnut Tree Cl Aston SG2 ....51 C6
 Cheshunt EN8 ....162 D8
 Hoddesdon EN11 ....135 A6
Walnut Tree Cres CM21 ....97 E3
Walnut Tree La LU4 ....58 E4
Walnut Tree Rd SG5 ....20 D3
Walnut Tree Wlk SG12 ....114 D8
Walnut Way SG5 ....21 E4
Walpole Cl HA5 ....176 A4
Walpole Ct SG2 ....69 C7
Walsh Cl SG5 ....34 D7
Walsham Cl SG2 ....69 C7
Walshford Way WD6 ....157 A1
Walsingham Cl
 Hatfield AL10 ....129 F6
 Luton LU2 ....45 D7
Walsingham Way AL2 ....142 C4
Walsworth Rd SG4 ....35 A8
Walter Rothschild Zoological Mus The HP23 ....100 A3
Walters Cl EN7 ....147 B6
Waltham Abbey EN9 ....163 C6
Waltham Cross Sta EN8 ....162 F5
Waltham Ct LU2 ....46 C3
Waltham Gate EN8 ....148 F5
Waltham Gdns EN3 ....162 C2
Waltham Holy Cross
 Cty Jun Sch EN9 ....163 D6
Waltham Rd ■ Hitchin SG4 ....34 F6
 Waltham Abbey EN9 ....149 F5
Walton Cl EN11 ....135 C8
Walton Gdns EN9 ....163 B6
Walton Rd
 Hoddesdon EN11 ....135 C8
 Ware SG12 ....114 D8
Walton St LU1 ....127 C5
Walverns Cl WD1 ....167 C3
Wandon Cl LU2 ....46 C4
Wannions Cl HP5 ....136 A1
Wansbeck Cl SG1 ....37 A3
Wansford Pk WD6 ....170 E5
Warburton Cl HA3 ....176 D4
Ward Cl
 Hammond Street EN7 ....148 A4
 Ware SG12 ....93 C2
Ward Hatch CM20 ....118 A3
Warden Hill Cl LU2 ....45 C8
Warden Hill Gdns LU2 ....45 C8
Warden Hill Inf Sch LU2 ....45 C7
Warden Hill Jun Sch LU2 ....45 C8
Warden Hill Rd LU2 ....45 C8
Wardown Cres LU2 ....45 D2
Wardown Ct LU2 ....45 D2
Ware Mus SG12 ....93 D1
Ware Park Rd SG14 ....113 E6
Ware Rd Hertford SG13 ....113 E6
 Hoddesdon EN11 ....115 A1
 Tonwell SG12 ....92 F6
 Watton at Stone SG14,SG12 ....71 C3
 Widford SG12 ....95 D4
Wareside CE Prim Sch SG12 ....94 E3
Wareside Cl AL7 ....111 B5
Warham Rd HA3 ....176 F1
Warmark Rd HP1 ....123 E5
Warminster Cl LU2 ....46 F1
Warneford Pl WD1 ....167 C3
Warner Rd SG12 ....114 D8
Warners Ave EN11 ....134 F4
Warners Cl SG2 ....51 C3
Warners End Rd HP1 ....124 B4
Warren Cl Hatfield AL10 ....130 B8
 Letchworth SG6 ....23 B8
Warren Dale AL8 ....89 D1
Warren Dell Prim Sch WD1 ....175 C7
Warren Dr The LU1 ....64 C1
Warren Gn AL10 ....130 B8
Warren Gr WD6 ....170 D5
Warren La Clothall SG7 ....24 D7
 Cottered SG9 ....39 B6
 Stanmore HA7 ....176 F6
Warren Park Rd SG14 ....113 D7
Warren Pl ■ SG14 ....113 D6
Warren Rd Bushey WD2 ....168 D1
 Luton LU1 ....62 F8
 St Albans AL1 ....141 C7
Warren Terr SG14 ....113 D8
Warren The
 Harpenden AL5 ....107 A6
 Radlett WD7 ....156 B6
 Royston SG8 ....7 D5
Warren Way AL6 ....89 C4
Warrenfield Cl EN7 ....162 A8

Warrengate La EN6 ....158 C8
Warrengate Rd AL9 ....144 C4
Warrensgreen La SG4 ....33 D5
Warton Gn LU2 ....46 E2
Warwick Ave EN6 ....146 D4
Warwick Cl Bushey WD2 ....168 E2
 Cuffley EN6 ....146 D4
 Hertford SG13 ....113 C4
Warwick Ct
 Chorleywood WD3 ....164 F6
 Luton LU4 ....63 B8
Warwick Dr EN8 ....148 D4
Warwick Rd
 Bishop's Stortford CM23 ....77 B6
 Borehamwood WD6 ....170 D6
 Enfield EN3 ....162 D1
 St Albans AL1 ....127 F5
 Stevenage SG2 ....51 C6
Warwick Rd E LU4 ....63 B8
Warwick Rd W LU4 ....63 B8
Warwick Way WD3 ....166 C5
Wash La Potters Bar,
 Dancers Hill EN6 ....158 C4
 Potters Bar, South
 Mimms EN6 ....158 C4
Wash The
 Furneux Pelham SG9 ....43 D5
 Hertford SG14 ....113 D4
Washington Ave HP2 ....124 E8
Watchlytes AL7 ....111 C6
Watchlytes Sch AL7 ....111 C6
Watchmead AL7 ....111 A6
Water End HP1 ....103 F2
Water End Rd HP1 ....123 C7
Water Hall Farm SG14 ....66 B6
Water La
 Abbots Langley WD4 ....139 B2
 Berkhamsted HP4 ....122 C4
 Bishop's Stortford CM23 ....76 F8
 Bovingdon HP3 ....137 C5
 Hertford SG14 ....113 C5
 Hitchin SG5 ....21 C1
 Stansted Mountfitchet CM24 ....59 E6
 Watford WD1 ....167 D5
Water Row ■ SG12 ....93 D1
Waterbeach WD2 ....154 A1
Watercress Cl SG2 ....51 D5
Watercress Rd EN7 ....148 D7
Waterdale SG13 ....113 C4
Waterdell La ■ SG4 ....35 A2
Waterend La
 Ayot St Peter AL4,AL6 ....88 E1
 Redbourn AL3 ....106 B5
Waterfield
 Chorleywood WD3 ....164 C2
 Welwyn Garden City AL7 ....111 B7
Waterfield Comm SG14 ....92 B2
Waterford Gn AL7 ....111 B6
Watergate The WD1 ....175 D8
Waterhouse Gate AL1 ....127 D3
Waterhouse La SG14 ....113 B6
Waterhouse The HP1 ....124 C3
Waterloo La SG5 ....21 A6
Waterlow Mews SG4 ....35 E3
Waterman Cl WD1 ....167 B3
Watermark Way SG13 ....113 D4
Watermead Rd LU3 ....44 D6
Watermill Ind Est SG9 ....40 E6
Watermill La EN7 ....148 A8
Waters Dr WD3 ....165 E1
Waters End SG5 ....11 E6
Waterside
 Berkhamsted HP4 ....122 D4
 Kings Langley WD4 ....139 A2
 London Colney AL2 ....142 E4
 Radlett WD7 ....156 B5
 Stansted Mountfitchet CM24 ....59 B1
 Welwyn Garden City AL7 ....90 B3
Waterside Ind Est EN11 ....135 D5
Waterside Pl CM23 ....98 A2
Waterslade Gn LU3 ....45 B6
Watersplash Ct AL2 ....142 F4
Watery La Flamstead AL3 ....84 E3
 Hatfield AL9 ....129 E4
 Marsworth HP23 ....79 F1
Watford Arches Ret Pk WD1 ....167 B4
Watford By-Pass WD6 ....169 C2
Watford Coll (annex) WD2 ....167 D6
Watford Coll of Art & Design WD2 ....167 D6
Watford County Ct WD1 ....167 C5
Watford Ent Ctr WD1 ....166 E3
Watford Field Jun Mix Sch WD1 ....167 C4
Watford Field Rd WD1 ....167 C4
Watford Football Gd WD1 ....167 B4
Watford General Hospl (Shrodells Wing) WD1 ....167 B4
Watford Gram Sch for Boys WD1 ....166 F5
Watford Gram Sch for Girls WD1 ....167 B5
Watford Heath WD1 ....167 F3
Watford Heath Farm WD1 ....167 F2
Watford High Street Sta WD1 ....167 C5
Watford Junction Sta WD1 ....167 C7
Watford Mus WD1 ....167 C5
Watford Nth Sta WD2 ....154 C2
Watford Rd
 Abbots Langley WD4 ....153 C6
 Chiswellgreen AL2 ....141 A6

Watford Rd continued
 Croxley Green WD3 ....166 B3
 Elstree WD6 ....169 C3
 Kings Langley WD4 ....139 A1
 Moor Park HA6 ....175 A2
 Watford WD4 ....155 F4
Watford Sch of Music WD1 ....154 A1
Watford Sta WD1 ....166 F6
Watling Cl ■ HP2 ....124 E6
Watling Ct WD6 ....169 D3
Watling Knoll WD7 ....155 F6
Watling St
 Park Street AL2 ....141 D6
 St Albans AL1 ....141 C8
Watling Vale AL1 ....141 C7
Watling View Sch AL1 ....141 D7
Watlington Rd CM17 ....118 D4
Watson Ave AL3 ....127 F6
Watson's Wlk AL1 ....127 D2
Watton at Stone Prim Sch SG14 ....70 D3
Watton at Stone Sta SG14 ....70 D3
Watton Ho SG14 ....70 D3
Watton Rd Knebworth SG3 ....69 A5
 Ware SG12 ....93 C3
 Watton at Stone SG3,SG14 ....70 D2
Watts Cl SG11 ....57 C2
Waulud Prim Sch LU3 ....44 D5
Wauluds Bank Dr LU3 ....44 E7
Wavell Cl EN8 ....148 E4
Wavell Rd AL4 ....128 A2
Waveney Rd LU3 ....44 F8
Waverley Cl SG2 ....69 A8
Waverley Gdns AL5 ....86 C3
Waverley Rd AL3 ....127 D5
Waxwell Cl HA5 ....175 D1
Waxwell La HA5 ....175 D1
Waxwell Rd HA5 ....175 D1
Wayfarers Dr CM23 ....77 B7
Waylands Dr CM23 ....77 B7
Wayne Cl CM17 ....118 C4
Wayne The CM17 ....118 C4
Waysbrook SG6 ....23 B5
Wayside Chipperfield WD4 ....138 B1
 Potters Bar EN6 ....159 D6
 Shenley WD7 ....156 D6
Wayside Ave WD2 ....168 D3
Wayside The HP3 ....125 C2
Waysmeet SG6 ....23 B4
Waytemore Castle CM23 ....77 A7
Weald Fst & Mid Sch HA3 ....176 F3
Weald La HA3 ....176 D2
Weald Rise HA3 ....176 F2
Wealdwood Gdns HA5 ....176 B4
Weall Gn WD4 ....154 B7
Weardale Ct EN6 ....171 C4
Weatherby AL5 ....44 D2
Weaver St CM23 ....76 C4
Weavers Rd HP4 ....122 C5
Weavers Way SG7 ....24 A8
Webb Cl SG6 ....23 C5
Webb Rise SG1 ....50 F7
Webber Cl WD6 ....169 D3
Wedgewood Cl HA6 ....174 D4
Wedgewood Gate SG1 ....37 C2
Wedgewood Rd SG1 ....35 B7
Wedgwood Cl SG1 ....37 C2
Wedgwood Gate SG1 ....37 B2
Wedmore Rd SG6 ....13 C4
Weedon Cl SG6 ....10 C5
Weighton Rd HA3 ....176 D2
Welbeck Cl WD6 ....170 A6
Welbeck Rd ■ LU2 ....107 D6
Welbeck Rise HA3 ....176 D2
Welbury Ave LU3 ....45 C7
Welch Pl HA5 ....175 C2
Welclose St AL3 ....127 C3
Welcote Dr HA6 ....174 D4
Welham Cl AL9 ....144 C7
Welham Ct AL9 ....144 C7
Welham Green Sta AL9 ....144 D8
Welham Manor AL9 ....144 C7
Welkin Gn HP2 ....125 C4
Well App HP1 ....124 D2
Well Croft HP1 ....124 B4
Well End Rd WD6 ....157 D1
Well Garth AL7 ....91 C4
Well Gn AL6 ....91 C4
Well La Harlow CM19 ....117 A1
 Mentmore LU7 ....61 B8
 Northaw EN6 ....145 F2
Well-Bsrn SG13 ....130 A7
Wellbrook Mews HP23 ....100 B4
Wellcroft LU7 ....80 F5
Wellcroft Rd AL7 ....111 A4
Wellcroft Rd LU7 ....80 F5
Wellen Rise HP3 ....138 E8
Wellers Gr EN7 ....148 A3
Wellesley Ave HA6 ....174 F5
Wellesley Cres EN6 ....158 E6
Wellfield Ave LU3 ....44 C8
Wellfield Cl AL10 ....130 A6
Wellfield Ct ■ SG1 ....37 B1
Wellfield Rd AL10 ....130 A7
Wellgate Rd LU4 ....44 D2
Wellhouse Cl LU1 ....63 E5
Wellhouse La EN5 ....171 D5
Wellingham Ave SG5 ....21 D1
Wellington Ave HA5 ....175 F1
Wellington Cl WD1 ....175 F7

Wellington Cotts SG11 ....73 B7
Wellington Ct ■ SG1 ....63 D6
Wellington Dr AL7 ....111 C5
Wellington Ho ■ WD1 ....167 C7
Wellington Pl
 Cheshunt EN10 ....148 C8
 St Albans AL1 ....128 B2
Wellington Rd
 London Colney AL2 ....142 D5
 Pinner HA5 ....175 F2
 St Albans AL1 ....128 B2
 Stevenage SG2 ....51 C5
 Watford WD1 ....167 B7
Wellington St
 Hertford SG14 ....113 B7
 Luton LU1 ....63 D7
Wells Cl
 Hammond Street EN7 ....147 C6
 Harpenden AL5 ....85 E4
 St Albans AL3 ....127 C8
Wells Yd ■ Ware SG12 ....93 D1
Wellside Cl EN5 ....171 C5
Wellstones WD1 ....167 B5
Wellswood Cl HP2 ....125 B4
Welsummer Way EN8 ....148 D3
Weltmore Rd LU3 ....44 F6
Welwyn Campus Liby (Tourist Information) AL8 ....110 D7
Welwyn Garden City Sta AL8 ....124 F7
Welwyn Hall Gdns AL6 ....89 C5
Welwyn North Sta AL6 ....89 F3
Welwyn Rd AL6 ....112 F7
Wendover Cl
 Harpenden AL5 ....86 D1
 St Albans AL4 ....128 C8
Wendover Ct AL6 ....89 C5
Wendover Dr AL6 ....89 C5
Wendover Ho WD1 ....166 E2
Wendover Way
 Bushey WD2 ....168 C3
 Luton LU2 ....45 F3
Wengeo La SG12 ....93 B2
Wenham Ct SG2 ....68 E8
Wenlock Jun Sch LU2 ....64 B8
Wenlock St LU2 ....64 B8
Wensley Cl AL5 ....107 D6
Wensleydale
 Hemel Hempstead HP2 ....124 F6
 Luton LU4 ....45 E1
Wensum Way WD3 ....165 D1
Wentbridge Path WD6 ....157 A1
Wentworth Ave
 Borehamwood WD6 ....169 F4
 Luton LU4 ....44 C6
Wentworth Cl
 Potters Bar EN6 ....159 A8
 Watford WD1 ....153 F1
Wentworth Cotts EN10 ....134 E1
Wentworth Dr CM23 ....76 D6
Wentworth Rd
 Barnet EN5 ....171 D6
 Hertford SG13 ....114 B6
Wenwell Cl HP22 ....99 A3
Wesley Cl Arlesey SG15 ....11 A4
 Goff's Oak EN7 ....147 C3
Wesley Rd AL3 ....83 E5
Wessex Cl EN5 ....171 C5
Wessex Dr HA5 ....175 E1
West Alley ■ SG5 ....34 E7
West Ave Baldock SG7 ....23 E8
 Chiswellgreen AL2 ....141 B6
West Burrowfield AL7 ....110 D4
West Chantry HA3 ....176 B3
West Common HP4 ....121 B4
 Harpenden AL5 ....107 A6
West Common Cl AL5 ....107 A5
West Common Gr AL5 ....107 A5
West Common Way AL5 ....97 E3
West Ct CM21 ....104 A8
West Dene HP4 ....104 A8
West Dr Arlesey SG15 ....11 B4
 Stanmore HA3 ....176 D4
 Watford WD2 ....154 B3
West Drive Gdns HA3 ....176 D4
West End Cl ■ AL9 ....4 C3
West End La Barnet EN5 ....171 D5
 Essendon AL9 ....131 C5
West End Rd
 Brickendon LU7 ....147 F8
 Bricket Wood 79 F7
West Herts Coll
 Cassio Campus WD1 ....154 A1
West Herts Coll
 Leggatts Campus WD2 ....154 A3
West Herts Coll
 Watford Campus WD1 ....167 A6
West Herts Coll
 Watford Campus Sch of Art & Design WD2 ....154 B1
West Hill SG13 ....34 D7
West Hill Rd
 Hoddesdon EN11 ....134 F8
 Luton LU1 ....63 E5
West Hyde La SL9 ....172 A4

West La Great Offley SG5 . . . . . .33 C2
Pirton SG5 . . . . .20 D5
West Lith HP23 . . . . .99 F1
West Lodge Cotts LU2 . . . . .46 D5
West Mead AL7 . . . . .111 B3
West Pas HP23 . . . . .100 A3
West Rd Berkhamsted HP4 . .122 A5
Bishop's Stortford CM23 . . . . . .76 E6
Harlow CM20 . . . . .36 E6
Sawbridgeworth CM21 . . . . .97 C3
Stansted Mountfitchet CM24 . .59 E6
West Reach SG2 . . . . .50 F2
West Riding
Bricket Wood AL2 . . . . .140 F1
Tewin AL6 . . . . .90 D5
West Side EN10 . . . . .148 E6
West Sq CM20 . . . . .117 C1
West St Hertford SG13 . . . . . . .113 C5
Lilley LU2 . . . . .32 D1
Ware SG12 . . . . .93 D1
Watford WD1 . . . . .167 B7
West Valley Rd HP3 . . . . .138 D7
West View Hatfield AL10 . . . . .130 A7
Letchworth SG6 . . . . .22 C5
West View Gdns WD6 . . . . .169 D3
West View Rd AL3 . . . . .127 D4
West Way Harpenden AL5 . . . .86 C2
Rickmansworth WD3 . . . . .165 B1
West Ways HA6 . . . . .175 A1
Westall Cl SG13 . . . . .113 C5
Westall Mews AL3 . . . . .113 C5
Westbourne Mews AL1 . . . . . . .127 D3
Westbourne Rd LU4 . . . . .45 B1
Westbrook Hay
Ed Trust Ltd HP3 . . . . .137 D7
Westbury EN8 . . . . .148 D1
Westbury Cl SG6 . . . . .34 D8
Westbury Gdns LU2 . . . . .45 E3
Westbury Jun Mix Inf Sch
SG6 . . . . .22 E5
Westbury Pl SG6 . . . . .22 E5
Westbury Rd
Moor Park HA6 . . . . .174 E7
Watford WD1 . . . . .167 B4
Westbush Cl EN11 . . . . .114 F1
Westcott AL7 . . . . .111 D7
Westcroft Cl EN3 . . . . .162 C1
Westell Cl SG7 . . . . .24 A8
Westerdale
Hemel Hempstead HP2 . . . . . .124 E6
Luton LU4 . . . . .44 B5
Western Ave SG16 . . . . .10 B3
Western Cl SG6 . . . . .11 E1
Western House Hospl
SG12 . . . . .93 E2
Western Rd
Lower Nazeing EN9 . . . . .135 C1
Luton LU1 . . . . .63 D6
Tring HP23 . . . . .99 F3
Western Terr EN11 . . . . .115 B1
Western Way SG6 . . . . .11 E1
Westfield
Welham Green AL9 . . . . .144 F8
Welwyn Garden City AL7 . . . . .111 A7
Westfield Ave
Harpenden AL5 . . . . .86 A3
Watford WD2 . . . . .154 D1
Westfield Cl
Bishop's Stortford CM23 . . . . . .76 E8
Cheshunt EN8 . . . . .162 E8
Hitchin SG5 . . . . .34 D7
Westfield Ct AL4 . . . . .128 D6
Westfield Dr AL5 . . . . .86 B4
Westfield Fst Sch HP4 . . . . . . .121 F5
Westfield Jun Mix Inf Sch
EN11 .134 F7
Westfield La AL5 . . . . .34 D7
Westfield Pk HA5 . . . . .175 F3
Westfield Rd AL5 . . . . .86 B4
Westfield Rd
Berkhamsted HP4 . . . . .121 F5
Bishop's Stortford CM23 . . . . . .76 E8
Harpenden AL5 . . . . .86 B4
Hertford SG14 . . . . .113 C8
Hoddesdon EN11 . . . . .134 F7
Pitstone LU7 . . . . .80 C3
Westfield Sch WD1 . . . . .166 F3
Westfield Wlk EN8 . . . . .162 E8
Westfields AL3 . . . . .141 A8
Westgate SG1 . . . . .50 D5
Westgate Cl EN3 . . . . .162 D4
Westholm SG6 . . . . .23 A8
Westholme SG6 . . . . .22 F8
Westland Dr AL9 . . . . .144 E4
Westland Rd WD1 . . . . .167 B7
Westlea Ave WD2 . . . . .154 E2
Westlea Cl EN10 . . . . .148 F8
Westlea Rd EN10 . . . . .148 F8
Westlecote Gdns LU2 . . . . .45 D4
Westly Wood AL7 . . . . .111 A7
Westmeade Cl EN7 . . . . .148 B2
Westmill La Hitchin SG5 . . . . .21 C2
Ickleford SG5 . . . . .21 C3
Westmill Lawns SG5 . . . . .21 D1
Westmill Rd Hitchin SG5 . . . . .21 D1
Thundridge SG12 . . . . .93 A3
Westminster Ct AL1 . . . . .127 C1
Westminster Ho 6 WD1 . . . .167 C7
Westmorland Ave LU3 . . . . . . .44 F5
Weston Ave SG8 . . . . .7 C7
Weston Cl EN6 . . . . .158 F7
Weston Jun Mix Inf Sch
SG4 . . . . .24 C1
Weston Rd Stevenage SG1 . . . .36 E1

Weston Rd continued
Stevenage SG1 . . . . .37 A3
Weston Way SG4 . . . . .23 C7
Westray HP3 . . . . .125 C1
Westridge Cl HP1 . . . . .123 F3
Westron Gdns HP23 . . . . .100 A3
Westrow Cl WD6 . . . . .169 D3
Westview Rise HP2 . . . . .124 D4
Westway LU2 . . . . .46 C4
Westwick HP2 . . . . .125 D2
Westwick Pl WD2 . . . . .154 C5
Westwick Row HP2 . . . . .125 E2
Westwood Ave SG4 . . . . .50 E2
Westwood Cl EN6 . . . . .145 A1
Wetherby Cl SG1 . . . . .51 C8
Wetherby Rd
Borehamwood WD6 . . . . .169 E8
Enfield EN2 . . . . .161 C1
Wetherfield CM24 . . . . .59 D7
Wetherly Cl CM17 . . . . .118 F4
Wetherne Link LU4 . . . . .44 C5
Wexham Cl LU3 . . . . .44 E8
Weybourne Cl AL5 . . . . .86 C2
Weybourne Dr LU2 . . . . .45 C7
Weymouth St HP3 . . . . .138 D7
Weyver Ct AL1 . . . . .127 E4
Whaley Rd EN6 . . . . .159 C6
Wharf La
Berkhamsted HP4 . . . . .121 C8
Rickmansworth WD3 . . . . .165 E1
Wharf Rd
 Bishop's Stortford CM23 . .76 F6
Hemel Hempstead HP1 . . . . . .124 B1
Hoddesdon EN10 . . . . .148 F8
Wharf Row HP22 . . . . .99 B4
Wharfdale LU4 . . . . .44 C5
Wharfedale HP2 . . . . .124 E6
Wheat Cl AL4 . . . . .128 A7
Wheat Croft CM23 . . . . .76 E4
Wheat Hill SG6 . . . . .22 F8
Wheatbarn AL7 . . . . .111 B7
Wheatcotes SG3 . . . . .69 C1
Wheatcroft EN7 . . . . .148 B3
Wheatcroft Prim Sch
SG13 .114 A7
Wheatfield Hatfield AL10 . . . .130 B6
Hemel Hempstead HP2 . . . . . .124 D5
Wheatfield Ave AL5 . . . . .107 A5
Wheatfield Cres SG8 . . . . .7 C6
Wheatfield Rd AL5 . . . . .107 A4
Wheatfields CM17 . . . . .118 D6
Wheatfields Inf Sch AL4 . . . .128 B7
Wheatfields Jun Mix Sch
AL4 . . . . .128 B7
Wheathampstead Rd
Harpenden AL5 . . . . .107 E8
Wheathampstead AL4 . . . . . . .108 A8
Wheathampstead Sch
AL4 . . . . .108 C7
Wheatlands SG1 . . . . .51 C7
Wheatley Cl
Sawbridgeworth CM21 . . . . . . .97 C1
Wheathampstead AL7 . . . . . . .111 A4
Wheatleys AL4 . . . . .128 C5
Wheatlock Mead AL3 . . . . . . .106 A5
Wheatsheaf Dr SG12 . . . . .93 B3
Wheatsheaf Rd SG12 . . . . .95 D1
Wheelers Cl EN9 . . . . .135 C1
Wheelers La HP3 . . . . .124 E1
Wheelright Cf WD2 . . . . .168 B3
Wheelwrights Cl CM23 . . . . . . .76 C4
Whempstead La SG12 . . . . .71 B6
Whempstead Rd SG12 . . . . .71 B7
Whetstone Cl AL6 . . . . .89 E8
Whinbush Gr SG5 . . . . .34 F8
Whinbush Rd SG5 . . . . .34 F8
Whippendell Hill WD4 . . . . . .138 C1
Whippendell Rd WD1 . . . . . . .166 F4
Whipperley Ct LU1 . . . . .63 C5
Whipperley Inf Sch LU1 . . . . .63 A6
Whipperley Ring LU1 . . . . .63 A6
Whipperley Way LU1 . . . . .63 C5
Whipsnade
Wildlife Animal Park LU6 .81 E7
Whisper Wood WD3 . . . . .165 B6
Whisperwood Cl HA3 . . . . .176 E3
Whit Hern Ct EN8 . . . . .148 C1
Whitby Rd LU3 . . . . .45 C1
White Bear CM24 . . . . .59 E8
White Craig Cl HA5 . . . . .176 A4
White Cotts SG5 . . . . .11 F6
White Gate Gdns HA3 . . . . . . .176 F3
White Hart Cl SG9 . . . . .40 E8
White Hart Ct HP2 . . . . .125 A2
White Hart Dr HP2 . . . . .125 A2
White Hart Rd HP2 . . . . .125 A2
White Hart St HP1 . . . . .138 D7
White Hedge Dr AL3 . . . . .127 C5
White Hill
Ashley Green HP5 . . . . .136 C7
Flamstead AL3 . . . . .105 B8
Hemel Hempstead HP1 . . . . . .123 F2
Rickmansworth WD3 . . . . .174 A4
Walkern SG2 . . . . .38 C2
Whipsnade
White Horse La
London Colney AL2 . . . . .142 E5
Markyate AL6 . . . . .90 C7
White House Cl SG14 . . . . .70 E3
White House The SG6 . . . . .23 B5
White La SG4 . . . . .49 C7
White Orchards N20 . . . . .171 F1
White Post Field CM17 . . . . . . .97 D2
White Stubbs La
EN10,SG13 . . . . .133 C2

White Way The SG6 . . . . .51 C7
Whitebarns SG9 . . . . .43 A5
Whitebarns La SG9 . . . . .43 A6
Whitebeam Cl EN7 . . . . .147 C5
Whitebeams
Chiswellfield AL2 . . . . .141 C3
Hatfield AL10 . . . . .130 A2
Whitebroom Rd HP1 . . . . .123 E5
Whitechurch Cl LU2 . . . . .46 D2
Whitechurch Gdns SG6 . . . . . .23 C3
Whitecroft AL1 . . . . .142 B8
Whitecroft Rd LU2 . . . . .64 A8
Whitefield Ho AL10 . . . . .44 C7
Whitefield AL10 . . . . .130 C7
Whitefield Inf Sch LU3 . . . . . . .44 E8
Whitefield Jun Sch LU3 . . . . . .44 E8
Whitefriars Ave HA3 . . . . .176 E1
Whitefriars Dr HA3 . . . . .176 E1
Whitefriars Fst & Mid Sch
HA3 . . . . .176 E1
Whitefriars Trad Est
HA3 . . . . .176 D1
Whitegale SG4 . . . . .35 A6
Whitegates Cl WD3 . . . . .166 A5
Whitehall Cl WD3 . . . . .135 E1
Whitehall Coll CM23 . . . . .58 E1
Whitehall La CM23 . . . . .58 E1
Whitehall Rd CM23 . . . . .58 E1
Whitehands Cl EN11 . . . . .134 F6
Whitehart Cross SG4 . . . . .136 F3
Whitehills SG6 . . . . .12 A1
Whitehill HP4 . . . . .122 E8
Whitehill Ave LU1 . . . . .63 D5
Whitehill Cotts AL6 . . . . .89 A3
Whitehill Ct HP4 . . . . .122 D5
Whitehill Jun Sch SG4 . . . . . . .35 A5
Whitehill Rd SG4 . . . . .35 A5
Whitehorse Ct SG8 . . . . .17 D4
Whitehorse St SG7 . . . . .23 F8
Whitehorse Vale LU3 . . . . .31 A1
Whitehouse Ave WD6 . . . . . . .170 B5
Whitehouse La EN9 . . . . .140 C4
Whitehurst Ave SG5 . . . . .21 F1
Whitelands Ave WD3 . . . . .164 C5
Whiteleaf Rd HP3 . . . . .138 C8
Whiteley Cl SG12 . . . . .71 E7
Whiteley Ls SG9 . . . . .27 C8
Whitesmead Rd SG1 . . . . .50 D7
Whitestone Wlk HP1 . . . . .124 A6
Whitethorn AL7 . . . . .111 B5
Whitethorn La LU3 . . . . .23 A4
Whitethorn Way LU1 . . . . .63 A6
Whitewaits CM20 . . . . .117 E1
Whiteway SG6 . . . . .23 C4
Whiteweaybottom La
LU2,SG4 . . . . .66 A3
Whitewebbs La EN2 . . . . .161 F4
Whitewebbs
Mus of Transport EN2 . .161 B4
Whitewebbs Park Cntry Pk
EN2 . . . . .161 D4
Whitewebbs Rd EN1 . . . . .161 C4
Whitewood Rd HP4 . . . . .122 A4
Whitfield Way WD3 . . . . .164 F1
Whitings Cl AL5 . . . . .86 D4
Whitings Hill
Barnet EN5 . . . . .171 C4
Whitings Rd EN5 . . . . .171 C4
Whitlars Dr WD4 . . . . .138 F3
Whitley Cl WD5 . . . . .154 A7
Whitley Ct EN11 . . . . .135 B8
Whitley Gn LU2 . . . . .46 D2
Whitley Rd EN11 . . . . .135 B8
Whitmores Wood HP2 . . . . . . .125 B4
Whitney Dr SG1 . . . . .36 C1
Whittingham Cl LU2 . . . . .46 F1
Whittingstall Rd EN11 . . . . . .135 C8
Whittington La SG1 . . . . .50 E4
Whittington Way HP2 . . . . .76 F3
Whittle Cl SG16 . . . . .10 B4
Whittlesea Cl HA3 . . . . .176 C3
Whittlesea Path HA3 . . . . .176 C2
Whittlesea Rd HA3 . . . . .176 C2
Whittlesea Sch HA3 . . . . .176 C3
Whitwell Cl AL5 . . . . .45 B8
Whitwell Rd WD3 . . . . .154 D4
Whitworth Jones Ave
SG6 . . . . .10 C5
Whitworth Rd SG1 . . . . .37 B3
Whomerley Rd SG1 . . . . .50 E4
Whydale Rd SG8 . . . . .7 F5
Whyngham Rd HP23 . . . . .100 C4
Wick Ave AL4 . . . . .108 D8
Wick Hill LU6 . . . . .82 F8
Wick Rd HP23 . . . . .120 D8
Wick The SG14 . . . . .92 C1
Wicken Fields SG4 . . . . .93 C3
Wickets End WD7 . . . . .156 E6
Wickets The LU2 . . . . .45 E1
Wickfield SG2 . . . . .69 A2
Wickfield Cl SG3 . . . . .69 A2
Wickham Cl EN3 . . . . .162 D1
Wickham Rd HA3 . . . . .176 C1
Wickham Way SG11 . . . . .55 E3
Wickhams Wharf SG12 . . . . . . .93 E1
Wicklands Rd SG12 . . . . .116 D8
Wickmere Cl LU2 . . . . .45 C7
Wickow Ave SG14 . . . . .44 E4
Wickwood Ct AL1 . . . . .128 B5

Widford Rd continued
Welwyn Garden City AL7 . . . . .111 B6
Widford Terr HP2 . . . . .105 A1
Widgeon Way WD2 . . . . .154 E2
Widmore Dr HP2 . . . . .125 E5
Wieland Rd HA6 . . . . .175 A3
Wiggenhall Rd WD1 . . . . .167 C4
Wiggington Bottom
HP23 .120 E8
Wight Ho WD1 . . . . .166 F4
Wigmore La LU2 . . . . .46 D2
Wigmore Park Ctr LU2 . . . . . . .46 E1
Wigmore Pl LU2 . . . . .46 E1
Wigmore Prim Sch LU2 . . . . . .46 E2
Wigmores N AL8 . . . . .110 D7
Wigram Way SG2 . . . . .51 B3
Wilbury Cl SG6 . . . . .22 C7
Wilbury Hills Rd SG6 . . . . .22 C7
Wilbury Jun Sch SG6 . . . . .22 D6
Wilbury Lodge SG6 . . . . .171 D5
Wilbury Rd SG6 . . . . .22 D6
Wilbury Way SG4 . . . . .22 A8
Wilbury Way SG4 . . . . .22 A3
Wilcot Ave WD1 . . . . .167 E2
Wilcot Cl WD1 . . . . .167 E2
Wilcox Cl WD6 . . . . .170 C8
Wild Cherry Dr LU1 . . . . .63 D5
Wild March Ct EN8 . . . . .162 E2
Wild Oaks Cl HA6 . . . . .174 F4
Wilderness The HP4 . . . . .122 C4
Wildhill rd AL9 . . . . .131 B2
Wildwood HA6 . . . . .174 E4
Wildwood Ave AL2 . . . . .140 F1
Wildwood Ct WD3 . . . . .164 F5
Wildwood La SG1 . . . . .50 E3
Wilford Cl HA6 . . . . .174 D3
Wilford Cl EN3 . . . . .162 E1
Wilkin's Green La AL4 . . . . . . .129 C4
Wilkins Gr AL8 . . . . .110 D5
Wilkinsgreen Terr AL4 . . . . . .129 B3
Wilkinson Cl EN7 . . . . .147 C6
Willenhall Cl LU3 . . . . .45 A7
William Austin Inf Sch
LU3 . . . . .45 C4
William Austin Jun Sch
LU3 . . . . .45 C4
William Covell Cl EN2 . . . . . .160 F1
William Ct HP3 . . . . .138 D7
William Pl SG2 . . . . .51 A3
William Ransom Prim Sch
The SG4 . . . . .35 B7
William St
Berkhamsted HP4 . . . . .122 D4
Luton LU2 . . . . .45 E1
Markyate AL3 . . . . .83 F8
Watford WD2 . . . . .167 D6
William Sutton Ct LU2 . . . . . . .46 B5
Williams Way WD7 . . . . .156 C4
Williamson St LU1 . . . . .63 E7
Williamson Way WD3 . . . . . . .165 A1
Willian Church Rd SG6 . . . . . .23 A2
Willian Rd
Great Wymondley SG4 . . . . . . .35 F7
Hitchin SG4 . . . . .22 E1
Willian Way Baldock SG7 . . . . .23 E6
Letchworth SG6 . . . . .23 A3
Willinghall CM9 . . . . .163 D7
Willison Rd LU2 . . . . .46 C2
Willoughby Cl EN10 . . . . .134 E2
Willoughby Ct SG5 . . . . .86 B4
Willoughby Way SG4 . . . . .35 A6
Willow Cl
Bishop's Stortford CM23 . . . . . .76 E8
Great Hormead SG9 . . . . .42 A8
Hammond Street EN7 . . . . . . .147 E5
Reed SG8 . . . . .16 D5
Willow Corner SG13 . . . . .132 F5
Willow Cres AL1 . . . . .128 C3
Willow Ct Harrow HA3 . . . . . .176 F2
Luton LU3 . . . . .44 E5
Willow Dean HA5 . . . . .175 D1
Willow Dene WD2 . . . . .168 E2
Willow Dr EN5 . . . . .171 E5
Willow Edge AL4 . . . . .139 A2
Willow End N20 . . . . .171 F1
Willow End HA6 . . . . .175 A4
Willow Gn WD6 . . . . .170 C4
Willow Gr AL8 . . . . .89 D3
Willow La Hitchin SG5 . . . . . . .34 D6
Watford WD1 . . . . .167 A4
Willow Mead CM20 . . . . .97 C2
Willow Path EN9 . . . . .163 E5
Willow Springs CM23 . . . . .76 D8
Willow Tree Way SG3 . . . . .25 F7
Willow Way
Chiswellgreen AL2 . . . . .141 A4
Harpenden AL5 . . . . .86 C4
Hatfield AL10 . . . . .129 F2
Hemel Hempstead HP2 . . . . . .124 B5
Luton LU3 . . . . .44 E5
Potters Bar EN6 . . . . .159 B6
Radlett WD7 . . . . .155 E3
Willow Wlk AL6 . . . . .89 D7
Willowby Ct AL2 . . . . .142 D5
Willowdene EN8 . . . . .148 C4
Willowfield Lower Sch
LU1 . . . . .62 F4
Willowgate Trad Est LU3 . . . .44 A8
Willowmead AL4 . . . . .113 B5
Willows Cl HA5 . . . . .175 C1
Willows Link
Stevenage SG2 . . . . .51 A1
Willows The
Buntingford SG9 . . . . .40 D8
Hemel Hempstead HP2 . . . . . .125 B5
Hitchin SG5 . . . . .35 A5
Rickmansworth WD3 . . . . .173 A8
St Albans AL3 . . . . .142 B7
Stevenage SG2 . . . . .51 A1

Willows The continued
Watford WD1 167
Willowside AL2 142
Willowside Way SG4 7
Willowtree Lo HA6 174
Wilsden Ave LU1 63
Wilshere Ave AL1 127
Wilshere Cres SG4 35
Wilshere Rd AL6 89
Wilshere-Dacre Jun Sch
SG5 34
Wilsmere Dr HA3 176
Wilson Cl
Bishop's Stortford CM23 76
Stevenage SG1 36
Wilsons La SG7 4
Wilstone Dr AL4 128
Wilton Cl CM23 77
Wilton Cres SG13 113
Wilton Ct WD1 167
Wilton Rd SG5 21
Wilton Way SG13 113
Wiltshire Rd SG2 51
Wimborne Cl CM21 97
Wimborne Gr WD1 153
Wimborne Rd LU1 63
Wimple Rd LU4 44
Winch Cl SG4 88
Winch St LU2 45
Winchells HP3 139
Winchester Cl
Bishop's Stortford CM23 76
Stevenage SG1 37
Winchester Ho AL3 127
Winchester Rd HA6 174
Winchester Way WD3 166
Winchfield Way WD3 165
Windermere Ave AL1 128
Windermere Cl
Chorleywood WD3 164
Hemel Hempstead HP2 125
Windermere Cres LU3 44
Windermere Ct 8 WD1 . . .167
Windermere Dr
Jun Mix Inf Sch SG1 128
Windhill
Bishop's Stortford CM23 76
Welwyn Garden City AL7 111
Windhill Old Rd CM23 76
Winding Hill SG10 75
Winding Shot HP1 124
Winding Shot SG14 91
Windmill Ave AL4 128
Windmill Cl Barkway SG8 17
Pitstone LU7 80
Waltham Abbey EN9 163
Windmill Dr WD3 165
Windmill Field SG12 114
Windmill Fields CM17 118
Windmill Hill
Buntingford SG9 40
Chipperfield WD4 151
Hitchin SG4 34
Windmill La Barnet EN5 170
Bushey WD2 168
Cheshunt EN8 148
Windmill Rd
Breachwood Green SG4 47
Hemel Hempstead HP2 124
Luton LU1 63
Markyate AL3 84
Windmill St WD2 168
Windmill Way
Much Hadham SG10 74
Tring HP23 99
Windmills SG12 93
Windmore Ave EN6 158
Windridge Cl AL3 127
Winds End Cf HP2 125
Windsor Cl
Borehamwood WD6 170
Bovingdon HP3 137
Chestnut EN7 148
Hemel Hempstead HP2 124
Northwood HA6 175
Stevenage SG2 69
Welwyn AL6 89
Windsor Ct LU1 63
Windsor Way WD3 165
Windsor Wood EN9 163
Windward Ct EN3 162
Windy Rise SG12 71
Windrof Dr EN10 134
Wingate Cl LU4 44
Wingate Gdns AL6 89
Wingate Rd LU4 44
Wingate Way AL1 128
Wingrave CE Comb Sch
HP22 60
Wingrave Rd Tring HP23 100
Wilstone HP23 79
Winifred Ho (Conv Hospl
for Children)
EN5 170
Winifred Rd HP3 138

field Cl LU4 . . . .44 B1
ington Rd EN3 . . . .162 C2
lon Ct **1** LU1 . . . .63 D6
lon Rd LU1 . . . .63 D6
ow Cl LU3 . . . .45 C4
ow Rd HP2 . . . .60 B3
ton Churchill Way
. . . .162 D6
on Cl Harrow HA3 . . .176 F4
in SG5 . . . .34 D7
on Cl HA3 . . . .176 B3
on Gdns HP4 . . . .121 F4
ton Way EN6 . . . .159 A6
on Rd WD6 . . . .170 A8
ers La SG2 . . . .38 C1
rscroft Rd EN11 . . .134 F7
on App WD3 . . . .166 C4
on Cl Letchworth SG6 . .23 D8
i LU2 . . . .45 D6
on Cres WD3 . . . .166 B4
on Dr Cheshunt EN8 . .148 E2
ny Green WD3 . . . .166 C4
on Rd SG12 . . . .93 F1
en Rd SG1 . . . .36 F1
nan Cl LU2 . . . .45 E7
mans Gdns CM21 . . .77 C1
ea Cres AL4 . . . .129 B1
ow Rd LU3 . . . .45 A6
nford AL7 . . . .111 D6
y Cl LU4 . . . .44 B4
y Pl AL2 . . . .143 C3
y Cl HA5 . . . .175 F4
and SG13 . . . .113 E1
er Ave SG5 . . . .21 E4
ton Cl LU2 . . . .45 D7
urn Ave CM23 . . . .76 C7
urn Cl Bushey WD2 . .168 C3
enage SG2 . . . .69 C7
urn Cl LU4 . . . .44 D5
croft Rd LU3 . . . .45 B6
on Park Sports & L Ctr
. . . .93 D4
sburg Ct **4** LU4 . . . .44 C5
ey Ave EN7 . . . .147 F2
ey Bsns Pk WD1 . . .166 D2
ey Mansions HA6 . . .174 C7
ey Rd
el Hempstead HP2 . . .124 D2
y Park HA6 . . . .174 D7
ton Cl LU1 . . . .63 C7
es Mere SG3 . . . .69 A2
escroft SG2 . . . .69 A2
i Cl LU3 . . . .130 B5
i Comm AL10 . . . .130 B8
d Cres HP3 . . . .124 E1
i Dr SG2 . . . .51 B2
i End AL2 . . . .141 C3
i End Cl HP2 . . . .125 C4
i End Hill AL5 . . . .85 D4
i End Jun Mix Inf Sch
. . . .85 D3
i End La AL3 . . . .104 E8
i End Rd AL5 . . . .85 D3
i Farm Rd HP2 . . . .124 E2
i Green Cl LU2 . . . .46 B5
i Green Rd LU2 . . . .46 C5
i Green Way EN6 . . .162 E8
i House La EN10 . . .134 A2
i La Birchanger CM23 . .59 E2
el Hempstead HP2 . . .124 D2
sden SG7 . . . .30 A6
d Lane End HP2 . . .125 B4
i St Barnet EN5 . . . .171 D5
n LU1 . . . .63 F6
i Vale AL10 . . . .130 B5
d View Cuffley EN6 . .146 E4
el Hempstead HP1 . . .124 B5
acre Dr AL6 . . . .90 A8
bine Gr EN2 . . . .161 D1
bridge Cl LU4 . . . .44 E4
brook Gdns EN9 . . .163 E6
bury Hill LU2 . . . .45 E2
cock Hill
mansworth WD3 . . .173 E4
ridge AL4 . . . .108 E1

Woodcock Rd Luton LU1 . . . .63 A7
Stevenage SG2 . . . .51 D2
Woodcote Cl EN8 . . . .148 C1
Woodcote Ho **1** SG4 . . . .34 F7
Woodcroft SG5 . . . .34 E6
Woodcroft Ave SG12 . . .115 E4
Woodfall Ave EN5 . . . .171 F4
Woodfield Ave HA6 . . .174 E6
Woodfield Cl CM24 . . . .59 E6
Woodfield Dr HP3 . . . .125 D1
Woodfield Gdns HP3 . . .125 D1
Woodfield La AL9 . . . .145 E8
Woodfield Rd
Radlett WD7 . . . .156 A3
Stevenage SG1 . . . .36 C1
Welwyn Garden City AL7 . .110 F6
Woodfield Rise WD2 . . .168 D2
Woodfield Sch HP3 . . .125 C1
Woodfield Terr CM24 . . .59 E6
Woodfield Way AL4 . . .128 C6
Woodfields
Stansted Mountfitchet CM24 . .59 E6
2 Watford WD1 . . . .167 C5
Woodford Cres HA5 . . .175 B1
Woodford Rd WD1 . . . .167 C7
Woodforde Cl SG7 . . . .4 E4
Woodgate WD2 . . . .154 B6
Woodgate Ave EN6 . . .160 B7
Woodgate Cres HA6 . . .175 A4
Woodgrange Ct EN11 . . .135 A5
Woodhall Ave HA5 . . .175 E2
Woodhall Cl SG14 . . . .113 C8
Woodhall Ct AL7 . . . .110 E5
Woodhall Dr HA5 . . . .175 E2
Woodhall Gate HA5 . . .175 D2
Woodhall Gr CM23 . . . .76 D6
Woodhall Ho AL7 . . . .110 F4
Woodhall La
Hemel Hempstead HP2 . . .124 E4
Shenley WD7 . . . .156 F4
South Oxhey WD1 . . . .175 E6
Welwyn Garden City AL7 . .110 E4
Woodhall Sch WD1 . . .175 E6
Woodham Way SG12 . . .115 C4
Woodhouse Eaves HA6 . .175 A5
Woodhurst Ave WD2 . . .154 D4
Woodland Ave
Hemel Hempstead HP1 . . .124 B2
Luton LU3 . . . .45 B2
Woodland Cl
Hemel Hempstead HP1 . . .124 B2
Tring HP23 . . . .99 F2
Woodland Dr
St Albans AL4 . . . .128 C4
Watford WD1 . . . .166 F8
Woodland La WD3 . . .164 D6
Woodland Mount SG13 . .113 F6
Woodland Pl
Chorleywood WD3 . . .164 F5
Hemel Hempstead HP2 . . .124 B2
Woodland Rd
Hertford Heath SG13 . . .114 C3
Maple Cross WD3 . . .172 D5
Woodland Rise
Studham LU6 . . . .82 B7
Welwyn Garden City AL8 . .110 C8
Woodland Way
Abbots Langley WD5 . . .139 F4
Baldock SG7 . . . .23 F6
Goff's Oak EN7 . . . .147 B3
Stevenage SG2 . . . .51 A1
Welwyn AL6 . . . .90 A7
Woodlands
Bishop's Stortford CM23 . . .77 C8
Brookmans Park AL9 . . .145 B4
Caddington LU1 . . . .62 E3
Chiswellgreen AL2 . . .141 C4
Harpenden AL5 . . . .85 E3
Radlett WD7 . . . .156 A5
Royston SG8 . . . .7 E6
Woodlands Ave HP4 . . .122 D3
Woodlands Cl
Borehamwood WD6 . . .170 B5
Hoddesdon EN11 . . .135 A5

Woodlands Dr
Abbots Langley WD4 . . .139 C3
Harrow HA7 . . . .176 F4
Woodlands Dr HA7 . . .176 F4
Woodlands Inf Sch WD6 . .170 A8
Woodlands Meade SG4 . . .37 B8
Woodlands Rd
Abbots Langley HP3 . . .139 A4
Enfield EN2 . . . .161 D1
Hertford SG13 . . . .113 F6
Thundridge SG12 . . . .93 D6
Watford WD2 . . . .167 E4
Woodlea AL2 . . . .141 A6
Woodlea Gr HA6 . . . .174 C4
Woodley Rd SG12 . . . .93 F2
Woodleys CM20 . . . .118 A1
Woodman Rd **4** HP3 . . .124 E1
Woodmere LU3 . . . .31 A1
Woodmere Ave WD2 . . .154 E1
Woodmill Mews EN11 . . .135 B8
Woodpecker Cl
Bishop's Stortford CM23 . . .76 C6
Bushey WD2 . . . .168 C1
Harrow HA3 . . . .176 F2
Hatfield AL10 . . . .129 F2
Woodridge Way HA6 . . .174 E4
Woodridings Ave HA5 . . .175 F2
Woodridings Cl HA5 . . .175 F3
Woods Ave AL10 . . . .130 B4
Woods Pl HP23 . . . .100 A3
Woods The Radlett WD7 . .156 B5
South Oxhey HA5 . . .175 A5
Woodshots Mdw WD1 . .166 D4
Woodside
Bishop's Stortford CM23 . . .77 D8
Borehamwood WD6 . . .169 F5
Cheshunt EN7 . . . .162 A8
Hertford Heath SG13 . . .114 C2
Watford WD2 . . . .154 A3
Woodside Farm
& Wildfowl Park LU1 . . .84 A8
Woodside Ho AL8 . . . .110 C7
Woodside Ind Pk SG6 . . .23 B7
Woodside La AL9 . . . .131 A1
Woodside Prim Sch EN7 . .147 B2
Woodside Rd
Abbots Langley WD5 . . .154 B8
Bricket Wood AL2 . . .140 F2
Welwyn AL6 . . . .89 F3
Woodside LU1 . . . .63 B3
Woodstock SG6 . . . .68 F3
Woodstock Ct SG13 . . .114 B4
Woodstock Rd
Bushey WD2 . . . .168 F2
Hoddesdon EN10 . . .134 E4
Woodstock Rd N AL1 . . .128 B4
Woodstock Rd S AL1 . . .128 B3
Woodvale EN8 . . . .162 C4
Woodville Court Mews
WD1 . . . .167 A7
Woodville Ct WD1 . . .167 A7
Woodville Pl SG14 . . .113 B8
Woodward Gdns HA7 . . .176 F3
Woodway WD1 . . . .167 C2
Woodwicks WD3 . . . .172 D5
Woolenwick Inf Sch SG1 . .50 B6
Woolenwick Jun Mix Sch
SG1 . . . .50 B6
Woolgrove Ct SG4 . . . .22 B1
Woolgrove Rd SG4 . . . .22 B1
Woolgrove Sch SG4 . . . .23 D5
Woolllam Cres AL3 . . .127 C7
Woollams AL3 . . . .106 A4
Woollard St EN9 . . . .163 C5
Woolmans Cl EN10 . . .134 F1
Woolmer Cl WD6 . . . .157 A1
Woolmer Dr HP2 . . . .125 C3
Woolmer Green
Jun Mix Inf Sch SG3 . . .69 A1
Woolmerdine Ct WD2 . .167 D6
Woolmers La SG14 . . .112 B2
Woolners Way SG1 . . . .50 C6
Woolston Ave SG6 . . . .23 A4
Wootton Cl LU3 . . . .45 B7
Wootton Dr HP2 . . . .124 F8

Worboys Ct SG8 . . . .1 F5
Worcester Cl AL1 . . .128 A2
Worcester Rd AL10 . . .129 F6
Worcesters Ave EN1 . . .162 A1
Worcesters Prim Sch
EN1 . . . .161 F1
Wordsworth Cl SG8 . . . .2 D1
Wordsworth Rd
Harpenden AL5 . . . .86 A3
Luton LU4 . . . .44 A2
Works Rd SG6 . . . .23 C7
Worley Rd AL3 . . . .127 D4
Wormley Ct EN10 . . .148 F7
Wormley Lodge Cl EN10 . .148 F8
Wormley Prim Sch EN10 . .148 E8
Worsell Way SG4 . . . .35 B7
Worsted La SG9 . . . .41 E7
Wortham Rd SG8 . . . .7 E4
Wortham Way SG2 . . . .51 B3
Wraglins The CM23 . . . .77 B5
Wratten Cl SG5 . . . .34 E6
Wratten Rd E SG5 . . . .34 E6
Wratten Rd W SG5 . . . .34 E6
Wrayfields SG5 . . . .12 B8
Wraysbury Cl LU4 . . . .44 D3
Wren Cl
Kimpton SG4 . . . .66 B1
Luton LU2 . . . .46 C6
Stevenage SG2 . . . .51 B6
Wren Cres WD2 . . . .168 C1
Wren Wood AL7 . . . .111 B7
Wrenbrook Rd CM23 . . .76 F6
Wrensfield HP1 . . . .124 B3
Wrestlers Cl AL10 . . .130 C7
Wrexham Terr SG8 . . . .7 D7
Wratten Cl AL4 . . . .108 E7
Wright's Bldgs WD1 . . .167 B7
Wright's Green La CM22 . .98 D8
Wrights Green La CM22 . .98 D7
Wrights Mdw SG2 . . . .52 B8
Wrights Orch SG2 . . . .51 E2
Wrotham Park EN5 . . .158 E3
Wrotham Rd EN5 . . . .171 E7
Wroxham Ave HP3 . . .124 D1
Wroxham Gdns
Crews Hill EN2 . . . .161 B4
Potters Bar EN6 . . . .158 D8
Wroxham Sch The EN6 . .158 D8
Wroxham Way AL5 . . . .86 C3
Wulfrath Way SG12 . . . .93 C3
Wulstan Pk EN6 . . . .159 D7
Wulwards Cl LU1 . . . .63 B6
Wulwards Ct LU1 . . . .63 B6
Wyatt Cl
Bushey WD2 . . . .168 C2
Ickleford SG5 . . . .21 D4
Wyatt's Cl WD3 . . . .165 A6
Wyatt's Rd WD3 . . . .165 A6
Wyburn Ave EN5 . . . .171 F6
Wych Elm CM20 . . . .117 C1
Wych Elm La AL6,SG3 . . .68 F2
Wych Elms AL2 . . . .141 B3
Wychdell SG2 . . . .69 C8
Wychford Dr CM21 . . . .97 C1
Wychwood Ave AL4 . . . .45 E3
Wychwood Way HA6 . . .174 F3
Wyciffe Cl LU3 . . . .45 C6
Wycliffe Ct WD5 . . . .153 E7
Wycombe Way
Luton LU3 . . . .45 A3
St Albans AL4 . . . .128 B6
Wyddial Gn AL7 . . . .111 B6
Wyddial Rd SG9 . . . .40 E8
Wye The HP2 . . . .125 A8
Wyedale AL2 . . . .142 F4
Wykeham Rise N20 . . .171 E1
Wyken Cl LU3 . . . .45 A7
Wyldwood Cl CM17 . . .118 C6
Wyllyotts Cl EN6 . . . .158 F7
Wyllyotts Pl EN6 . . . .158 F7
Wymondley
Jun Mix Inf Sch SG4 . . .35 E4

Wymondley Rd
Hitchin SG4 . . . .35 B6
Letchworth SG6 . . . .23 A1
Wynches Farm Dr AL4 . .128 D3
Wynchgate HA3 . . . .176 E3
Wynchlands Cres AL4 . .128 D3
Wynd Arc The SG6 . . . .22 F6
Wynd The SG6 . . . .22 F6
Wyndham Rd LU4 . . . .44 C2
Wyndhams End AL7 . . .110 F2
Wynlie Gdns HA5 . . . .175 B1
Wynn Cl SG7 . . . .13 A6
Wynyng Dell SG6 . . . .23 A3
Wysells Ct SG6 . . . .22 D7
Wyton AL7 . . . .111 D6
Wyvern Cl LU4 . . . .44 E3

Y

Yardley SG6 . . . .23 C4
Yardley Ave LU7 . . . .80 D4
Yardley Ct **8** AL5 . . . .86 B1
Yarmouth Rd
Stevenage SG1 . . . .50 A7
Watford WD2 . . . .154 C1
Yately Cl LU2 . . . .45 D7
Ye Cnr WD1 . . . .167 E3
Yearling Cl LU3 . . . .114 F7
Yeatman Ho WD2 . . . .154 B3
Yeats Cl SG8 . . . .2 D1
Yeomanry Dr SG7 . . . .13 A1
Yeomans Ave AL5 . . . .85 D3
Yeomans Cl CM23 . . . .76 D6
Yeomans Dr SG2 . . . .51 E2
Yeomans Ride HP2 . . .105 A1
Yeovil Ct LU2 . . . .46 B2
Yeovil Rd LU2 . . . .46 B2
Yew Cl EN7 . . . .147 E4
Yew Gr AL7 . . . .111 C5
Yew Tree Cl Botley HP5 . .136 A1
Pitstone LU7 . . . .80 E5
Yew Tree Ct HP1 . . . .124 A1
Yew Tree Dr HP3 . . . .137 B3
Yew Tree Pl CM23 . . . .76 F8
Yew Wlk EN11 . . . .135 A5
Yewlands Hoddesdon EN11 . .135 A5
Sawbridgeworth CM21 . . .79 C1
Yewlands Dr EN11 . . .135 A5
Yews Ave EN1 . . . .162 B3
Yewstone Ct WD1 . . .167 A6
Yewtree End AL2 . . .141 B4
York Cl WD4 . . . .139 A2
York Cres WD6 . . . .170 D7
York Ho AL3 . . . .127 C2
York Mead Prim Sch
. . . .166 A4
York Rd Cheshunt EN8 . .162 E6
Hitchin SG5 . . . .34 E8
Northwood HA6 . . . .175 A1
St Albans AL1 . . . .127 F4
Stevenage SG1 . . . .36 F1
Watford WD1 . . . .167 C4
York St LU2 . . . .63 F8
York Terr EN2 . . . .161 C1
York Way
Hemel Hempstead HP2 . . .124 E2
Royston SG8 . . . .7 B8
Watford WD2 . . . .154 E3
Welwyn Garden City AL6 . .89 C3
Yorke Gate WD1 . . . .167 A7
Yorke Rd AL3 . . . .166 A3
Youngfield Rd HP1 . . .123 F4
Youngs Rise AL8 . . . .110 C6
Youngsbury La SG12 . . .93 E8
Yule Cl AL2 . . . .140 F1

Z

Zambesi Rd CM23 . . . .76 F5

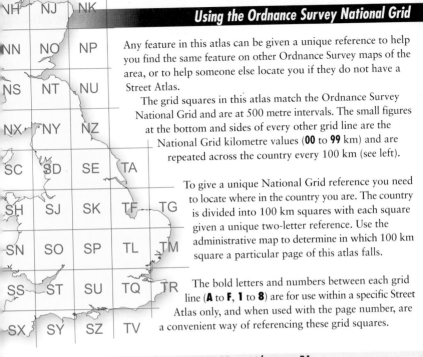

Any feature in this atlas can be given a unique reference to help you find the same feature on other Ordnance Survey maps of the area, or to help someone else locate you if they do not have a Street Atlas.

The grid squares in this atlas match the Ordnance Survey National Grid and are at 500 metre intervals. The small figures at the bottom and sides of every other grid line are the National Grid kilometre values (**00** to **99** km) and are repeated across the country every 100 km (see left).

To give a unique National Grid reference you need to locate where in the country you are. The country is divided into 100 km squares with each square given a unique two-letter reference. Use the administrative map to determine in which 100 km square a particular page of this atlas falls.

The bold letters and numbers between each grid line (**A** to **F**, **1** to **8**) are for use within a specific Street Atlas only, and when used with the page number, are a convenient way of referencing these grid squares.

ample *The railway bridge over DARLEY GREEN RD in grid square B1*

p 1: Identify the two-letter reference, in this ample the page is in **SP**

ep 2: Identify the 1 km square in which the ilway bridge falls. Use the figures in the southwest rner of this square: Eastings **17**, Northings **74**. is gives a unique reference: **SP 17 74**, accurate 1 km.

ep 3: To give a more precise reference accurate 100 m you need to estimate how many tenths ong and how many tenths up this 1 km square e feature is (to help with this the 1 km square is vided into four 500 m squares). This makes the ridge about **8** tenths along and about **1** tenth up om the southwest corner.

his gives a unique reference: **SP 178 741**, accurate 100 m.

Eastings (read from left to right along the bottom) come before Northings (read from bottom to top). If you have trouble remembering say to yourself "Along the hall, THEN up the stairs"!

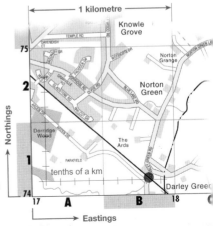

Addresses

Name and Address	Telephone	Page	Grid reference

Name and Address	Telephone	Page	Grid reference

Street Atlases from Philip's

Philip's publish an extensive range of regional and local street atlases which are ideal for motoring, business and leisure use. They are widely used by the emergency services and local authorities throughout Britain.

Key features include:

◆ Superb county-wide mapping at an extra-large scale of 3½ inches to 1 mile, or 2½ inches to 1 mile in pocket editi...

◆ Complete urban and rural coverage, detailing every name... street in town and country

◆ Each atlas available in two handy sizes – standard spiral and pocket paperback

'The mapping is very clear... great in scope and value'

★★★★ **BEST BUY**   **AUTO EXPRESS**

1 Bedfordshire
2 Berkshire
3 Birmingham and West Midlands
4 Bristol and Bath
5 Buckinghamshire
6 Cambridgeshire
7 Cardiff, Swansea and The Valleys
8 Cheshire
9 Derbyshire
10 Dorset
11 County Durham and Teesside
12 Edinburgh and E... Central Scotland
13 North Essex
14 South Essex
15 Glasgow and We... Central Scotland
16 Gloucestershire
17 North Hampshire
18 South Hampshire
19 Hertfordshire
20 East Kent
21 West Kent
22 Lancashire
23 Leicestershire and Rutland
24 London
25 Greater Manchest...
26 Merseyside
27 Northamptonshire
28 Nottinghamshire
29 Oxfordshire
30 Somerset
31 Staffordshire
32 Surrey
33 East Sussex
34 West Sussex
35 Tyne and Wear and Northumberland
36 Warwickshire
37 Wiltshire and Swindon
38 East Yorkshire and Northern Lincolnshi...
39 North Yorkshire
40 South Yorkshire
41 West Yorkshire

How to order

The Philip's range of street atlases is available from good retailers or directly from the publisher by phoning 01903 828503